Wartime Women

Recent Titles in
Contributions in Women's Studies

Wartime Women:
SEX ROLES, FAMILY RELATIONS, AND THE STATUS OF WOMEN DURING WORLD WAR II

★ Karen Anderson ★

Contributions in Women's Studies, Number 20

GREENWOOD PRESS
WESTPORT, CONNECTICUT ● LONDON, ENGLAND

Library of Congress Cataloging in Publication Data

Anderson, Karen, 1947-
    Wartime women.

    (Contributions in women's studies ; no. 20 ISSN 0147-
104X)
    Bibliography: p.
    Includes index.
    1. Women--United States--History--20th century.
2. World War, 1939-1945--Social aspects--United States.
I. Title. II. Series.
HQ1420.A65   305.4'2'0973   80-1703
ISBN 0-313-20884-0 (lib. bdg.)

Library of Congress Catalog Card Number: 80-1703
ISBN: 0-313-20884-0
ISSN: 0147-104X

First published in 1981

Greenwood Press
A division of Congressional Information Service, Inc.
88 Post Road West, Westport, Connecticut 06881

Printed in the United States of America

10 9 8 7 6 5 4 3 2 1

CONTENTS

ACKNOWLEDGMENTS

I wish to thank Otis Pease of the University of Washington for his assistance and advice in the early stages of this project. Mary Rothschild of Arizona State University also provided sound editorial advice and, more importantly, a sustained encouragement and personal friendship for which I am deeply grateful.

This study owes a great deal to the resources and staff of the National Archives, especially to Tom Gedosch, who was always willing to provide prompt assistance.

Finally, I wish to express my gratitude to James Sabin of Greenwood Press for his faith in my work and for his editorial contributions to this book.

Wartime Women

1

WORLD WAR II
AND THE CHANGING STATUS
OF AMERICAN WOMEN

In recent years the significance of World War II as a catalyst for long-term change in the status of American women has engaged the attention of historians. The historiographical debate that has developed has revealed a great deal not only about women's experiences during the war and the postwar period but also about scholarly assumptions concerning the nature of social change as it affects gender role defini-tions. In determining the social impact of the war, historians have had to assess the relative importance of ideology and economic trends in fostering or inhibiting change in women's status; they have had to determine whether short-term changes in conduct and circumstances can lead to long-term modifications of cultural values regarding appro-priate sex role behaviors. Throughout the debate, the central issue has been whether to stress the widening of opportunities for women in paid work or the persistence of sexist values and discriminatory practices in the economy, the family, and the society in general.[1]

For women, the liberative potential of wartime changes is undeniable because the dislocations of a nation at war have always created important challenges to traditional assumptions and practices. Because men are siphoned into the war machine right when the productive demands on society are greatest, the conventional distinctions between "women's" work and "men's" work are put under great stress. In order to provide the materials necessary to prosecute the war and meet civilian needs as well, women have assumed economic roles traditionally ascribed to men, undercutting conventional notions regarding their abilities. Wartime imperatives have generally created a substantially greater need for the coordination of community and national efforts in numerous areas; as a result, women have also left the private sphere of the home to participate in such public organizational work.[2]

In spite of the amount of historical literature documenting the extent of short-term change generated by wars in American history, few claims have been made for the long-term liberative effect of war on American women, except in the case of World War II. Because of its duration and the extent of civilian participation it fostered, no war in American history has had as profound an effect on American society and American women. World War II marked a temporary retreat from prevailing notions of women's capabilities and proper roles. The manpower demands of the industrial and war machine created a situation in which the employment of large numbers of women became mandatory. Moreover, employers in many job classifications that traditionally had been male were hiring significant numbers of women for the first time. Government, industry, the media, women's clubs, and other voluntary organizations joined in urging women to do their patriotic duty by taking a job. By 1943 the reserve of single women had been exhausted and recruitment was aimed more directly at married women. Whether motivated by patriotism, necessity, the availability of a multiplicity of jobs at high wages, or the independence, social interaction, and other rewards to be gained from working, American women responded to the call. At the wartime peak in July 1944, 19 million women were employed, an increase of 47 percent over the March 1940 level.[3]

A closer look at the composition of the wartime female labor force will reveal more fully the extent of change created by the national emergency. Because single women were already participating in the labor force in considerable numbers and because the percentage of single women in the female population declined in the war years, they represented a labor pool too small to meet the wartime demand for women workers. Consequently, married women constituted a significantly larger proportion of the wartime increase in female employment than did single women. Between April 1940 and March 1944, the number of married women gainfully employed increased by 2 million, 72.2 percent of the total increase. For the first time in U.S. history, married women outnumbered single women in the female work force.

Their labor force participation rate jumped from 15.2 to 23.0 percent. Thus, although still strong, societal reservations about wives working were waived to some extent in the war years.[4]

Despite this willingness to deviate from the established norms for women, the claims of home and family remained strong. Wives of servicemen away from home were three times as likely to work as wives with their husbands present. Women over thirty-five accounted for over 60 percent of the increase in the female labor force, and girls between fourteen and nineteen added another 17.3 percent to the total. In contrast, women between the ages of twenty-five and thirty-four who were in the main childbearing years, exceeded their expected numbers in the labor force by less than one-half of one percent. This stability at a time when all other women were entering the job market in large numbers can be attributed in part to Selective Service dependency regulations and allotments and, more importantly, to the increased marriage and birth rates beginning in 1940, which resulted from the war-induced prosperity. Between 1940 and 1944 the number of young married women relative to single women increased, as did the ratio of married women with young children to those without young children. Public resistance to the idea of working mothers also held down the labor force participation rate of women aged twenty-five to thirty-four. War Manpower Commission Chairman Paul McNutt reflected this sentiment in a directive issued in 1942, which stated that "no women responsible for the care of young children should be encouraged or compelled to seek employment which deprives their children of essential care until all other sources of supply are exhausted." Even in major war production areas, where the labor shortage was most severe and the increases in female employment were even greater than the national average, the number of working mothers was surprisingly low. A Women's Bureau survey of ten such areas revealed that only 32 percent of the women workers who were married, widowed, or divorced had children under fourteen and that over half of those had only one child. Thus, although the war caused an unprecedented expansion of the female labor force, it was women whose housekeeping and child care responsibilities were lightest who contributed most to that expansion.[5]

Not only did the war bring large numbers of newcomers to the labor force, it also provided an unparalleled opportunity for upward mobility for millions of women with previous work experience. The wartime system of labor priorities enabled many women to escape the low-paying female-dominated fields of domestic and personal service and to obtain jobs in the burgeoning war industries or in the government. Between 1940 and 1944 the number of women employed in manufacturing increased 141 percent, while those in domestic service declined by 20 percent. Women's share of the jobs increased from 22.0 percent to 32.7 percent in manufacturing and from 19.4 percent to 38.4 percent in government. Former saleswomen, waitresses, and maids took over jobs as riveters, welders, taxicab drivers, and drill-press operators, demonstrating women's capabilities in these and a host of other activities previously assigned almost exclusively to men. Wartime imperatives were thus undermining somewhat the sex-segregated labor market and the ideas that perpetuated it, long an impediment to economic advancement for women.[6]

Some long-standing inequities in pay were also disappearing. In 1942 the National War Labor Board established an equal pay principle when it decided that the same rates should be paid to women when the work they did was the same or substantially the same as work done by men. Further definition of the board policy weakened its commitment to equal treatment. Union contracts containing inequitable pay were allowed to remain in force; pay scales for jobs traditionally performed by women were presumed to be acceptable; and pay differentials were allowed in some cases when men's jobs were classified as "heavy" and women's jobs as "light". Despite these loopholes, some firms did pay women equally, and the disparities betweeen men's and women's average earnings narrowed somewhat during the war years, primarily because of the increased demand for women workers and the changes in their occupational distribution.[7]

The drastic increase in the number of women in the work force, especially those with family responsibilities, focused national attention on the special problems faced by women workers and prompted some public programs designed to assist them. The most important and controversial of these was the federally subsidized child care system begun under the provisions of the Lanham Act. Although at its peak the program cared for 130,000 children in 3,000 centers, it did not begin to meet the need created by the employment of large numbers of mothers.

If the child care system was inadequate, other programs to provide community services to women workers were, for all practical purposes, nonexistent. As Eleanor Straub has noted, the federal government never created a policy to deal with the mobilization of large numbers of women, relying instead on "a mosaic of experiments, make-shifts, and temporary expedients." The lack of central direction placed added burdens on the local communities, which often lacked the resources, imagination, or experience to devise such programs.[8]

The federal government's failure to deal with the implications of the significantly increased employment of women reflected its preference for voluntarism over social compulsion and, more important, its perception of the war as a temporary, emergency situation from which significant changes were neither wanted nor expected. Yet, in fact, many of the changes created by the war became permanent once the nation had readjusted to peacetime living. Despite public pressure to return to the home and their competitive disadvantages in the marketplace caused by discriminatory union and employer practices, their unfavorable seniority ratings, and preferential hiring of veterans, many women elected to stay in the labor force after the war—even though it meant accepting jobs at skill and pay levels considerably below what they had become accustomed to—as the sex-segregated labor market was reestablished during the reconversion period.[9]

Although the postwar employment rate for women was considerably less than the wartime peak, the labor force participation rate of women over the age of sixteen jumped from 28.9 percent to 33.0 percent during the 1940s and continued to rise thereafter. It reached 37.4 percent in 1960, and by 1968 it was 41.0 percent. Moreover, the wartime transition from a female work force dominated by young, single women to one in which the majority of workers were older and married became a permanent change in the postwar period. Whereas in 1940 41.6 percent of all women workers were over the age of thirty-five, by 1968 women in this age group represented 58.5 percent of the female labor force. The biggest jump in labor force participation during the 1940s occurred among women aged forty-five to fifty-four, whose rate increased from 24.5 to 37.1 percent. Equally significant was the increase in the number of married women working: their labor force participation rate rose from 16.7 percent in 1940, to 24.8 percent in 1950, and 31.7 percent in 1960.[10]

Historians and other scholars disagree on the significance of these changes. In his work, *The American Woman*, William Chafe contends that the changing work habits of American women during and after World War II make the 1940s "a turning point in the history of American women." Chafe does observe, however, that the changes of the postwar period involved serious contradictions. Conventional attitudes regarding woman's place and discriminatory practices against women persisted in the postwar era without generating any significant increase in advocacy of women's rights. In fact, the 1950s witnessed an increased emphasis on home and family life and on traditional femininity. Thus, although American women were taking paid employment to a greater extent than ever before, they were also marrying younger and having larger families. Chafe explains this paradox by noting that Americans were willing to accept women in the work force as long as the changes could not be interpreted as a threat to traditional sex role divisions. Because women's work was justified as a patriotic necessity during the war and as a means of improving the family standard of living afterward, it coincided with other values important to Americans, and thus antifeminist opposition was muted.[11]

Two critics of Chafe's turning point theory question his conclusion that the war promoted an acceleration of trends in women's labor force participation. According to Paddy Quick, labor force statistics exaggerate wartime changes because the 1940 census undercounted discouraged workers, who were predominantly female, with the result that the 1945 statistics represented a more reliable count of working women and a more accurate barometer of women's work preferences. His analysis, however, suffers from his assumption that women's work orientation is solely determined by economic circumstances and his consequent failure to take into account the cultural dimension of women's work decisions and experiences both before and during the war. Although she agrees with Chafe that the postwar period was characterized by an increased propensity among women to work for pay, Leila Rupp in her *Mobilizing Women for War* contends, unconvincingly, that the war had no bearing on this development and that long-term economic trends, including the expansion of the service sector, accounted for the changes.[12]

Not surprisingly, economists investigating the post-1940 period also attribute the changes in the postwar period to ongoing economic forces.

In his *Married Women in the Labor Force: An Economic Analysis*, Glen Cain warns that the "impact of World War II should not be exaggerated." He points out that many of the wives joining the postwar work force were too young to have been in the wartime labor force, indicating that longer-run forces were more important. He fails, however, to pinpoint which forces caused the postwar changes. Juanita Kreps, in *Sex in the Marketplace: American Women at Work*, contends that the postwar labor market had changed significantly in that the demand for workers in traditionally female fields had outstripped growth in other fields. Clarence D. Long's *The Labor Force Under Changing Income and Employment* attributes the rise in females working to the aging of the female population, labor-saving devices, a shorter workweek, and, most importantly, expanding opportunities for women in clerical and service occupations.[13]

Despite their general confidence in the significance of long-term forces in increasing female labor force activity, several economists also expressed confusion over the contradictions of the postwar period. Many circumstances that had historically operated to impede women from working assumed greater importance in the period from 1940 to 1960, creating a perplexing situation. While the real wages for employed adult males grew 36 percent from 1940 to 1956, the employment of wives, which is usually inversely related to husbands' income, also increased substantially. Although the relationship between the presence of children and work rates is consistently negative, the extraordinarily high fertility rates of the period between 1946 and 1960 were accompanied by increasing work rates for women, especially including those with children. Thus, the long-term trends utilized by most economists to explain women's work force activity were modified significantly by postwar events.[14]

Recent historical works on women in the pre-1940 period also stress the importance of prewar trends in beginning the accommodation between women's work and family roles that is especially characteristic of postwar years. According to Winifred Bolin, the decades preceding World War II witnessed the expansion of white-collar work opportunities for middle-class women and the growing acceptance of the values of a consumer society, both of which promoted the entrance of middle-class married women into the labor force. Moreover, they abetted the development of a new concept of family need, which insisted that the maintenance of a certain standard of living was more important than conformity to the dictates of conventional sex role prescriptions. Thus, married women sought paid employment in the 1930s despite a hostile public sentiment and inhospitable economic circumstances. Lois Scharf's study of married women workers during the Depression also supports this thesis, contending that in the 1930s unfavorable circumstances restrained an upward trend in married women's propensity to seek paid work.[15]

It is not necessary, however, to revise notions about the prewar period in order to raise questions about the amount of change generated by the war. Those who doubt the war's liberative effects stress the extent to which wartime circumstances increased the attention and prestige accorded male social roles and contributions, accommodated traditional beliefs and practices even in a theoretically uncongenial situation, and created considerable anxiety regarding the retention of conventional values and roles. Eleanor Straub, for example, in a well-researched and convincingly argued work contends that "the extent to which old institutions, values, and modes of thought remained intact" is more significant than the changes caused by the war. Rupp's study of wartime propaganda also stressed ideological continuity in the war period, pointing out that the appeals used to mobilize women workers emphasized the temporary and aberrant nature of the situation and "allowed the public to accept the participation of women in unusual jobs without challenging basic beliefs about women's roles." Moreover, as Richard Polenberg and others have noted, the changes in women's roles caused by the war created considerable anxiety about the stability and durability of the family, as working mothers were blamed by many for a rising divorce rate, child neglect, an ostensibly increasing rate of juvenile delinquency, and a host of other ills supposedly exacerbated by women's newly acquired independence.[16]

D'Ann Campbell pointed out that the tendency of historians to focus on Rosie the Riveter has distorted the analysis of the nature of wartime changes. Because most American women remained homemakers during the war, Rosie was not the typical wartime woman. Campbell suggests that the wartime housewife, who stayed out of the labor force despite considerable pressure to do otherwise and who experienced great difficulty in accomplishing her traditional tasks, received little real recognition for her efforts and may have undergone considerable status anxiety as a result. The note of condescension in the almost obligatory praise for the homemaker during the war betrayed the fact that the real prestige was conferred only on women who assumed previously male responsibilities, not on those who performed traditionally female functions. An examination of the changes wrought in the homemaker role and the social effects of its deteriorating status is thus important to understanding the contradictions of the postwar period.[17]

Although she was not typical, Rosie could have been in the vanguard of social change for women, and there have been several attempts to explain her failure to assume this role. Lisa Anderson and Sheila Tobias note the extent of private and public discrimination against women workers in the reconversion period and suggest that the war's liberative potential was thwarted by postwar policies. Straub and Alan Clive cite a lack of feminist leadership and, more significantly, the failure of women themselves to lodge important protests against their treatment. In a study of feminist organizations during the war years, Susan Hartmann concludes that within the small women's movement, the continuing divisions based on issues of class and race prevented a unified effort to capitalize on the gains of the war years.[18]

The reservations these works raised regarding the revolutionary effects of the war years suggest that a reliance on labor-force statistics as barometers of the social consequences of war is too simplistic an approach to the question. In order to understand more clearly the significance of the early 1940s, it is important to explore more fully women's daily lives, both at home and on the job, and the cultural response to changing roles for women. The question of the war's effect on women's consciousness of themselves as women and as workers must be addressed, along with the extent to which war-induced innovations promoted an erosion of sexist prejudices. The young women of the war years were raised in the increasingly male-defined post-Jazz Age era, yet the question of the changes they experienced as a result of living in a society with a male deficit remains largely unexplored. In addition, the effects of war on sex role socialization and family structure and role divisions have been treated only cursorily.

This study is an attempt to address these issues by focusing on three major defense production areas—Baltimore, Seattle, and Detroit—and thereby providing a closer examination of the forces contributing to social change and social stability during and after the war. A focus on the local community facilitates a closer examination of the effects of national trends and federal government policies and enables the historian to determine the relative importance of local institutions and cultural values in promoting or impeding an altered social role for women. The three areas selected for this study vary in terms of their peacetime economic structures, their political ideologies, and their religious, ethnic, and social composition. Although they did share in the changes and dislocations caused by defense spending, they diverged in their political and social responses to the problems and opportunities of the war years.

For all three communities, the imperatives of war created myriad problems. Rapid population growth caused by the in-migration of large numbers of people from all areas of the nation created housing shortages and transportation problems, placed added burdens on municipal and commercial services, and contributed to social tensions as new elements were assimilated into the population. Vast community and individual resources were called upon to cope with the new wartime realities, but they frequently proved inadequate in areas where human and physical resources were greatly overtaxed.[19]

Although much attention has been focused on federal policies during the war years, their successful implementation was frequently dependent on local initiative and cooperation. This dependency was most apparent in the areas of greatest controversy, including, for example, any policies that promoted greater racial or sexual equity. In some cases the necessary cooperation was impeded by a general suspicion of federal authority; more frequently, a hostility to the specific goals of the programs and policies being implemented prevented effective action. Because local leaders were often reluctant to countenance fundamental changes in social relations, even on a temporary basis, the myopia, confusion, and contradictions of federal policies were compounded by infighting and inertia at the local level.[20]

The three areas selected for study typified in many ways the experiences of war boom communities. The Detroit-Willow Run area, which included Wayne, Macomb, Oakland, and Washtenaw counties in the State of Michigan, experienced a 400,000-person increase in its labor force as a consequence of its crucial role in the industrial war machine. Described by journalist Agnes Myer as "a no-man's land sprang up, a nightmare of substandard living conditions," Willow Run itself became a symbol for the extreme dislocations fostered by war. The Baltimore area, which included the city of Baltimore, southern Baltimore County, eastern Howard County, and northern Anne Arundel County in Maryland, suffered a chronic labor deficit throughout the war exacerbated by shortages in housing and other basic community services and facilities so serious that there were more out-migrants than in-migrants by mid-war. Smaller than the other two areas under study, the Puget Sound area in the State of Washington, which included King, Pierce, and Kitsap counties, experienced dramatic growth during the war years; its population increased 25.0 percent and its labor force 83.6 percent between April 1940 and May 1944.[21]

By any standards, the Puget Sound area was one of the major war boom communities in the nation. It received $3,450,061,000 in government supply contracts through 1944 and $315,396,000 to finance expansion of local war plants, excluding project orders for the Puget Sound Navy Yard in Bremerton. These contracts alone were worth over ten times as much as products manufactured in King and Pierce counties in 1939. All indices of economic activity, including retail sales, manufacturing employment, and bank debits and deposits, reflected the war-induced expansion. The only brake on the area's growth during the war was its chronic inability to meet its labor requirements; almost anyone who wanted a job could get one and could expect to receive relatively good wages.[22]

Prior to the economic expansion caused by wartime spending, the Puget Sound economy had been based primarily on its position as a commercial center for the Pacific Northwest. Located on the shores of Puget Sound and endowed with a good natural harbor, Seattle served as a collection point for the agricultural products of eastern Washington and the timber resources of the Cascade Mountains and as an outlet to the markets of Alaska and the Far East. In addition, its scenic location between Lake Washington and Puget Sound, with the Cascade and Olympic mountains towering in the distance, made it a center of tourism. As a result, manufacturing was relatively less important and trade and transportation relatively more important in Seattle's economic structure than in other cities of its size. This was true also of Pierce County and its main population center, Tacoma, whose manufacturing sector was limited primarily to the processing of lumber products. In contrast, in Kitsap County, which had by far the smallest population of

the three counties, 38.2 percent of its workers were engaged in manufacturing, primarily shipbuilding in Bremerton and shipbuilding and
timber products in the rest of the county. In the area as a whole, transportation equipment and basic timber industries accounted for over half
of all manufacturing employees.[23]

In 1940 the Puget Sound area was just beginning to recover from
the Great Depresssion, which had affected it even more adversely than
the nation as a whole. Primarily because the area's timber industry was
closely tied to the national construction industry, the area had experienced a severe setback in the early years of the Depression. Throughout
the 1930s the Puget Sound area lagged behind the nation as a whole in
its number of manufacturing employees and value of manufactured
products, relative to 1929. Because of its heavy reliance on timber
products, Tacoma fared the worst in the area, with an unemployment
rate of 16.8 percent as late as 1940. In Bremerton, where the navy yard
had already begun expanding its work force, the unemployment rate
was only 6.9 percent. [24]

Wartime defense spending, however, abruptly reversed the economic
situation for the Seattle area. The war-induced expansion began early;
according to chamber of commerce figures, Seattle had received almost
$600 million in defense contracts by December 1940, and by 1941 it
ranked first among major cities in per capita defense spending. Department store sales reflected the impact of the infusion of capital, rising
30 percent in Seattle and 32 percent in Tacoma between 1940 and
1941.[25]

While many other war boom communities of the nation were converting their local industries from civilian to defense production, Seattle
area defense output relied heavily on the expansion of existing facilities,
especially those in aircraft and shipbuilding, to attract government
contracts. In King County two-thirds of the federal supply contracts
were for aircraft, with most of the rest going for ships. Most of the
federal contracts in Pierce and Kitsap counties were granted for shipbuilding. Between April 1940 and November 1943, the number of
persons employed in shipbuilding and repairs in the area increased
from 8,000 to 92,000, and the number making other transportation
equipment increased from 6,300 to 40,500.[26]

As a result of the great expansion in the transportation industries, the
manufacturing sector of the local economy assumed exaggerated impor-

tance during the war years. Because the defense contractors were given priorities on labor and materials, businesses in other sectors of the economy suffered a relative decline in importance during the war years. While the number of persons holding civilian nonmanufacturing jobs increased by 35.7 percent between April 1940 and November 1943, the number in manufacturing positions more than doubled. Whereas 51.7 percent of King County workers had been employed in service and trade in 1940 and 20.0 percent in manufacturing, by 1944, 37.4 percent were employed in manufacturing and 37.0 percent in service and trade. Logging, mining, and domestic service were especially hard hit by the competitive advantages of war industries.[27]

The expansion of civilian jobs at the various military installations in the area contributed significantly to growth in the nonmanufacturing sectors of the economy. Nonmanufacturing civilian jobs at area installations increased from 1,400 in April 1940 to 26,500 in September 1944. The major government establishments employing large numbers of civilians included the Sand Point Naval Air Station in Seattle, the Seattle Port of Embarkation, and the Army base at Fort Lewis, south of Tacoma. The dramatic growth in government employment as well as shipbuilding and aircraft production underscores the importance of federal defense spending in the area's remarkable economic development during the war years.[28]

A city built on the American love affair with the automobile, Detroit had grown along with the industry that served as its economic backbone. Described as a "one-industry, man-employing city," by 1940 Detroit had a higher proportion of its workers engaged in manufacturing than any other American city of comparable size. While manufacturing jobs engaged 47.1 percent of the Detroit labor force, 17.1 percent were employed in wholesale and retail trade, 6.7 percent in professional and related activities, and 7.3 percent in service work. Almost 65 percent of the manufacturing employees were in the auto industry, with another 15 percent in the related areas of machinery and iron and steel. As a result of the demand created for white male blue-collar workers within the local economy, their entry level wage rates were considerably higher than the national average. Clearly, the economic fate of Detroit was tied inextricably to that of the automakers.[29]

In contrast to the situation in Seattle, war-created expansion in Detroit was predicated on the conversion of existing industries from civilian to military production. Because of the initial resistance of the auto industry to such a conversion, much of the early economic growth of Detroit in the defense period was based on a brisk civilian market for automobiles rather than any defense-related expansion. Although its unemployment rate was still high (14.7 percent) and its proportion of manufacturing employees substantially below that of 1929, Detroit had begun recovering from the Depression in 1939, when the auto industry experienced increasing demand for its products. Citing the high costs and risks of overexpansion and increasing federal intervention in company affairs, the automakers had delayed converting to defense production until federal policies introduced a new element of compulsion and assumed much of the financial risk involved. Despite its slow start, Michigan ranked seventh in defense contracts as early as February 1941.[30]

As was true elsewhere in the nation, the contract allocation policies of the federal government increased the industrial concentration already characteristic of Detroit's economic structure. Between June 1940 and July 1943, Detroit-area war plants received over $11 billion in war contracts, with more than two-thirds of them going to three companies and a subsidiary of one of them. Considering that the value of all products manufactured in the area was less than $3 billion in 1939, federal spending clearly dominated the local economy during the war, with aircraft and aircraft parts accounting for the largest proportion of federal contracts.[31]

As a result of the area's central role in war production, its civilian labor force increased 30 percent, with the 64 percent rise in manufacturing employment coming at the expense of the other sectors of the economy. Attracted by the prospect of high-paying jobs in war industries, thousands of migrants poured into the area, swelling the population by 26 percent during the war years. For some of those hopeful job-seekers the promise of war-generated opportunities was stillborn because employer preference for white male workers remained more intractable in Detroit than elsewhere despite a persistent labor shortage throughout the war.[32]

By contrast with the officials in Baltimore, the business and political leaders in the Detroit area were quite willing to turn to the federal government for financial and other aid during the war on the grounds that the local changes required were a product of national circumstances and that the local government should not be expected to assume the responsibilities or risks involved. Although such a position implied an acceptance of considerable federal authority, local leaders frequently disregarded federal dicta, especially in employment policies. The business leadership of the community demonstrated that its innovations in manufacturing and marketing techniques were not to be replicated in civic affairs. Commenting on the situation, Edsel Ford told Agnes Myer that the corporate leadership of the auto industry had been so preoccupied with its business interests that it had never had the time to develop a sense of civic responsibility.[33]

Filling the gap left by the business leaders was a well-organized, experienced group of private activists who faced extremely difficult problems within their community. A city plagued by racial, religious, and economic antagonisms, Detroit provided a spawning ground for extremists and demagogues of every sort during the war years. Long-standing problems, including violent antipathies between labor and management and a racial hostility whose explosive potential was realized in the bloody race riot of 1943, eclipsed all other social issues. An impediment to full war production, the internecine conflict dividing the city also militated against a translation of the war-induced economic gains into greater equity and opportunity for disadvantaged groups, including blacks and women.[34]

Baltimore had a more diversified economy in the prewar period than did Detroit and Seattle. Because of its location on the Chesapeake Bay, Baltimore had served as an important port since its founding. Later its low rail rates to the West had increased its favorable position as a commercial depot. The growth of industry in the twenty-five years preceding World War II had promoted its transition from a trading to a manufacturing center. By 1940, 29 percent of the civilian labor force in the Baltimore area were employed in manufacturing, while 40 percent were engaged in trades and service occupations. Even within the industrial sector, diversification characterized Baltimore's development; only 24 percent of its manufacturing employees were found in iron and steel work, its largest single industrial category. An additional 26 percent were working in the clothing and food industries, where job opportunities for women were greater than in most manufacturing categories.[35]

Although it still had a 10 percent unemployment rate, Baltimore had made a substantial recovery from the Depression by 1940, experiencing employment gains even in the 1937–39 period, when the nation as a whole slumped. Once the defense period began, Baltimore expanded faster than the national rate and outstripped every comparable Eastern area except Hampton Roads. Unlike Detroit, Baltimore began its war-related expansion early. Between June 1940 and August 1941, Baltimore received nearly $500 million in defense contracts, most in aircraft and shipbuilding. As a result, the number of persons employed in manufacturing rose by 33 percent. By 1945, the area would witness a 20 percent jump in population and a 32 percent increase in its labor force.[36]

Baltimore's pattern of diversification was undermined to some extent by the national demand for ships and aircraft, although the amount of distortion was not as great as elsewhere. By 1945, 42 percent of the area's civilian labor force was employed in manufacturing, with 35 percent remaining in trades and service work. The share of manufacturing workers claimed by the aircraft and shipbuilding industries jumped from 12 percent in 1940 to 39 percent in 1945. Except for the clothing industry, which declined during the war, all manufacturing categories shared in the war-induced expansion. Although some large employers, most notably the Glenn L. Martin Aircraft Company, received a disproportionate share of war contracts, many small operators also benefited from federal allocation policies.[37]

An ethnically diverse city in which blacks represented about one-fifth of the population, Baltimore maintained throughout the war a surface harmony in social relationships that was based on a settled system of racial accommodation and control rather than any progress toward equality. As noted in Hamilton Owen's sympathetic history of Baltimore, the city was Northern in its commercial and industrial life but Southern in its social relations. Blacks in Baltimore represented a reservoir of unskilled labor available to fill the least desirable jobs and to prevent successful unionization, thus keeping wage levels low. A determination to maintain this situation despite the wartime labor shortage fueled some employer resistance to federally mandated open employment policies.[38]

A stubborn insistence on doing things in their own way characterized public and private actions in Baltimore throughout the war, much to the despair of federal officials. An Office of Community War Services report in 1943 observed that Baltimore was noted for disregarding the advice of outsiders and rather automatically refusing to follow the examples of other communities confronting similar situations. The OCWS recreation adviser in Baltimore, P. N. Binford, complained constantly about the discourtesy and hostility of Baltimore officials to federal authorities. Ironically, Baltimore's insistence that problem solving was best left to local and private groups belied its own inertia in dealing with war-created difficulties.[39]

The wartime boom transformed communities almost overnight, creating a situation conducive to rapid and significant changes in social and economic institutions. At the same time, however, it produced an artificial economic context with an uncertain legacy for the postwar period and serious social strains whose imperatives sometimes inhibited innovations in the social structure. The purpose of this study is to examine the nature and degree of the wartime changes as they affected the status of women and the development of family life and values and thus to aid in determining the importance of the war as a force for social change.

Notes

1. William Chafe, *The American Woman: Her Changing Social, Economic, and Political Roles, 1920-1970* (New York: Oxford University Press, 1972), pp. 135—95; Leila Rupp, *Mobilizing Women for War: German and American Propaganda, 1939-1945* (Princeton: Princeton University Press, 1978); Paddy Quick, "Rosie the Riveter: Myths and Realities," *Radical America* 9 (July-August 1975); Sheila Tobias and Lisa Anderson, "Whatever Happened to Rosie the Riveter?" *Ms.* (June 1973); Eleanor Straub, "Government Policy Toward Civilian Women During World War II" (Ph.d. diss., Emory University, 1973); Joan Ellen Trey, "Women in the War Economy," *Review of Radical Political Economics*, 4 (July 1972).

2. Peggy R. Sanday, "Female Status in the Public Domain," in *Woman, Culture, and Society*, Michelle Rosaldo and Louise Lamphere, ed. (Stanford, Calif.: Stanford University Press, 1974), pp. 189-206; Carl Degler, "The Changing Place of Women in America," in *The Woman Question in American History*, ed. Barbara Welter. (Hinsdale, Ill.: Dryden Press, 1973), pp. 138-39.

3. Chafe, pp. 135-46; U.S. Department of Commerce, Bureau of the Census, *Current Population Reports: Labor Force*, Series P-57, No. 60, "The Monthly Report of the Labor Force", June 10, 1947, Table 1.

4. U.S. Department of Labor, Women's Bureau, Bulletin No. 211, "Employment of Women in the Early Postwar Period with Background of Prewar and

War Data" (Washington, D.C.: Government Printing Office, 1946) [hereafter cited as WBB 211], pp. 10-11; International Labour Office, *The War and Women's Employment: The Experience of the United Kingdom and the United States* (Montreal: International Labor Office, 1946), p. 176.

5. WBB 211, p. 7; International Labor Office, p. 175; *Employment Security Review* (October 1942): 1; *Monthly Labor Review* (November 1945): 845.

6. WBB 211, pp. 4, 5; U.S. Department of Labor, Women's Bureau, Bulletin No. 209, "Women Workers in Ten War Production Areas and Their Postwar Employment Plans," (Washington, D.C.: Government Printing Office, 1946), pp. 37, 38 [hereafter cited as WBB 209].

7. Chafe, pp. 154-58; International Labour Office, pp. 218-23.

8. Chafe, pp. 158-72; National Manpower Council, *Womanpower* (New York: Columbia University Press, 1957), p. 147; U.S. Office of War Information, "Advance Release," August 9, 1943, Women's Bureau Archives, RG 86, Box 1540, National Archives, Washington, D.C.; Eleanor Straub, "United States Government Policy Toward Civilian Women During World War II," *Prologue* (Winter 1973): 254.

9. Straub, "United States Government," *Prologue*, 254; WBB 211, p. 13; "Employment of Women— Notes for Use of Staff," February 11, 1946, RG 86, Box 1536, NA; Mary Waggaman, *Women Workers in Wartime and Reconversion* (New York: Paulist Press, 1947), pp. 4-9.

10. U.S. Department of Labor, Women's Bureau, Bulletin No. 294, "Handbook on Women Workers" (Washington, D.C., Government Printing Office, 1969), pp. 10, 17, 18, 26.

11. Chafe, pp. 194-95, 217-25; U.S., Department of Labor, Bureau of Labor Statistics, *Handbook of Labor Statistics* (Washington, D.C.: Government Printing Office, 1973), p. 28.

12. Quick, pp. 115-32; Rupp, pp. 176-181.

13. Glen Cain, *Married Women in the Labor Force: An Economic Analysis* (Chicago: University of Chicago Press, 1966), pp. 43, 118, 119; Clarence D. Long, *The Labor Force Under Changing Income and Employment* (Princeton: Princeton University Press, 1958), p. 268; Juanita Kreps, *Sex in the Marketplace: American Women at Work* (Baltimore: Johns Hopkins University Press, 1971), pp. 34-38.

14. Cain, pp. 1, 16, 118; Long, pp. 117, 207; Kreps, p. 20; Valerie K. Oppenheimer, *The Female Labor Force in the United States* (Berkley: University of California Press, 1970), pp. 25-29, 36, 37.

15. Winifred Bolin, "Past Ideals and Present Pleasures: Women, Work and the Family, 1920-1940" (Ph.D. diss., University of Minnesota, 1976); Lois Scharf, "The Employment of Married Women During the Depression, 1929-1941" (Ph.D. diss., Case Western Reserve University, 1977).

16. Straub, "Government Policy Toward Civilian Women," pp. 162, 358; Rupp, pp. 175-81; Susan Hartmann, "Women's Organizations During World War II: The Interaction of Class, Race, and Feminism" (paper presented at the convention of the Organization of American Historians, April 1978); Richard Polenberg, *War and Society: The U.S., 1941-1945* (Philadelphia: Lippincott, 1972).

17. D'Ann Campbell, "Unorganized Women: Housewives in World War II" (paper presented at the convention of the Organization of American Historians, April 1978).

18. Tobias and Anderson; Straub, "Government Policy," p. 358; Alan Clive, "The Society and Economy of Wartime Michigan, 1939-1945" (Ph.D. diss., University of Michigan, 1976), pp. 540-46; Hartmann, passim.

19. U.S., Department of Labor, Bureau of Labor Statistics, "Impact of the War on the Detroit Area," Industrial Area Study No. 10, July 1943, Records of the Office of Community War Services [hereafter cited as OCWS], War Area Reports and Correspondence [hereafter cited as WARC], RG 215, Box 10, National Archives, Washington, D.C. [hereafter cited as "Impact of the War on the Detroit Area"]; U.S., Department of Labor, Bureau of Labor Statistics, "The Impact of the War on the Seattle-Tacoma Area," Industrial Area Study No. 19, January 1945, National Archives, Washington, D.C. [hereafter cited as "Impact of the War on the Seattle-Tacoma Area"].

20. "Some Observations on the Federal Program for Care of Children of Employed Mothers," Mary Keeley, Day Care Division, OCWS, December 29, 1943, OCWS, Director's Subject File, RG 215, Box 2, NA.

21. 'Impact of the War on the Detroit Area"; "Impact of the War on the Seattle-Tacoma Area"; Agnes Myer, *Journey Through Chaos* (New York: Harcourt, Brace, 1943), p. 34; Supplementary Report on War Area, Baltimore, Maryland, July 10, 1943, OCWS, Community Reports, RG 215, Box 4, NA.

22. Seattle Chamber of Commerce, *The Postwar Labor Market in the Seattle Area* (Seattle: Chamber of Commerce, 1944), p. 12; Dun and Bradstreet, Inc., "Seattle: Study of Economic and Financial History of Seattle," 1948, pp. 18, 22; *Northwest Industry* (December 1943): 2, 3, and (March 1948): 108; U.S., War Manpower Commission, "Adequacy of Labor Supply in Important Labor Market Areas," April 1, 1944, October 1, 1944, July 1, 1945; "Impact of the War on the Seattle-Tacoma Area," pp. 2, 60, 67.

23. "Impact of the War on the Seattle-Tacoma Area," pp. 1, 6, 8, 61-63, 66.

24. Ibid., pp. 6, 8, 9.

25. *Seattle Times,* July 24, 1941, August 10, 1941, September 24, 1941; *Seattle Business,* December 19, 1940; Grant I. Butterbaugh, "A Review of Business Activity in the Puget Sound Area for the Year 1941," *Northwest Industry* (January 1942); 6-9; "Impact of the War on the Seattle-Tacoma Area," p. 43.

26. University of Washington, Bureau of Business Research, *Federal Expenditures in Washington* (Seattle: University of Washington Press, 1956), pp. 36, 38; Butterbaugh, pp. 6, 7; *Seattle Business*, August 1, 1940; "Impact of the War on the Seattle-Tacoma Area," pp. 2, 60.

27. Seattle Chamber of Commerce, *The Postwar Labor Market in the Seattle Area*, pp. 12, 13; "Impact of the War on the Seattle-Tacoma Area", p. 60; Washington, Employment Security Division, *Labor Force and Employment*, August 1947, p. 4, Washington State Library.

28. "Impact of the War on the Seattle-Tacoma Area," pp. 2, 41; "Composite Report on the Puget Sound Area," May 15, 1944, pp. 41, 46, OCWS, RG 215, Box 17, NA.

29. Tobias and Anderson, p. 92; "Impact of the War on the Detroit Area."

30. "Impact of the War on the Detroit Area"; Clive, pp. 57, 64-70.

31. "Impact of the War on the Detroit Area."

32. Ibid.

33. *Detroit News*, February 1, 1942; Clive, pp. 118, 223, 372; Myer, p. 40.

34. "Detroit is Dynamite," *Life*, May 17, 1942; Clive, pp. 381, 438.

35. Consolidated Gas Electric Light and Power Company of Baltimore, *Second Industrial Survey of Baltimore* (Baltimore: Consolidated Gas Electric Light and Power Company of Baltimore, 1939); Hamilton Owens, *Baltimore on the Chesapeake* (Garden City, N.Y.: Doubleday, Doran, 1941), pp. 5-7, 22, 317; Labor Market Developments Report, Baltimore, November, 1945, Records of Bureau of Employment Security [hereafter cited as BES], RG 183, Box 162, National Archives, Washington, D.C.

36. "Recent Migration Into Baltimore, Maryland," November 14, 1941, FWA, BES, RG 183, Box 165, NA; "Preliminary Report," Baltimore Area, War and Post-War, April, 1942, OCWS, Community Reports, RG 215, Box 4, NA, "Supplementary Report on War Area, Baltimore, Maryland," July 10, 1943, OCWS, Community Reports, RG 215, Box 4, NA.

37. Ibid.

38. "Summary Report, Baltimore Labor Market Area," May 9, 1942, OCWS, WARC, RG 215, Box 7, NA; Owens, pp. 3, 317.

39. "Summary Report, Baltimore Labor Market Area," May 9, 1942, OCWS, WARC, RG 215, Box 7, NA; Baltimore, Maryland, December 10, 1943, OCWS, General Classified, Maryland (Region IV), RG 215, Box 124, NA; Memo, P. N. Binford to John Neasmith, March 2, 1943, OCWS, General Classified, Maryland (Region IV), RG 215, Box 124, NA.

2

"WOMAN'S PLACE IS IN THE HOME —AND IN THE FACTORY, TOO"

The rapid expansion of local economies while large numbers of young men were being withdrawn into the armed forces created a labor shortage so severe that it facilitated a rapid improvement in the status of women in the labor force. The war years thus provide an indication of the strength of prejudice in the face of economic trends subversive of traditional employer and cultural biases in favor of white male workers. By 1943, the shortage of preferred workers had toppled many sex, race, and age barriers, creating jobs for those previously considered hard to place and opening up many traditionally male fields to women. As a result, women could choose from many more types of work and command considerably higher wages than before. The greatly increased number of women in unionized jobs were able to take advantage of the improved pay and working conditions provided by union contracts. Although the greatest benefits accrued to women engaged in previously male work, many women employed in traditionally female fields also benefited from their new competitive labor market position and experienced improvements in wage levels and working conditions.

Although the economy operated more nearly equally in regard to women during the war than at any time before, many employers persisted in discriminatory practices, even in the face of unmet labor requirements. Some refused to hire women while many others set unnecessarily low hiring quotas for women or were unimaginative and inflexible in assigning women to tasks previously undertaken only by men. For women with labor market liabilities in addition to that of sex, job prospects diminished appreciably. Thus, young white women experienced considerably more mobility during the war than older or minority group women.[1]

In the early stages of the war boom, however, traditional ideas as to appropriate sex role divisions worked to inhibit the employment of women. The belief that men should be the primary or sole bread-winners in the family was especially significant in limiting women's job opportunities as long as unemployed men were still available to fill labor needs. In January 1942, the *Seattle Times* editorialized against any immediate hiring of women because "it is fairly obvious that the chance of a man to get a job may be delayed if a woman gets there first." A letter to the editor of the *Seattle Star* from "C.J.N." supported this position, adding, "I don't want my wife to take a man's job as long as I am still able to work for our living." Masculine pride in the role of provider was also evidenced in a letter from Walter V. Marquis, who commented, "I never let my wife work, and I know she is a far sweeter woman than many women who have been coarsened by having to get out in the business world. I say, let's keep the women out of industry and out of the war."[2]

Hampered by these conventional attitudes, women found their competitive disadvantages in the labor market further increased because most of the job openings were in employment classifications traditionally reserved to men. The greatest labor demand came in the manu-facturing sector, especially in skilled positions, which required appropriate training and experience. In Baltimore, for example, 90 percent of the new jobs in shipbuilding immediately after Pearl Harbor were for skilled workers. Moreover, the nature of the changeover to war production created male unemployment in those industries being curtailed or converted. This was especially true in Detroit, where auto industry shutdowns in early 1942 cost thousands their jobs and created a special initial demand for skilled workers to undertake the necessary retooling.[3]

Because of the legacy of the sex-segregated dual labor system in the American economy, the skills and experience of the women seeking work did not match the requirements of most of the openings. Women in the labor force in the areas under study were heavily concentrated in low-paying, traditionally female fields, such as retail trade and domestic service. Only 10.7 percent of the persons employed in manufacturing in the Seattle-Tacoma area in 1940 were women; the comparable figures were 11.1 percent and 19.8 percent for the Detroit and Baltimore metropolitan areas, respectively, with the higher proportion in the latter accounted for by the relative importance of textiles, foods, and other light industries in the Baltimore area manufacturing sector. Of the 4,324 women registered as available for work in the active file of the Seattle office of the United States Employment Service in April 1941, only 244 were listed as being qualified for skilled manufacturing work, and fully two-thirds of them were over forty-five years of age. In Detroit, only 593 unemployed women were designated as skilled industrial workers, and most of them were dressmakers.[4]

It was not only the lack of the requisite skills that prevented women from benefiting from the economic upturn of the early defense period. Unconvinced that the level of growth would be so extensive as to exhaust available male labor supplies and skeptical of women's ability to undertake work requiring physicial strength or mechanical aptitude, employers refused to modify traditional hiring practices. They also cited the costs of providing facilities for women workers and of reeingineering industrial equipment so that it could be readily utilized by women as reasons for their discriminatory policies. As a result, women were among the last hired in the early stages of the war boom. Over 90 percent of the 17,239 requests for employees made to the Seattle Employment Service in 1941 were for men only. During the conversion period in the first half of 1942, women workers accounted for only 12 percent of the employment increase in Detroit.[5]

The slowness of employers in hiring women caused a corresponding lag in the opening of federally sponsored vocational training courses to women. Because federal appropriations for defense training had required that training programs be tied to the specific needs of defense contractors, the refusal of such contractors to hire women contributed to women's exclusion from vocational programs. Nationally, women accounted for only 32,075 of the 687,697 enrolled in preemployment and refresher courses by the end of February 1942. Because of the dislocations created by Detroit's late conversion to war production, women were still barred from defense courses operated by the Detroit schools as late as April 1942. Prior to Pearl Harbor, women were also excluded from the federal program centered in Seattle's public schools and limited to training as waitresses in the Seattle National Youth Administration job training center.[6]

Once the nation entered the war, however, hesitant steps were taken to equip the women of Baltimore and Seattle with the job skills they would need to contribute to wartime production requirements. On December 14, 1941, Baltimore officials decided not to accept any more men for defense training courses in aircraft riveting, small parts assembly, and related skills because the men would be vulnerable to the draft. At the time, women constituted approximately 1 percent of the enrollment in Maryland vocational training courses. In January 1942, Washington State Superintendent of Public Instruction Pearl Wanamker announced that a limited number of women would be trained for the aircraft industry in the state's vocational program. Within three months the first thirty women to finish the training had taken their places on the assembly lines at the Boeing Aircraft Plant in Seattle. It was not until mid-1942 that large numbers of women were recruited for the aircraft classes and that shipfitting classes were opened for women wanting to work in the shipyards.[7]

These developments were a product of the realization that the pool of available men was rapidly being exhausted while the demand for workers was skyrocketing. Despite the insistence of federal officials that employers rely on locally available labor supply, employer preference for in-migrant white male workers continued in the early war period. The acute housing shortage and strains on municipal services created by the already large in-migration to defense centers meant that a further reliance on imported labor contributed to further social dislocations and an unnecessary level of civilian deprivation. In Baltimore and, to a lesser extent, Detroit, the unsatisfactory living conditions caused by rapid growth and wartime shortages made the retention of in-migrant workers a growing problem; many decided to leave when they could not find adequate housing for their families or found the difficulties of living in a war boom community not worth the work opportunities. Baltimore officials estimated that 35,000 people migrated to Baltimore in the first eight months of 1944, while 61,000 left the area.[8]

Thus, employers were ultimately forced to abandon some of their discriminatory policies. In Detroit, for example, Ford Motor Company and the other automakers finally gave women access to the single largest source of employment in the area when they agreed to hire them for production work. As a result, women constituted 90.8 percent of the new hires in 185 Detroit war plants by February 1943. Similar changes occurred across the nation as women increased their share of industrial jobs from 14.6 percent in May 1942 to 27.2 percent in May 1943.[9]

While demand for women workers was increasing, however, numerous disincentives were operating to limit the available female labor force. The high male wages and declining availability of consumer goods meant that economic pressure was becoming less important in women's work decisions. Women in the preferred younger age groups were marrying and having children in greater numbers, thus assuming greater family responsibilities and becoming less likely to be available for employment. Cultural biases, including the social stigma attached to factory work for women and to married women working outside the home, had to be overcome. Many women were also afraid that factory work was too heavy or dirty for them to do. Moreover, many married women feared that announcing their availability for work or taking a job would jeopardize their husbands' draft status.[10]

Various expedients, including propaganda campaigns and registration drives, were tried to enlist the required number of women. All three cities launched door-to-door solicitation drives to survey prospective workers and encourage women to take war jobs. These drives involved thousands of hours of volunteer work, mostly done by women, and accomplished very little. The Baltimore survey began with 259,850 questionnaires and directly yielded 255 women referred to war jobs and thirty-two in training courses. Seattle and Detroit reported equally discouraging results from their registration campaigns. Other efforts, however, were more successful. Baltimore experimented with the establishment of three neighborhood recruitment centers, one of which was for blacks, and a War Manpower Commission–sponsored heavy propaganda campaign. Despite the participation of Martin Aircraft, the largest single employer of women in wartime Baltimore, which sent representatives to the centers to answer questions and demonstrate the kind of work women were doing at the plant, the publicity campaign was much more successful than the centers.[11]

In addition to patriotism, which figured prominently in mobilization themes in Baltimore and elsewhere, the availability of economic opportunities, a glamorization of war work, a stress on women's capacities for nontraditional work, and attempts to allay specific fears regarding women and industrial work characterized recruitment programs. Ads for Martin Aircraft, for example, contended that "work at Martin's is simplified, light and your co-workers are young, congenial." In Seattle an advertisement sponsored by I. Magnin & Company attempted to reassure women that they were physically capable of factory work, observing that "an American homemaker with the strength and ability to run a house and raise a family . . . has the strength and ability to take her place in a vital War industry." Not only that, but according to Martin war work was "a lot more exciting than polishing the family furniture." In its zeal to attract women workers, Martin also claimed that its pay was high, promotion for women rapid, and that women would have a postwar future at Martin.[12]

Not surprisingly, mobilization literature also stressed a woman's duty to take a war job, if at all possible, in order to do her part in the war effort. A Boeing advertisement pointed out, "The Fortresses—and the men who fly them—are fighting for you—your home—all the things you hold dear," and then asked, "Are you doing your part?" Newspaper stories described the various industrial jobs women were taking on and praised them for their help in "bringing their menfolk back home alive." "Sister, you'd better reform" was the message the *Baltimore News Post* had for Baltimore women in a 1943 editorial. Citing with approval an article in *Vogue*, the newspaper agreed with author Philip Wylie that women's record of homefront sacrifice had better match up to that of the men in the battle zones.[13]

Although patriotism was certainly an important inducement for many women to sign up for war work, it was only one of many motivations for such actions. Economic necessity, the excitement and challenge of war work, the need to cope with the loneliness and anxiety caused by having husbands and sons overseas, a disaffection from housework, a desire for more social independence, the sense of purpose accompanying productive work, and other such personal considerations complemented the desire to help in the war effort. Seattle city bus driver Josephine Bucklin typified the complex motivations of her peers, commenting, "We do feel we're doing something concrete for the war effort," and adding, "Besides that, it's thrilling work, and exciting, and something women have never been allowed to do before."[14]

For some women the war provided an opportunity for a socially sanctioned respite from full-time housework. A hand driller employed at Eastern Aircraft in Baltimore told a Women's Bureau representative that she needed diversion when her husband entered the service and that "staying at home—emotionally and temperamentally does not suit me." Another Baltimore woman, who had quit her factory job at her husband's insistence, told the interviewer that her return to domesticity had made her so nervous and irritable that her doctor ordered her back to work. Similarly, a government secretary in Detroit commented, "[I] would just die if I had to stay home and keep house." Freda Philbrick, who worked at the Puget Sound Navy Yard, observed that "somehow the kitchen lacks the glamor of a bustling shipyard."[15]

Financial necessity or the desire to improve their economic circumstances provided a dominant motive for many of the women who entered war industries. Evelyn Knight, a former cook, signed on at the Navy Yard because "after all, I've got to keep body and soul together, and I'd rather earn a living this way than to cook over a hot stove." A Baltimore machine operator found her new job a welcome relief from the drudgery and insecurity of her previous life as a coal miner's wife in West Virginia. For Josephine Palmer, a widow and mother of twelve children, the war boom provided the means to put her children through school. Many others, including Leola Hougland, a welder at Associated Shipyards in Seattle, and Mary Guinn, a lumber mill worker, worked to pay for the family home. Josephine McKee, a mother of nine employed at Boeing, typified those who took advantage of the new opportunities for women to pay off bills accumulated in less prosperous times. Of those interviewed by the Women's Bureau, many indicated that the illness or disability of husbands and fathers made it necessary for them to work.[16]

Although the range of motives inducing women to take war jobs remained the same from place to place, the relative importance of specific incentives varied. This was especially true in the area of economic necessity, which seemed to be a more significant factor in Baltimore and Detroit than in Seattle, where the general population and the female labor force in particular was more often white, middle-class, and well-educated than in the other two cities. Among those working women living in family groups and contributing regularly to family expenses, the Women's Bureau found that Seattle women used 59 percent of their earnings for family requirements; in Detroit and Baltimore the figures were 62 and 64 percent, respectively. The discrepancy was especially pronounced in regard to single women, whose responsibility for family maintenance was considerably less in the Pacific Northwest defense area. In all three cities, however, over 90 percent of the women workers living in family groups contributed systematically to family upkeep, accustoming their families to the increased financial security and material comforts that their additional income could provide.[17]

Women's wartime earnings accelerated income and property mobility for American women and their families. Among the economic goals most frequently mentioned by working women were the purchase of home, land, business, or furniture. Although it is impossible to determine the extent to which their plans were realized, that they were in some cases is clear. In Baltimore, for example, the proportion of owner-occupied dwelling units, fueled by the increased wartime earnings of both men and women, rose from 43 percent in 1940 to 51 percent in 1947. Once financial obligations for a home, farm, or other possessions were assumed, a second income in the family could remain a necessity long into the postwar period. Thus, the reassessment of the concept of family need, which began in the decades prior to the war, was accelerated by the wartime boom and its economic opportunities for women. The material dimension of the American dream was expensive, and even husbands initially hostile to their wives' employment could find the financial benefits quite seductive, with the result that traditional mores and family patterns were further undermined.[18]

In order to encourage the fullest utilization of women workers, the War Manpower Commission and the Women's Bureau did yeoman work to overcome the objections of employers to the hiring of women. They did studies of the technology and skills required for certain operations and the changes that could be made through job breakdown and reengineering so that women could be introduced into heretofore male industrial job classifications. They also did surveys in similar plants located elsewhere to determine which jobs women could do. Moreover, they encouraged local employers to undertake their own experiments. When the provision of guidance and reassurance was insufficient for its purposes, the WMC also used its labor stabilization program as an incentive for the hiring of women by putting ceilings on the number of males who could be hired and leaving the maximum number of women to be hired at the discretion of the employer. The latter policy, instituted late in the war, had little impact on employment opportunities for women.[19]

Because of the WMC's reliance on voluntary compliance and its resultant willingness to accept discriminatory job orders, many employers continued their unreasoning attitudes long after the male labor supply was exhausted, sacrificing output to prejudice. This was especially true in Detroit, where war plants were chronically understaffed in the last eighteen months of the war while some women remained unemployed. As late as May 1943, a Detroit USES study showed that 70 percent of the employer's orders specified men for semiskilled work that could be done by women. The following February, Detroit employment officials received 8,462 employer requests for male workers and only 144 for women in the unskilled job categories.[20]

The problem of female unemployment in Detroit, which began at least as early as January 1944, was a product of the strong prejudice in favor of male workers, whom the automakers were certain they could acquire by encouraging in-migration, and a calculated attempt on the part of the automakers to ensure an oversupply of labor (male) in the postwar period. Joblessness among women was intensified by the fact that women were more likely than men to lose their jobs when war industries completed government contracts and were forced to lay off workers. Employment officials reported special difficulties in placing these women, who had industrial experience, because they refused to accept jobs in the understaffed service sector as long as better-paid factory work was still available, if only to men.[21]

As a result of the differences in local economic structures, the availability of male labor, and the extent of employer willingness to hire women in nontraditional work, market demand for women workers varied from place to place during the war years, as did the proportion of women hired in various industries. In shipbuilding, for example, the proportion of women hired ranged from 4 percent in Baltimore to 16 percent in Seattle. The discrepancy between the figures for the two cities is largely explained by the greater availability of previously excluded black male workers for the heavy shipyards work in Baltimore. In Detroit, where aircraft production was hampered by the labor shortage, the proportion of women in such jobs reached only 20 percent, with employers contending that any greater concentration was not feasible. At Boeing Aircraft in Seattle, however, women comprised 47 percent of the labor force and would have reached an even greater proportion had not a system of branch plants and subcontracting made it unnecessary.[22]

Even within the same city, employer policies varied greatly. In Baltimore, the proportion of women among total employees ranged from 19 percent at Bartlett-Hayward to 59 percent at American Hammered Piston Ring. Women's share of jobs in the private shipyards of Seattle ranged from 1.8 percent at Todd-Seattle Dry Docks to 21 percent at Associated Shipbuilders.[23]

Despite the persistence of discrimination in the war centers, the wartime economy provided the first serious assault on the sex-segregated labor market in the areas under study. For the first time ever larger numbers of women were taking jobs as welders, riveters, security guards, cab drivers, and in a variety of other hitherto male occupations. Women became a significant part of the labor force in the aircraft plants, lumber mills, foundries, shipyards, and many other industries. The number of women employed in manufacturing in Baltimore rose from 26,100 to 78,600 between 1940 and 1945; the figures for the Seattle-Tacoma area jumped from 6,200 to 40,800 in the same period. In the latter area, the shipyards alone accounted for over 10,000 women workers in 1943. Reflecting the unusual importance of manufacturing in its local economy, Detroit registered the largest absolute increase among women factory workers with a wartime growth from 46,800 to 215,000.[24]

The gains that some experienced in the manufacturing sector came partially at the expense of the trade and service sectors, which generally were not competitive with war industries in terms of the pay level or the patriotic sanction accorded the work. In Seattle the percentage of working women employed in manufacturing increased from 11 percent to 33 percent, while trade and service jobs experienced a decline from 67 percent to 42 percent of women workers. Compared to Detroit and Baltimore, however, Seattle remained a city where traditional female-employing work claimed a sizable share of the women workers. Manufacturing jobs, which occupied a larger proportion of women workers in the two eastern cities prior to the war, claimed 48 percent of the female labor force in Baltimore and 56 percent in Detroit by 1944.[25]

Of the traditionally female fields, only clerical jobs maintained a majority of their prewar workers and managed to attract a significant proportion of the new women workers. The field remained attractive because it had shorter hours than factory jobs, was less strenuous physically than the assembly lines, offered the status of a white-collar job, provided more job security than the war-inflated manufacturing sector, and, at least among those employed by war industries, managed to keep its pay competitve with that for factory operatives. The pay differential was smallest in Seattle, where clerical workers' take-home earnings in the war plants averaged $36.25 a week and those working on assembly lines averaged $39.90 a week. Despite these incentives and the relative popularity of the work, the demand for office workers exceeded the supply throughout the war because of the tremendous expansion in this job category. The shortage was especially acute for civilian employers because the federal government had raised its wages and lowered job quality standards in order to attract the office help it required. This created special problems in Baltimore, which competed for workers with the Washington, D.C., economy.[26]

In contrast to the clerical workers, women in the poorly paid fields of service and trade reacted to the widening of their options by leaving their jobs in great numbers. Some quit their jobs to allow their husbands to provide support for the family; others took industrial or office jobs. In Seattle the war years witnessed the shift of 62 percent of the women who had been employed in sales before the war and 54 percent of those in service to other occupational groups. Except for those employed in eating and drinking places, pay scales for women employed in trade and service were considerably lower than for factory operatives. Women employed in the retail and wholesale trade in Seattle, for example, made an average of $26.40 a week in take-home pay. Not surprisingly, these factors indicate that women were responding to labor market mechanisms in the same way that men did; high wages and higher status attracted them from other sectors or into the labor force for the first time. Although many patriotic exhortations were made in order to get women to shore up the labor-starved service and trade sectors, they consistently refused to do so as long as wages there remained low.[27]

The effects of these changes in the distribution of women workers were felt early; by February 1942, R. W. Dale, president of the Washington State Restaurant Association, was announcing a shortage of waitresses. According to Dale, Seattle alone needed 400 to 500 immediately. Despite efforts to raise wage levels and institute part-time work shifts, an estimated one-third of the restaurants in Detroit had closed by late 1943, and other retail establishments had had to curtail services. Although the situation was less drastic in Baltimore, which experienced initial gains in employment in traditional female-employing service jobs in the defense period, it was also faced with personnel shortages in laundries, hotels, and other retail outlets by mid-1943.[28]

Even domestic servants experienced considerable widening of opportunities as a consequence of the war boom. This was especially true in Seattle, where service was not so fully an adjunct of the system of racial control as elsewhere. By April 1942, the Seattle office of the USES had discontinued placing persons as domestic workers and was referring those formerly employed as domestics to war industry jobs. In Baltimore, by contrast, local employment officials continued to refer black women for service jobs despite the persistent female labor shortage and the complaints from black women regarding this form of discrimination. For those women who took such work, the conditions of their employment improved dramatically during the war. In Baltimore, wage levels rose from $8-12 a week in the prewar period to $18-25 by late 1943, and the number of hours worked declined from seventy-two to fifty a week. Nevertheless, the number of Baltimore women employed as domestics declined by about one-half during the war, and many of them were in-migrants accepting such work as a stopgap measure.[29]

The exodus of women from service jobs created difficulties for other women who also desired to take advantage of high-paying war industry jobs. Historically, when men have entered the labor force they have relied on the unpaid labor of their wives or the poorly paid labor of women in service and trade jobs to take care of such household duties as cooking, cleaning, laundry, and child care. When economic opportunities outside of traditionally female fields opened up for women, they had nowhere to turn for such services. Nora Eck, an assistant manager at a Seattle employment agency, said that no one was available for work as domestic servants, adding, "Although we have hundreds of requests every week, sometimes frantic, tearful ones, we simply have no one to place." The lack of such services thus deterred some women from seeking employment and greatly inconvenienced others who did work.[30]

For a few women, notably those with college degrees in mathematics, engineering, and other scientific or technical fields, the wartime economy provided opportunities for professional jobs that would otherwise have been closed to them. By September 1942, the Seattle Boeing plant had five women employed as engineers. Martin aircraft marvelled in a 1944 ad that "even Engineering is done by girls." After holding out as long as it could, the Puget Sound Navy Yard hired eight women to do drafting work in March 1943. Soon thereafter an on-the-job drafting course was begun for selected women employees, which, when completed, led to a promotion to junior engineering draftsman. In addition, the yard employed fifteen women as chemists. In Detroit, the Lawrence Institute of Technology opened its doors to women for the first time, offering a free course in drafting, and was inundated with applicants. Generally, however, women's share of such technical work remained small during the war years. In 1943, the University of Maryland program designed to meet shortages of engineers, chemists, physicists, and production supervisors numbered only 912 women among its 7,836 enrollees.[31]

The occupational changes experienced by women during the war years meant improved pay, a greater range of choice regarding their work, and a somewhat enhanced status within American society. Because their traditional wage levels were so low, women frequently experienced a greater proportional increase in their earnings than did male workers. A study done in 1945 of some workers at the Willow Run Bomber Plant revealed that one-third of the women experienced pay increases of at least 100 percent, while only one-ninth of the men could report such a gain. Moreover, the woman who took a war job shared in the status accorded male activities because she was doing "men's" work and because she was providing essential support to that most important of male undertakings, the making of war. As *Life* put it in 1942, the woman war worker had "acquired some of the glamor of the man in uniform."[32]

Despite the opening of new job categories to women, the war did not eliminate the segregation of work by sex within the American labor force. The Detroit Edison Company's response to the labor shortage typified employer reaction to the prospect of hiring women. The utility decided to shift some men out of clerical work, substituting women for them, and to use women in light indoor work when it became necessary to hire them in nontraditional categories. Although many women in production jobs worked equally alongside men, industrial employers continued to categorize work by sex to the extent that circumstances allowed, placing women in jobs requiring dexterity, concentration, and speed and shifting men to heavier and more skilled work. In addition, service, clerical, and other work historically done by women retained their "feminine" labels.[33]

In addition to changing the occupational distribution of women workers, the wartime economy also altered the composition of the female labor force. In light of the fact that from 45 to 54 percent of the women employed in the war centers under study had not been in the labor force before the war, these changes should not be surprising. As was true among working women in the nation as a whole, the female labor forces in these areas changed from the prewar pattern, in which single women predominated, to a pattern in which married women constituted the largest group, as in Seattle and Detroit, or substantially closed the gap with single women, as in Baltimore. Married women, especially those engaged as homemakers prior to the war, constituted an especially important element of the work force in wartime Seattle, largely because it also experienced the most drastic proportional increase in the female labor force of the three cities. While the percentage of all women in the Seattle labor force jumped from 33.4 percent in 1940 to 47.4 percent in 1944, the labor force participation rate of married women almost doubled with an increase from 15.7 to 29.8 percent. According to a Women's Bureau study, 54 percent of the Seattle-area female work force was married, while the figures for Baltimore and Detroit were 43 and 45 percent, respectively.[34]

If married women were becoming more commonplace and accepted in the wartime labor force, mothers of small children remained a small minority within the working population. Although the labor force participation rate of married women having one or more children under the age of ten doubled in both Detroit and Seattle, only about one-eighth of those women chose to take paid employment during the war. Not surprisingly, mothers in the younger age groups, whose children would also be younger, were less likely to join the work force than those over thirty-five. Although all areas experienced a considerable increase in the proportion of older women entering the labor force, Seattle's reliance on older women to fuel the expansion of the female work force was especially significant. Despite the persistence of some discrimination against older women in Seattle, Women's Bureau figures indicate that women over forty accounted for 35 percent of women workers by 1944. The comparable figures for Baltimore and Detroit were 16 and 20 percent, respectively.[35]

The critical labor shortage created by the war did not mean that all barriers had been toppled. Discrimination against black women proved to be one of the most unyielding of prewar practices. Even employers willing to hire black men and white women balked at changing their practices to include black women, indicating that the intersection of sexism and racism in American society had produced a prejudice even more deep-seated and invidious than either of its constituent elements. In both Detroit and Baltimore, where black women constituted 17 to 19 percent of the female labor force, employment officials continued to refer them primarily for service jobs, and many war plants either refused to hire them, employed them only for limited kinds of work, and/or segregated them on the job. In Baltimore, for example, black women were still being referred to jobs in hospitals, food services, and domestic service in mid-1943, when the female labor shortage was impeding defense production. At the same time, the Fair Employment Practices Commission estimated that 25,000 black women were available for work in Detroit defense plants but were unable to secure such jobs.[36]

The reason most commonly given by employers for the retention of discriminatory practices was the fear that the introduction of black women into their operations might provoke resistance on the part of white workers. Martin Aircraft, for example, cited the walk-outs and other difficulties experienced at the Edgewood Arsenal near Baltimore when black women were first employed as a justification for its own exclusionary policies. Although those who espoused such a position had some basis for their fears in that co-worker hostility to integration was a very real problem, their stance clearly meant the abrogation of any management responsibility to educate employees to the necessity and justice of equal hiring practices.[37]

Not surprisingly, the situation was most acute in Detroit, where the introduction or upgrading of black women prompted five separate hate strikes in one two-week period. When white women workers participated in such walk-outs, their rationale was more social than economic. They objected to sharing bathroom and other facilities with black women, whom they tended to regard as dirty, diseased, and uncongenial. Specifically, they feared that the women were infected with venereal disease, indicating that an important persisting dimension of racism that was particularly divisive among women was the virgin/whore dichotomization of feminine personality expressed in racial terms. Such prejudice was not limited to women, however. The white male management of Detroit industries shared this stereotypic notion, regarding black women, in the words of historian Alan Clive, "as so many refugees from Porgy and Bess or Harlem's Cotton Club."[38]

In order to circumvent government-mandated fair employment practices, employers resorted to several devices. Some turned in requests for employees without the proscribed "whites only" designation but then told black women applicants that there were no current openings. Others hired women employees only at the gate, thus avoiding obvious discrimination against black women referred by the U.S. Employment Service, an action which could jeopardize their war contracts or employee quotas. Bendix Radio and Bethlehem-Fairfield Shipyards canceled their worker orders when the USES referred blacks for the positions.[39]

In the early stages of the war black women in Baltimore had special difficulties in securing admittance to training programs because of employer refusal to hire them and because of racial discrimination in the funding of such courses by the Baltimore public schools. Local school officials used federal grants earmarked for vocational training programs for blacks in the white programs or refused to spend the money at all. Even once they had received training, black men and women had trouble getting hired. When Hazel Coates and Margaret Ruffine, who had completed training in acetylene burning and welding classes, applied for work at three Baltimore shipyards, they were refused, even by Bethlehem-Fairfield, the only one to employ women in significant numbers.[40]

Because of the kinds of jobs created by the defense boom, the extent of employer preference for male workers, and the depth of the prejudice against black women, black male workers generally faced less difficulties in securing employment during the war than black females. Ford Motor Company, for example, had utilized black men in production work even before the war and increased their numbers in order to meet wartime needs but had to be coerced by the WMC into hiring black women. In Baltimore, employment officials noted that unemployment among black men had been eliminated by mid-1943, whereas black women remained available for defense work. The male labor force was more racially flexible during the war years than the female labor force largely because minority group men could fill hot, heavy jobs in the foundries and shipyards, where opportunities were limited for women.[41]

The availability of work in heavy female-employing industries, however, did not necessarily result in the hiring of black females even when female labor was scarce. Martin Aircraft, for example, never employed more than 4 percent blacks despite a persistent labor shortage. The

Chesapeake and Potomac Telephone Company also refused to hire a black women despite continuous job openings and protests from the Total War Employment Committee, a wartime group formed in Baltimore to fight racial discrimination in jobs, and from other Baltimore civil rights groups. In Detroit, Sears lowered its barriers against black women enough to employ them in the wrapping and stock departments but refused to hire them for sales work, which would have involved contact with the public.[42]

Although black women had much greater access to light industrial work than did black men during the war, to some extent they shared in the racial designation of hot, dirty, arduous, or otherwise disagreeable work as more appropriate for blacks. The Pennsylvania Railroad in Baltimore, for example, hired about fifty black women in 1943 for work that was hot, heavy, and sometimes dangerous. Some of the women served as water and fire tenders, keeping up the fire and steam in the locomotives, while others did various general labor jobs. One of the black women interviewed by the Women's Bureau in Baltimore indicated that her job as a loader at the Edgewood Arsenal entailed lifting fifty-five-pound boxes of TNT all day for a salary of $18 a week. In Detroit, the meat-packing industry hired a significantly greater number of black women in order to fill positions others has spurned. The city of Baltimore, which first tried to fill positions as city street cleaners with black men when white men became unavailable, finally resorted to black women in April 1943.[43]

The persistence of discrimination against minority women was particularly irrational in communities wishing to utilize local labor resources because black women proved more responsive to the call for women workers than did white women. In Detroit, for example, the labor force participation rate of all women aged eighteen to sixty-four increased from 29.5 to 39.7 percent from 1940 to 1944, while the rate for nonwhite women rose from 31.6 to 48.8 percent. Baltimore labor officials also reported a greater willingness for black women to enter the labor force. Had not the increase been constrained by the persistence of racial discrimination, especially in the higher-paying war industries, black women workers could have formed an even more important part of the wartime work force than they did and could have reaped more of the benefits from the war-induced prosperity.[44]

Black women's greater willingness to enter the labor force during the war years reflected the higher level of economic need of their families, even in boom times, and the greater cultural acceptance of an economic role for women within the black community. Although precise statistics are not available, accounts of individual women workers in the records of the Women's Bureau indicate a considerable level of responsibility for the support of others on the part of black working women in Baltimore. Moreover, at least one columnist for the *Baltimore Afro-American* expressed considerable anxiety regarding those black women who chose to withdraw from the labor force, especially if they did so in order to live on their allotments as servicemen's wives. Complaining that "too many young women would rather live on the 'fortune of soldiers' than to accept jobs at any price," Captain H. A. Robinson, a black U.S. Army chaplain, wrote that servicemen found it demoralizing for their wives to refuse to work and worried that former domestic servants who had made intemperate parting remarks to their former employers upon quitting would regret having done so once the temporary wartime prosperity was over. Robinson's remarks seemed to indicate a special concern that black women were abdicating their economic obligations and that such "women of leisure" were especially vulnerable to moral perils.[45]

Despite Robinson's remarks to the contrary, black women frequently displayed courage and resourcefulness in seeking access to jobs on an equal basis. According to Geraldine Bledsoe, chief of the minority section of the WMC in Detroit, black women, who were confronted with an especially hostile employment situation in the Motor City, were more willing to take chances in job seeking than were black men. Despite the fact that many minority females who had completed high school and 700-800 hours of defense training were being turned away from Detroit defense plants, they would often go up to as many plants as it took to land a job, even though that might mean up to thirty prior rejections. When one Detroit company resorted to hiring at the gate in order to circumvent WMC orders against discrimination, black women formed long lines at the gate and turned back white female applicants by telling them that only blacks were being hired. The disgruntled employer then agreed to hire on a nondiscriminatory basis all women referred by USES. In Baltimore, black women cooperated with the Urban League and the Total War Employment Committee in securing evidence of discrimination and in picketing the C&P (Chesapeake and Potomac) Telephone Company. Significantly, black women turned to civil rights groups and federal agencies, including the President's Committee on Fair Employment Practices (FEPC), rather than to the Women's Bureau or any other feminist organizations when they needed help in fighting employment discrimination.[46]

Because of their low seniority ranking and the persistence of discrimination, black women were especially vulnerable to unemployment resulting from layoffs caused by the completion of war contracts or the need for temporary cutbacks. At the Continental Can Company in Baltimore, for example, a large number of black women lost their jobs in September 1944 as a result of seasonal cutbacks. In several such cases, black women contended that white women were not also being laid off and that seniority, the official management reason for the firings, was a smoke screen for discrimination. Once they were discharged, minority group women were rarely rehired. As a result of such practices, they were disproportionately represented among those who experienced discontinuous employment patterns.[47]

Despite the persistence of discrimination, urban work opportunities for minority women improved considerably during the war years, and many women and their families experienced a new mobility and some level of security as a result. Given the somewhat expanded range of choice provided by the economic expansion, some women chose to withdraw from the labor force while others left domestic service and other low-paying jobs to take defense and other better work. Even those who remained in the service sector took advantage of wartime conditions to improve their pay and hours. Not surprisingly, the war produced a large number of individual success stories. Women's Bureau interviewers in Baltimore found former domestic servants working at Western Electric and elsewhere for $48-52 a week and a file clerk at the Social Security office who had been promoted from charwoman after passing the appropriate civil service examination.[48]

Despite the upward mobility experienced by some black women during the war, their relative position within the American economy remained the same. In many cases they were not seriously considered as a source of labor until shortages of white women and black men developed and/or pressures from federal officais forced a revision of policies. As a result, the economic upturn of the war years meant an improved status within the civilian sector for minority women, especially in service jobs outside the household. In the better-paid manufacturing area, their late claim on production jobs left them with the least seniority of any group; consequently, they were the most vulnerable to wartime and postwar cutbacks.[49]

Nonwhite women were not the only women to experience discrimination during the war years; older women also experienced greater difficulties than others in claiming their share of defense work. Some civilian defense jobs at Seattle-area military installations were limited to women under the age of thirty-five. Because they believed that women over forty could not stand the work as well as younger women, Boeing officials limited the number of older women hired. In addition to employment discrimination, older women faced unequal opportunities for advancement once they were on the job at Boeing. Officials of local employment offices and training schools in Seattle often advised older women to take lower-paying sales and service jobs. Celia Shelton, the women's counselor at the Edison Vocational School, stated that she encouraged younger women to go into war industries and older women to take civilian jobs such as dressmaking or cooking. The Seattle Works Progress Administration (WPA) training school paid women aged eighteen to twenty-five to take training courses while those over twenty-five received no pay. In Detroit the prejudice against hiring women over forty meant that the vast majority of mothers hired had younger children, a situation which seriously aggravated the day-care problem.[50]

Many older women expressed resentment at the discriminatory practices. Seattlite Clara Smart wrote a letter of protest to the National Youth Administration (NYA) training school objecting to the age limit on employment at Boeing and contending that women over fifty could do the work as well as those aged thirty-five to forty. She added that she had no intention of taking domestic work so that a younger woman could get higher-paid defense work. The 15,000 to 16,000 applications for work received at Boeing from women over fifty-five in the first year of the war indicated that Smart was not alone in her stand. Moreover, 62 percent of the women who expressed interest in defense training courses in the Seattle Civilian War Commission's registration of women in 1942 were over the age of forty. Baltimore officials estimated that 60 percent of the women there available for employment were over forty-five. Despite such findings, employment authorities did little to discourage age discrimination on the part of war industries.[51]

Another more subtle form of discrimination unique to the war years was the employer attempt to "upgrade" its female labor force at the same time that it expanded it by giving preference to middle-class women who applied for factory work. Daniel W. Siemon, Martin Aircraft personnel chief, stated that his company always sought "a high type of woman, especially those with better educations." Noting with pride that the Ford Highland Park plant had 600 college graduates among its women workers, Edsel Ford commented that women employees were "superior in intelligence and general education to the men" and that "they have dignified the idea of working in a factory." Whether this policy was also part of a conscious effort to ensure an easier elimination of women from industrial work after the war is not clear, although it certainly operated to facilitate that goal.[52]

Despite Ford's sanguine statement, class prejudices deterred some middle-class women from factory work, its higher pay and patriotic sanction notwithstanding. For them, referral to the production line rather than the clerical work force once they were hired by a war industry produced a keen disappointment and sense of lost status. Even retaining the trappings and appearance of office workers remained important to some. At the Detroit Highland Park Plant women office workers responded to a company order mandating slacks for all women workers by wearing dresses to work. Bernice Clark, a secretary, explained the women's refusal to go home and change after they were ordered to do so by commenting that "we want to feel like ladies."[53]

Even when women workers had expressed no desire to be treated like "ladies" on the job, some employers limited women's work duties in order to protect them from perceived moral or physical hazards. Girls and women hired to deliver telegraph messages in Seattle worked only during the day, made only short deliveries, and were not sent to "taverns, second-class hotels, and the like." At the Puget Sound Navy Yard, women truck drivers did not load the trucks as their male counterparts did. Women commissioned as plant guards at the Bendix plant in Baltimore carried riding crops instead of guns, and their principal duty was to guide visitors through the plant. Similarly, women guards at Boeing did not carry firearms and were instructed to call one of the men if a situation requiring the use of force arose, although their duties were otherwise essentially the same as those of male guards.[54]

The introduction of women into jobs previously held exclusively by men provoked a variety of reactions from unions, employers, and male co-workers. Many accepted the hiring of women as an unavoidable necessity created by the labor shortage. Others, however, including longshoremen, shipbuilders, and cab drivers, reacted with hostility and ridicule to the suggestion that women take jobs in their fields, contending that women could not perform in their occupations and that it would be physically harmful to women to engage in such activities. Such antagonism toward women workers was most intense among workers in fields most associated with attributes traditionally considered "masculine."[55]

Nowhere was the pained outcry of workers fighting to maintain their male preserve louder than at the shipyards. When the International Brotherhood of Boilermakers and Iron Shipbuilders held a national referendum on the admission of women to their union in August 1942, members of Seattle Local 104 vociferously denied that the shortage of men was so great that women should be brought into the shipyards and ridiculed the idea that women could handle the work. Bill Miller, recording secretary of the local, told women who applied for jobs at Seattle shipyards that the work was "tough", commenting,

Some of them want the silliest jobs. At the aircraft factories they use the Buck Rogers' riveter, driving 3-16th rivets. They don't understand that in the yards they'd be using an outfit that drives rivets 10 to 20 times bigger. If one of these girls pressed the trigger on the yard rivet guns, she'd be going one way and the rivet the other.

As the comment indicates, the boilermakers did not take the aspirations of the women job seekers seriously.[56]

Congruent with their identification of their jobs with masculinity, the yard workers seemed most confortable with traditional sex role divisions. Boilermaker Leo Miller suggested, "There are many things women can do to help just the same as men, such as: repairing sox, o'alls, meals on time, well-cooked economically provided and supervised; maintaining a clean home so that male will stay home . . . saving more than will be produced by them in the yards." Another commented that the change was all right by him if they let him pick his own partner. Many foresaw marital discord resulting from the introduction of women into the yards as wives reacted jealously to the idea of their husbands working closely with the women. Others claimed that working with women would be a distraction to men on the job. Such responses revealed the inability of the men to perceive women outside of the roles of housewife and sex object.[57]

Given the nature and extent of the opposition to the admission of women, it is not surprising that Local 104 voted overwhelmingly against amending the international's constitution. When the votes were counted, the women had lost by a five-to-one margin in Seattle and by a three-to-one margin in Local 568 in Tacoma. On the national level, however, the majority of locals approved the change, but the number of votes cast was not sufficient to validate the election. As a result, the international executive board, convinced that they had a mandate from the locals and that the employment of women was essential to meeting defense contracts, ordered the locals to admit women to the union. Although they argued that the executive board action was illegal, the Puget Sound locals acquiesced in the decision. By November 1942, when the draft was taking hundreds of men from the yards every month, they began accepting women for jobs in the shops, usually as welders.[58]

An equally unsuccessful effort to bar women was made by Seattle's cab drivers beginning in the spring of 1942. Confronted with a shortage of drivers, the Seattle Taxicab Owners' Association announced in March 1942 that it would hire women between the ages of twenty-one and thirty-five for jobs as drivers. The owners, however, had not consulted with the Taxicab Drivers' Union prior to their announcement and were surprised to find that the drivers adamantly opposed the move. According to Dave Beck of the Teamster's Union, there were enough men drivers to meet the owners' needs, cab driving posed moral hazards to women, and drivers were vulnerable to robbery, assault, and murder. B. I. Bowen, secretary-treasurer of the Taxicab Drivers' Union, agreed, adding that driving was "not a woman's job. Taxicab drivers are forced to do things and go many places that would be embarrassing for a woman to do."[59]

In the meantime the owners had selected twenty-seven women from among their applicants for jobs as drivers. When they were rejected by the union, the women responded angrily that they had as much right to the jobs as anyone else. "Let us women handle our own morals," demanded Peggy Miller, adding that she had worked nights in a Yesler Way restaurant for several years without any difficulty. She also observed,

"What's the difference between a drunk man and a sober one? Well, when he's drunk, you have the advantage." When told that the union would not accept her, Erma Hawke challenged, "I'd like to see them stop me." She added, "Beck says taxicab driving isn't women's work, and I'd like to ask him about the women who are doing riveting and welding and performing other jobs in defense plants." They were supported in their position by the four women in Bremerton who had been accepted by the union there and were driving cabs. The Bremerton women contended that the customers gave them no trouble and that the objections raised by Seattle drivers were not valid.[60]

Despite the Bremerton example, the Seattle union staunchly defended its position. In late March 1942, they reached an agreement with the owners that women would not be hired for the time being and that, when it became absolutely necessary to employ women, only unemployed and self-supporting women would be hired. By October 1942, the owners had lost at least 100 drivers to the armed forces and several to war industries, so the union relented and voted to admit women. In order to protect women drivers as much as possible, they decided to assign them only to the day shift, which paid less and offered less opportunity for overtime than the night shift. As one last gesture in the direction of traditional womanhood, the union also voted to require that women drivers not wear slacks.[61]

Other attempts to prevent women from entering new occupations were more successful. Local 119 of the Longshoremen's and Warehousemen's Union refused to admit women on the grounds that the work was too hazardous for them. Chief Dispatcher Dan O'Connell said that he opposed hiring women for the docks because "I respect them too much." Other longshoremen contended that the women would distract male workers (a common apprehension) and, more importantly, that the men did not want women taking their jobs. One union official summed up the opposition, declaring, "No, no, no. Women longshoremen? I'm ag'in' it just on principle." Equally successful in holding the line against women was Local 487 of the Bartenders' International League. Secretary-Treasurer Judd Squire contended that a bar was no place for a woman, adding, "Supposing some difficult patron tries to start a fight? An experienced man bartender knows how to handle a situation like that without getting fussed. And a woman would have a hard job tapping a keg of beer properly." The *Seattle*

Times editorially supported this position, observing that the talk in taverns was "not always such that milady should listen to." Thus, notions of proper moral conduct for women combined with conventional attitudes regarding their physical capabilities to limit women's access to certain jobs.[62]

The lifting of restrictions against women in jobs traditionally reserved to men did not necessarily mean that hostility to their employment had abated. Mary Pitts, a novice driver for the Yellow Cab Company in Seattle, stated, "The hardest thing about the job was to overcome the hostility of men toward women driving." Reportedly, the most common response of men employed at Boeing who were asked what they disliked about their job was, "wages and women." Willie Wilson, a Boeing employee, commented, "About 10 percent of the women are good mechanics. The rest are all right to stand around and talk to." A co-worker, Connie Straub, agreed, saying that women did not belong in his shop because "when we really swing into production, they won't be able to take it." According to Gerry Colson, a columnist for the *Aero Mechanic*, the degree of male resentment against the new women workers was so great that it had caused some women to quit their aircraft jobs.[63]

A woman's success and happiness in an industrial job depended in part on her acceptance by male co-workers and supervisors and their willingness to help her learn her job and do it well. Most of the women taking industrial jobs had never done that kind of work before and had had only a minimal training program, if any. Moreover, many lacked confidence in their abilities to handle "men's work." One young woman working at Boeing decided she had to quit or be transferred to a different shop because, she said, "I'm so afraid of drilling the wrong thing or wrecking a plane that I dream about it at night." The self-consciousness and lack of confidence of many women workers was most pronounced in industries and shops that were hiring women for the first time. Whistles and catcalls followed the women as they attempted to do their jobs; some workers charged that the presence of women was distracting to the men. One Boeing mechanic commented, "You'd think those fellows down there had never seen a girl. Every time a skirt would whip by up there, you could hear the whistles above the riveting, and I'll bet the girls could feel the focus of every eye in the place." Lili Solomon described her feelings as she began work in the shipyards as follows:

Maybe you think it didn't take nerve for women to make that first
break into the yards . . . I never walked a longer road in my life than
that to the tool room. The battery of eyes that turned on my jittery
physique, the chorus of "Hi, sisters" and "tsk-tsk" soon had me
thinking: "Maybe I'm wrong. Maybe I'm not just another human.
Maybe I am from Mars."[64]

Although Solomon was able to regain her bearings in short order,
others were not so lucky, especially when confronted with hostility from
those who were supposed to be teaching them their jobs. One woman
told *Seattle Times* reporter Anne Swennson that she had been fired from
Boeing, explaining as follows:

I had to work with a man who had never had a woman helper before.
He hated me. He was supposed to show me how to do the work, but
he would sort of get around a corner where I couldn't see him,
then when I had to do it, I couldn't, and I got so nervous I went to
pieces. I spoiled stuff—you know how it is.[65]

Others experienced similar difficulties. A woman riveter at Boeing
described her situation as a beginner at the plant: "At first I was a
bucker, and worked with a man who didn't like women, and who
watched every move I made without trying to teach me the job." She
expressed relief that she had been promoted to riveter and had "some
responsibility, and no one breathing over my shoulder every move I
make." These complaints about the attitudes of male riveters were
especially significant because most of the women employed at Boeing
began as rivet buckers whose job was to supply the riveter with the
rivets and tools he or she required. In addition, the riveter was to teach
the bucker the job of riveting. Consequently, close cooperation between
the two was important so that the job would be done efficiently and the
novice would learn the necessary skills.

At Martin Aircraft the sexual hostility manifested in this training
situation became so extreme that new training operations had to be
devised early in the war. In fact, amicable relationships between male
riveters and female buckers were so unusual that the *Baltimore Evening
Sun* featured one such harmonious duo as a conspicuous exception to

the rule. As the novelty of working with women wore off, some of the tension and hostility between workers abated, and as a result working conditions for women improved.[66]

Taking on an industrial job for the first time created other adjustment problems for women as well. The size and impersonality of the industrial establishment, the nature and physical demands of the work, the tedium of the assembly line, the long hours on their feet, the noise, and, in the shipyards, the necessity of working outdoors regardless of weather were new experiences for most of the women workers. A woman employed at Boeing complained, "There's not a place to relax. We even eat our lunches standing up at counters across the street. We wash our hands in troughs, and if we want to smoke we have to go off the grounds or down into the tunnels." She added, "It's sort of like being in the Army." A machine operator at McCord Radiator in Detroit complained to a Women's Bureau interviewer that the noise and "men yelling" made her nervous on the job.[67]

More than anything else the necessity of combining paid employment with household responsibilities created serious problems for women workers. Before or after spending long hours on the job, many women had to cook, clean, and shop for their families as they always had. At the same time, the shortages of civilian goods, the inconveniences and overcrowding of a war boom community, and the necessity to conserve essential resources made the traditional chores of the homemaker all the more complicated and time-consuming. While taking responsibility for the daily needs of her family, the woman also remained the one in the household who had to take over in case of illness or other family emergencies. In contrast to their male co-workers, whose obligations to their employers were rarely subordinated to such considerations, many women workers could not devote the time, energy, or undivided attention to their jobs that ideally they should have.[68]

The high rates of turnover and absenteeism among female employees provide the most compelling evidence of the hardships created by the dual responsibilities of women workers. A study of absenteeism in Seattle war industries in 1943 showed that women were 2.2 times more likely to be absent from work than men. According to those investigating the problem, the difficulties of working a six-day week while also managing a household contributed significantly to the differential. The

WMC concluded that 100,000 worker hours a month were lost in Detroit because of women taking the day off to do the laundry. Women workers also had an unusually high rate of turnover in their jobs; in Baltimore, the monthly quit rate for women was 6.16 in August 1943, compared to 4.78 for men. Seattle Chamber of Commerce statistics showed that 65 percent of the workers who left Boeing in the first six months of 1943 were women. In the opinion of Harold J. Gibbon, president of Local 751 of the International Association of Machinists (IAM), the turnover among women was so high because they "cannot stand the strain of factory work and carry on with home work, too."[69]

Although local and federal officials gave some attention to the problem of increasing services so that working women could be recruited and retained more easily, little was actually done beyond encouraging businesses to stay open later on some evenings and to save some scarce items for sale later in the day. Plans for shopping services, hot carry-out meals, and other innovations important to working homemakers rarely got beyond the stage of speculation. The Willow Run service center, for example, did not open until February 1944, and was not at all as extensive as originally planned. The situation was especially serious in war boom communities experiencing rapid growth, where population increases outstripped the provision of even minimal commercial services. By comparison with the British, who provided considerable support services and allowed working women released time so that they could do their shopping and housework, American policy makers were inflexible, unimaginative, and not especially helpful in confronting the issues raised by women's dual burden.[70]

Exacerbating the problem for women workers were the long hours on the job required by most employers. Because the federal government hoped to maximize the output of those in the labor force, most major war industries operated on the basis of a mandatory six-day, forty-eight-hour week. In addition, frequent overtime was not unusual, especially in the shipyards. In the Puget Sound area, 53.4 percent of the women employed worked a forty-eight hour week, while 80.8 percent worked at least forty hours a week. At the Navy Yard, employees worked thirteen days straight and then took the fourteenth day off. Moreover, the serious transportation problems created by wartime shortages further extended the number of hours a working woman had to spend outside the home. Some employees at Martin Aircraft had to spend two to three hours a day just in transit to and from work. A woman employed at Boeing in Seattle observed that "it takes me two hours sometimes, just going to work. Only place I could find to live is so far out. I make two transfers before I get the Boeing bus. I don't get so tired on the job, but this bus riding wears me out."[71]

Despite pressure from the WMC, the Women's Bureau, and local officials, war plants generally refused to experiment with part-time shifts so that larger numbers of women could be drawn into the labor force. According to these employers, part-time shifts were unworkable on assembly line operations. By contrast, some employers in the civilian clerical and service sectors turned to part-time workers as the solution to an otherwise hopeless labor shortage.[72]

Some employers made special efforts to facilitate a satisfactory adjustment to industrial life on the part of their women employees. In Baltimore, war industries cooperated in a mandatory two-week orientation course for women who had never worked in a factory before. The most important vehicle for such efforts involved the hiring or upgrading of women to supervise and counsel female factory workers. At the Briggs Manufacturing Company in Detroit women counselors were given a six-week training course and then delegated the responsibility for inducting new women employees; handling loans, insurance, and recreational programs for women workers; and providing counseling for women in the plant. The counselors had no disciplinary authority and served in an advisory capacity for both women employees and management. Similar groups were established at Packard, Hudson, and other automobile companies. In order to provide support for these supervisory systems, the local Council of Social Agencies provided a consultant to women's counselors in Detroit war plants.[73]

The success of these counseling programs varied according to the amount of authority given to the women supervisors, their competence and willingness to familiarize themselves with the problems of the women employees, and their accessibility to women on the job. In Seattle, for example, the program at the Puget Sound Navy Yard and in those private shipyards which adopted the idea involved no mandatory contact between the workers and the supervisors, whose offices were often located far from the shops where the women worked. Women employees in one of the private yards complained that women's counselor Alta Dobyns did not spend enough time in the yards learning the real difficulties they experienced on the job. Muriel Job, the women's director at the Navy Yard, did not go into the shops to meet the women or learn about their work, although she said that she was always available to them. Moreover, the supervisory system at the Navy Yard suffered because of the lack of definition in the responsibilities and lines of authority of the women monitors, which led to serious management errors. In the plating shop, for example, the monitor was required to clean out the men's and women's restrooms. The situation prompted Women's Bureau representative Jennie Mohr to ask, "I wonder how much authority she might develop?"[74]

Another source of special difficulty for the women's supervisory groups was the tendency for some employers, including Ford Motor Company and Boeing, to utilize some of the supervisors as matrons whose primary purpose was actually to provide a level of surveillance over women on the job which was not thought necessary for male employees. A particular source of grievance for women workers in such places was the use of monitors whose function was to minimize the amount of time women employees spent in the restrooms. The petty harassment of the workers inherent in such a system contributed needlessly to alienation between management and female employees.[75]

Yet many employers found the reliance on women to supervise women workers an improvement over the use of male foremen. According to Mabel Mosler, the head of the supervisory group at Boeing, the system was an improvement because women were more likely to reveal their fears and problems to other women. At the Seattle-Tacoma Shipbuilding Corporation women field representatives exercised meaningful authority and served effectively as intermediaries between the women workers and the foremen. At the Packard Motor Company, where women supervisors were required to have been to college while many foremen had not gone beyond the sixth grade, the foremen asked for an extension of the female supervisory system. Whether this request was an expression of support or a means of avoiding responsibility for women workers is not clear.[76]

The subtle differences between supervisory systems devised for women and those in existence for men revealed important differences in attitudes toward male and female employees and the delegation of authority to them. Women workers were assumed to pose special social and moral difficulties while male workers were thought to have problems that were more directly work-related. A paper on "Women in Industry" used at the Seattle-Tacoma Shipyards for guidance in supervising women workers typified the conventional wisdom regarding women workers. According to this paper, women's greater emotional volatility created supervisory problems and women workers had to be treated differently because women disliked competition and were less assertive than men. As a result, the responsibilities of women supervisors were defined more in the social-emotional realm and usually involved limited authority to be exercised only over women workers. Foremen, on the other hand, exercised disciplinary authority over workers of both sexes and handled in-plant situations rather than providing social welfare or counseling services.[77]

Although the creation of these supervisory groups generated some opportunities for advancement for women workers, upgrading through the established ranks in the various war industries was often impeded by overt and subtle discrimination on the part of unions and employers. This discrimination reflected their failure to take women's career aspirations seriously or to evaluate their skills without bias and their unwillingness to accept the wartime changes as anything but temporary expedients to be limited as much as possible so as to prevent women from threatening the skilled jobs traditionally reserved to men.[78]

At Boeing, where both labor and management claimed to be treating women workers equally in all regards, hostility toward women workers by the foremen who rated them and made recommendations on promotions played an important role in keeping women in the lower classifications. In some cases consideration for promotion by the supervisors went to the younger and more attractive women rather than to those whose work merited it. Although the *Aero Mechanic* stated that advancement decisions were based on the seniority and job performance of workers and told women not to believe their supervisors when they said advancement was not possible for women, it was, in fact, those supervisors who determined a worker's chances for upgrading. The IAM's unwillingness to recognize the problem amounted to an acceptance of the restriction of most women to the lower-paying job categories. In May 1943, only 3,062 of the 14,435 women employed at Boeing were in semiskilled and 109 in skilled positions.[79]

As bad as the Boeing situation was in regard to promotions, women workers still found it much preferable to that at the Puget Sound Navy

Yard or the commercial shipyards. Although the Navy Yard had promised when it was recruiting women workers that advancement for them would be rapid and based on job competence, local Navy officials had set upper limits on women's advancement based on their estimates of how many women they would have to hire and at what positions. They justified their policy on the grounds that the employment of women beyond those job categories where they would be immediately needed was not necessary. In July 1943, however, the policy was officially reversed when the Navy Department directed the navy yards to increase the number of women employed in skilled group III. Despite this directive, the number of women promoted thereafter was small, and most of them were given positions in the women's supervisory group rather than improved ratings in their particular mechanical skills.[80]

Not surprisingly, in the commercial shipyards in Seattle, where the Boilermakers Union held jurisdiction over many of the jobs, women's chances for advancement were also seriously limited. Because Local 104 of the Boilermakers Union accepted women into their union only as temporary mechanics, their upgrading into more skilled job classifications was effectively blocked. Attempts by the women to work within the union to revoke the discriminatory policy failed, as did the intercession by a Women's Bureau representative, who tried to get the Seattle Metal Trades Council to support the women's position. As a result, women remained largely in unskilled and, to a lesser extent, semiskilled job categories at the major shipyards in the Puget Sound area. At the Seattle-Tacoma Shipbuilding Corporation, for example, no women had been advanced out of the unskilled categories by May 1943.[81]

Closely related to the question of promotion was the availability of training so that women workers could develop the skills necessary for advancement to the higher-paying job classifications. By the time a few women were completing defense training courses in mid-1942 the demand for workers exceeded the supply of trained workers to such an extent that most war industry employers, including Boeing, Martin Aircraft, Ford Motor Company, and the Navy Yard, decided to rely primarily on in-plant training programs rather than making the pre-employment courses offered under federal auspices a prerequisite for employment. In the commercial shipyards the pre-employment training requirements were kept for some job categories, including welders, but by mid-1943 the number of hours to be spent in the courses had been drastically reduced. As a result many workers chose to forgo the training courses so that they would not lose the wages they would receive if they learned their skills on the job. Thus, the vast majority of women hired in these industries had had little or no training or previous experience in industrial jobs.[82]

Those women employed in major war industries who wanted to take supplementary training courses once they had become competent in their basic skills encountered important obstacles that made it more difficult to complete such training. In general, since the workers who were to take additional training were selected by their foremen and/or shop stewards, there was the possibility of the kind of discrimination already described. Moreover, the supplementary training had to be taken on the employee's own time because few such courses were offered as part of in-plant training programs. This meant that four to eight hours in classes would be added to a work week that was already at least forty-eight hours long for the majority of workers. Because the training centers were frequently located in residential areas rather than near the plants, the chronic transportation problems of a war boom community compounded the difficulties and added to the time required for those wanting to go through the extra training. In addition, many women preferred not to go out at night during the frequent dim-outs. As a result of these disadvantages, many women, especially those with families, did not participate in the supplementary programs. Enrollment in Baltimore-area supplementary classes in early 1944 included 2,050 white males, 242 white females, 87 black males, and 187 black females. Of the 1,214 Seattle Boeing employees in such courses in January 1943, only 249 were women.[83]

Because the unions occupied a position of strength in key war industries, especially in Seattle and Detroit, the status of women within those industries depended in part on their status within their unions. Once the question of whether to hire women was settled by the exigencies of the war, the unions had to decide questions regarding pay scales, advancement opportunities, and seniority provisions for women workers. Their decisions in these matters generally reflected their perceptions as to what would most benefit the interests of their current membership, including those who would be returning to their jobs after service overseas.

Because they feared that women could be used by management to undercut existing union wage scales and working conditions, local labor organizations generally accepted women as full dues-paying members and safeguarded the principle of equal pay for equal work. Women members of the IAM and the UAW, for example, entered their locals with the same dues and benefits as male members. When the shipyards in Seattle began hiring women at the gate and paying them at the office rate of 65 cents per hour, the Boilermakers Union intervened to ensure that it would dispatch all workers, including women, and that the prevailing wage for the job would be paid to women. Although there were some exceptions, the entry of women workers into previously male work meant the protection of wage levels in that work by the unions.[84]

While supporting the principle of equal pay, the unions could utilize the seniority provisions of their labor contracts to protect the job security of the male membership or to limit women's access to certain jobs. At the Bethlehem Steel Company in West Seattle the seniority provisions of the union agreement worked to limit the assignment of jobs to women because the lighter jobs that they could do were rated higher than the heavier jobs from which they were barred. In the auto industry, the UAW supported a system whereby seniority remained plant-wide or an employee retained seniority in her or his prewar job regardless of wartime job assignment. At the same time, it remained inflexible regarding the assignment of male workers to heavier work or that involving undesirable shift assignments when such changes would have facilitated the increased hiring of women. Seattle Local 104 of the Boilermakers Union protected male jobs by putting women on a separate seniority list, classifying them as temporary mechanics. When women members contested this in 1944, the local voted two to one against them. Although few other locals adopted such blatantly discriminatory policies, women, whose tenure in their jobs was invariably short, would find that their much-discussed equality in regard to seniority in the IAM, the UAW, and other unions was not particularly meaningful when the postwar cutbacks came.[85]

Despite their acceptance of equal pay in principle, unions did little about the pattern of inequality institutionalized in the discrepancy in pay levels between "women's" and "men's" work and exacerbated by discrimination in promotion. As a result, women war workers earned considerably less than their male counterparts. Among auto industry workers, women averaged $44.91 a week in earnings in 1943, compared to $62.65 for male workers, who worked an average of 3.5 hours a week more than the women. At the Ford Willow Run plant those women workers who had sufficient seniority to survive the drastic cutbacks in the spring of 1945 averaged $2,928 in annual earnings compared to $3,363 for the remaining male workers.[86]

Within the local organizations women achieved varying levels of participation and influence. These depended in part on the proportion of women in the wartime membership, the ideological or political heritage of individual unions, and the personalities of key leaders. In Seattle, the unions with jurisdiction in the shipyards retained their masculinist view of the workplace and severely limited the role of women in their organizations, although some women did become shop stewards in Local 104 of the Boilermakers and Local 79 of the IAM. In contrast, Seattle Local 9-26 of the International Woodworkers of America conducted an educational campaign among its male members on the need to accept wholeheartedly the new women members and soon had one woman shop steward and five women on the executive board of the union.[87]

Logically, women workers acquired the greatest voice in those unions in which they constituted an appreciable part of the membership during the war. Fearing that the indifference or hostility of new women members could jeopardize union gains, the UAW and IAM actively courted their new constituency, if not with unambiguous enthusiasm. The ambivalence of UAW President R. J. Thomas, when he noted in 1944 in the union publication, *Ammunition,* that 60 percent of the votes in an upcoming union election would be cast by women, typified this response to wartime changes. Thomas conceded that the men in the union had made some mistakes when women first entered in large numbers but stated that their support of equal pay and other issues important to women indicated that they had improved. He urged the women to vote and called for more women in leadership positions.[88]

More so than most unions at the time, the UAW sought to encourage women's participation in union affairs and to overcome the hostility of some women members, many of whom had no previous experience with urban industrial life or with labor organizations, to the idea of a closed shop and mandatory dues. In order to better understand the problems of working women and to foster their loyalty to the union, the

UAW established a women's bureau in its War Policy Division. In addition, under pressure from women delegates, its 1944 convention passed a resolution supporting the addition of women organizers, especially in regional offices. Despite its success in elevating some women to leadership positions, even the UAW had very few women officers on bargaining or grievance committees. Mirroring national patterns in large unions, many of the women leaders in the Detroit UAW locals were found on social welfare committees, although Mildred Jeffrey and Lillian Hatcher did serve in the Fair Practices Department.[89]

Despite some encouragement from the *Aero Mechanic*, women members of the Seattle IAM, which had a closed shop agreement with Boeing, found that institutionalized barriers and prejudice limited their participatory role. In the early stages of the war women found their participation impeded by a rule requiring that union officers be members of the union for one year before taking office. Some members suggested rescinding the regulation and at least one, Margaret Driggs, recommended that women be elected as "honorary trainees" who would have a voice but not a vote so that they could run in the January 1943 elections. Her suggestion prompted one male member, C. Buchanan, to write and recommend that the requirement be extended to three years because being a union officer "is a He-man's job" and that women's "feminine way of handling things . . . does not go in grievance cases or other Union business." He added that it would not be fair to the union for women to serve as officers "when it takes a man with 'innards' to hold the job." Edith Dugro reacted to his assertions in a letter to the *Aero Mechanic* contending that there were women at Boeing "who have the intelligence, experience, and ability to organize as well as any man." The debate was resolved by a decision to retain the one-year requirement. Consequently, women did not run for office until December 1943, when at least twenty entered the races and two were elected to office. Thereafter, the number of women in such positions within the union remained small, although by 1945 Lorraine Summers, a local officer from the Renton division and a delegate to the Washington State Federation of Labor, became the first woman to be chosen for the district council.[90]

The IAM's encouragement of women to participate in union affairs was often couched in terms exhorting them to safeguard union interests so that union jobs and working standards would be maintained for returning veterans. The *Aero Mechanic*, for example, editorialized as follows:

The WOMEN WHO ARE NOW TAKING THE MEN'S JOBS IN THE WAR PRODUCTION PLANTS SHOULD NEVER FORGET THE FACT THAT A LABOR UNION MAN gave up his job to them so that he could put on a uniform and fight the battle that may cost him his life. He expects you to be loyal to your union and his union.

It also reminded the women that they might be supported by a union man after the war was over.[91]

If the *Aero Mechanic* accurately reflected official union sentiments, few in leadership positions doubted that the returning servicemen had a greater claim on aircraft production jobs than the women employed during the war. According to the union publication, the "men will take back their jobs when they come marching home and well they should." Women who wrote or spoke for the union often echoed this sentiment. In a speech on the "751" lunchtime radio broadcast, Jane Stokes told the listeners:

When this war is over—I'll get a manicure, put on the frilliest dress I can find, pour a whole bottle of cologne over my head, and THEN, I'll be GLAD to give up my Union chair in the Eagle Aerie Room to some boy who comes marching home deserving it.

According to the Aero Woman's Page, the women would gladly surrender their jobs to the men after the war was over. Columnist Gerry Anderson agreed that this was true and added that the postwar period would bring no conflict between the sexes over jobs because of "woman's constant unconscious consciousness of her real place, which is, as fate will have it, in the home." The only dissenting opinion came from columnist Jack Bradford, who described the women war workers as "self-reliant, energetic, capable" and concluded that "modern women aspire to a higher level in life than that of being a cross between a household drudge and a pampered 'baby doll'."[92]

In general, however, wartime unions extended union benefits to women only to the extent that was necessary to safeguard the pay, seniority, and other labor standards guaranteed in union contracts. They acquiesced in the violation of supposedly sacrosanct union principles, especially those involving seniority-based job security and promotion, when such practices meant a preference for male workers in skilled job categories and enhanced the possibility that women would be excluded from "male" jobs once the war was over. The long-term needs of male workers took precedence over the prerogatives of women workers, as the postwar period would soon demonstrate.

Despite some improvements in women's labor force status during the war years, wartime changes did not signal any radical revision of conventional ideas regarding women's proper social and economic roles. Media depictions of the "New Woman" created by the war expressed a special concern that the economic changes caused by the war not be allowed to diminish traditional femininity or threaten women's fulfillment of their family responsibilities. Although women were exhorted to take war jobs as a patriotic necessity, they were also warned that men do not want to marry career women and that competence in "woman's realm," the home, was a woman's greatest asset. A *Seattle Times* article, for example, warned that "a woman must not go berserk over the new opportunities for masculine clothing and mannish actions" or else she would forfeit her femininity and thus her happiness. In their rules for women workers, the women's counselors at the Navy Yard included the exhortation to "be feminine and ladylike even though you are filling a man's shoes."[93]

In addition, the women's sections of union and employer publications included advice on homemaking, personal appearance, and personal relationships, notably those involving men. The *Martin Star*, a monthly publication at Martin Aircraft, offered a Women at War page providing homemaking and beauty tips for busy women workers. In the July 1943 issue, for example, information was given on fixing a proper lunch for herself and her husband so that *he* could be head man on the production line. The Production Girl's Diary by Jane Stokes, which appeared as a regular feature in the *Aero Mechanic*, devoted most of its attention to the author's romantic problems. The *Aero Mechanic* also published a series of questions to enable women workers to determine their "FQ" (Femininity Quotient); those who managed to combine their industrial work with traditional concepts of femininity in attire, tastes, and behavior off the job scored highest. In order to aid women employed at Boeing in maintaining their "FQ", the Women's Recreational Activity Council scheduled charm courses, which offered instruction in proper dress and makeup, poise, and personality development.[94]

Such media treatment of women workers contributed to the confusion in the images of Rosie the Riveter. In an article on "Girls in Uniform," *Life* pictured Boeing worker Marguerite Kershner with a caption contending that "although Marguerite looks like a Hollywood conception of a factory girl, she and thousands like her are doing hard, vital work." Spelling out the imperatives of the new role for women, the popular publication continued its preoccupation with the physical appearance of those responsible for meeting military production goals:

> Now, at day's end, her hands may be bruised, there's grease under her nails, her make-up is smudged and her curls out of place. When she checks in the next morning at 6:30 a.m. her hands will be smooth, her nails polished, her makeup and curls in order, for Marguerite is neither drudge nor slave but the heroine of a new order.

The ultimate expression of this glamorization of the woman war worker occurred at the Bendix Friez plant in Baltimore, where women employees formed the Friez Rockettes to give performances at nearby military installations.[95]

Moreover, the demonstration by women that they could perform jobs hitherto assigned primarily or solely to men caused a reassessment not of the nature of women but rather of the nature of the jobs they were doing so that they conformed more closely to traditional preconceptions regarding women. Whereas critics of the employment of women had emphasized the physical strength required for war jobs, those interpreting women's abilities in war industries frequently stressed the close resemblance between traditional women's work and their new industrial jobs. In explaining the success of women at Boeing, the *Boeing News* noted "that it's only a short step from homemaking to plane making" and gave examples of the similarities between the operations involved in each. It compared spotwelding to sewing, stamping and piling parts in the heat treat department to cutting cookies, and ordering parts from the parts store to shopping at a bargain counter. In a full-page advertisement for Martin Aircraft, prospective women employees were told that "domestic skills, such as sewing, can be readily adapted to varied phases of airplane manufacturing." Describing welding as a "meticulous handicraft" (rather than a physically strenuous labor), Cliff Daving, the welding instructor at Associated Shipbuilders in Seattle observed, "The best prerequisite for a course in welding is a deft hand, and the hand that formerly did needlework, measured flour or rocked the cradle is usually better at welding than a man's hand."[96]

Women were also credited with superior abilities in repetitive, tedious jobs, particularly those involving detailed work, because they ostensibly had more patience and manual dexterity than men. An advertisement for Martin Aircraft repeated a persistent wartime theme when it commented that "women surpass men in many fields where nimble fingers and a light touch are needed." According to *Aero Mechanic* columnist Gerry Anderson, "Because of past experience at sewing and knitting, women have become conditioned to monotony." Charlotte Cates, a former office worker who made cartridge dies during the war, agreed, observing, "This is tedious work but it's the kind for which women are particularly suited."[97]

Although the tenacity of such stereotypes, including the belief that women had less mechanical aptitude than men, could be taken to indicate that they were not performing up to previous standards in the industrial and other jobs they had taken over, it is difficult to determine accurately how well women actually did in their new occupations. Several employers praised their women workers for being competent, conscientious, obedient, and responsible. Edsel Ford noted that the women at his River Rouge Plant were "doing the hardest work, such as welding battle tanks, as well as the finest kind of instrument work, and they are doing both jobs superbly. They are every bit as good as the men." A. H. Wenck, manager of the Yellow Cab Company of Seattle, which employed sixty women by mid-1943, joined in praising the women workers. "They have tact and honor," he commented, "and their accident rate is very, very low. We never made a better move than when we employed these women." That some of this praise was empty rhetoric designed to lure women workers in times of shortage would become clear once the postwar economy permitted a return to previous discriminatory practices.[98]

A more reliable measure of the job performance of women workers was the level of efficiency in woman-employing war industries, a standard which indicated that the female work force was discharging its responsibilities quite ably. At the Willow Run Bomber Plant, a factory plagued by high turnover and absenteeism and considerable worker disaffection with management policies, the number of worker hours per bomber was reduced from a 1941 industry average of 200,000 per ship to less than 18,000 by 1945. Approximately 29 percent of the plant's work force was women. Boeing Aircraft in Seattle increased its monthly output four times between 1942 and 1944 and decreased the cost of its B-17 despite its large numbers of inexperienced workers, continuous changes in airplane design, and greater overhead caused by higher wages. At the same time, its labor force remained the same size. In both cases a program of simplification of individual jobs accounted for the improvement in output per worker.[99]

Many of the women who pioneered in nontraditional fields during the war took pride in their individual and collective accomplishments and expressed confidence in the abilities they had acquired. A woman welder at the navy yard commented, "Some of us had our doubts at first, but now after we've gotten into it, we found it's fascinating, probably because there is so much to learn. Then, too, there's a thrill in turning out a good piece of welding." Anna Nelson, a coremaker in a foundry, agreed that industrial work was rewarding, observing, "You're proud of your work when it's done—like an artist with a picture." An older Baltimore woman who had returned to paid employment after years as a homemaker agreed, commenting on her job in assembly work at Bendix Friez Company: "I love my job and I hate the idea of giving it up. Sometimes I can hardly wait to get there. Never thought I could do such exacting work—and I'm real proud." Margie Lacoff, a war widow who worked as a helper electrician at the Navy Yard, summed up the feeling of many women employed in war jobs when she said prophetically, "I like my work so much that they'll have to fire me before I leave."[100]

For the millions of women who took their places in the wartime economy, many of whom were entering the labor force for the first time, the meaning of the wartime experience was as individual as the women who lived it. The Margie Lacoffs found greater choice in lifestyles and career opportunities than had ever been available before and were happily surprised with the personal reward afforded them in work hitherto closed to women. Despite the physical demands and frequent inconvenience of industrial work in a war boom community, they valued the economic independence, sense of accomplishment, and social contacts made possible by expanded job opportunities. Others, however, entered war plants out of a sense of duty and dreamed of the cottage surrounded by flowers, "an adorable curly-headed baby and a romantic mate."[101] For them the war meant deferred marriage or motherhood and, often, separation from their husbands. Many shouldered dual responsibilities at home and on the job and felt unequal to the task; the long hours at work and the shortages in products and services caused by war conditions created great difficulties for these women and made the work experience a less attractive option for many of them.

Because of the opportunities it created and the changes it generated in the life experiences of millions of American women, the war period became an important time of testing for women. Employers, co-workers, and the general public would be judging the women's performance in order to assess its meaning for the return to a "normal" postwar world, and the women themselves would be evaluating their experiences and measuring them against more traditional alternatives.

Whatever the individual conclusions drawn in response to the changes wrought by the war, those changes did further confuse the social definition of appropriate sex roles. As a result of their culture's attempt to graft certain "masculine" attributes onto an otherwise conventional model of womanhood, American women received conflicting signals during the war. They were urged to demonstrate physical strength, mechanical competence, and resourcefulness for eight hours a day, while being told to be "feminine" and attractive, weak and dependent on men during their free time. The contradictory images of working woman created perplexity and facilitated an anachronistic retreat into the "feminine mystique" of the postwar period.

Moreover, the women who took part in labor force activities found that the persistence of prejudice and its pervasive institutionalization created barriers to any change not mandated by the economic imperatives of the war machine. As a result, industrial technology, job classifications and pay scales, seniority arrangements, and union leadership and policy frequently retained their male bias despite the increased employment of women. Although attenuated during the war years, the segregation of the labor force by sex remained the rule, and the cultural and monetary overvaluation of "men's" work persisted, even when it was performed temporarily by women. Women engaged in traditional "women's" work found that the pay and status they received, despite some improvements, remained low by comparison with other work. To a large extent, working women had to accept the American labor force on its own terms, not revise them to meet their own needs.

Such a revision would have required strong feminist leadership at a time when feminist organizations remained engaged in a fruitless internecine strife which blinded them to the possibilities of the war years. Moreover, they retained a focus on national rather than local efforts which removed them from any contact with the working women who experienced the greatest change during the war and who were thus essential to a wartime feminist renascence. Lacking a feminist perspective and frequently unable to rely on women's groups for support, working women with grievances turned to other institutions—unions, civil rights organizations, and federal agencies. These groups, however, subordinated women's issues to a variety of male-defined goals and policies and constrained the amount of change generated by the war. Consequently, no vehicle for retaining wartime gains and improving women's status as workers emerged as a result of the war experience.[102]

Thus, the historical picture of the war years as a period of unequaled economic opportunity and resulting social advance for women requires considerable qualification. Even in a war boom community like Detroit, prejudice limited and defined the extent of change created in social, sexual, and racial arrangements as a consequence of a "full employment" economy. The lack of ideological and institutional accommodation for those women who did break with convention and attempt to combine work and family responsibilities helped determine their response to their new experiences and accustomed employers and public policy makers to imposing most of the social cost of change on the working woman herself. For all the improvement in her absolute status during the war, the working woman would find that her relative position within the American economy and its ideological concomitants remained unaltered by the wartime experience.

Notes

1. Eleanor Straub, "Government Policy Toward Civilian Women During World War II" (Ph.D. diss., Emory University, 1973), pp. 33, 158; "Labor

Market Developments Report," Baltimore, July 1943, BES, RG 183, Box 161, NA; "Report on Special Field Visits Regarding Need for Day Care of Children of Women Employed in Defense Industries," April 6, 1942, OCWS, RG 215, Children's Division, Box 3, NA; "Problems of Women War Workers in Detroit," WPB, August 20, 1943, OCWS, RG 215, WARC, Box 10, NA.

2. *Seattle Times*, January 26, 1942; *Seattle Star*, January 12, 1942, January 20, 1942; *Catholic Northwest Progress*, April 24, 1942.

3. Alan Clive, "The Society and Economy of Wartime Michigan, 1939-1945" (Ph.D. diss., University of Michigan, 1976), pp. 166-67; *Baltimore Sun*, December 26, 1941; *Detroit News*, February 1, 1942; "The Impact of the War on the Seattle-Tacoma Area."

4. Special Survey of the Employment Service Active File in the Detroit Central Placement Area, by Age, Sex, Color, and Occupation, As of December 7, 1940," Michigan Unemployment Compensation Commission, BES, RG 183, Box 18, NA; "Labor Market Developments Report, Detroit Labor Market Area," Month Ending July 31, 1946, BES, RG 183, Box 184, NA; U.S., Department of Commerce, Bureau of the Census, Series P-LF, No. 5, "Report on the Labor Force of Baltimore, Maryland," October 1946, BES, RG 183, Box 166, NA; "Monthly Reports," Office of Unemployment Compensation and Placement [hereafter cited as OUCAP], Arthur B. Langlie Papers, RG 11-12, Box 12-21, Washington State Archives, Olympia, Wash. [hereafter cited as WSA].

5. "Current Trends in the Employment of Women in Michigan's War Industries," December 24, 1942, BES, RG 183, Box 184, NA; "Survey of the Employment Situation in Detroit, Michigan," February 1941, BES, RG 183, Box 161, NA; "Seattle-Tacoma-Bremerton Labor Market Survey," February 1942, BES, RG 183, Box 415, NA; *Seattle Times*, February 18, 1942.

6. U.S., FSA, SSB, Bureau of Employment Security, "The Employment of Women in War Production," May 1942, WBA, RG 86, Box 1534, NA; "Report on Special Field Visits Regarding Need for Day Care of Children of Women Employed in Defense Industries," April 6, 1942, OCWS, RG 215, Children's Division, Box 3, NA; *Seattle Times*, October 5, 1941, December 27, 1941.

7. *Baltimore Sun*, December 14, 1941, December 28, 1941; *Seattle Times*, May 1, 1942, May 10, 1942, June 15, 1942, June 16, 1942; *Bremerton Sun*, January 16, 1942.

8. "Problems of Women War Workers in Detroit," WPB, August 20, 1943, OCWS, RG 215, WARC, Box 10, NA; Memo, Frank M. Landers to William F. Schaub, May 31, 1943, CCPA, RG 212, Box 48, National Archives, Washington, D.C., Memo, Henry B. Steeg to Corrington Gill, June, 1943, CCPA, RG 212, Box 51, NA; "Labor Market Developments Report, Baltimore," March 1943, BES, RG 183, Box 161, NA; "Statistical Tables, Baltimore Area," October 30, 1944, BES, RG 183, Box 162, NA.

9. "Special Labor Market Survey, Baltimore," March 1942, BES, RG 183, Box 165, NA; "Current Trends in the Employment of Women in Michigan's War Industries," December 24, 1942, BES, RG 183, Box 184, NA; "War Program News," DHWS, Region IV, October 9, 1942, OCWS, RG 215, General Classified, Region IV, Box 9, NA; Day Care News, No. 9, March 1943, OCWS, RG 215, WARC, Box 10, NA; "Composite Report, Detroit," OCWS, RG 215, Community Reports, Box 5, NA.

10. "Outline of Proposed Drive to Recruit Women for War Work in Wayne County Area," OCWS, RG 215, General Classified, Michigan (Region V), Box 134, NA; Clarence R. Innis to Corrington Gill, June 6, 1944, CCPA, RG 212, Box 95, NA; "Where Can We Get War Workers?" Public Affairs Pamphlet No. 75, 1942, BES, RG 183, Box 162, NA.

11. "Outline of Proposed Drive," OCWS, RG 215, General Classified, Michigan (Region V), Box 134, NA; "Women's War Work Recruiting program, WMC, Baltimore Area," OCWS, RG 215, WARC, Box 7, NA; "Labor Market Developments Report, Baltimore," September 1942, BES, RG 183, Box 161, NA; Baltimore Sun, September 23, 1943; Letter, Kenneth Douty to Robert O. Bonnell, August 21, 1943, War Records Collection, RG 2010, Box 72, Maryland Historical Society, [hereafter cited as MHS]; Straub, "Government Policy Toward," pp. 107-39; Seattle Times, August 6, 1942, October 21, 1942, July 28, 1943, March 7, 1944, April 9, 1944; U.S., Department of Commerce, Bureau of the Census, Population Series CA-3, No. 8, "Characteristics of the Population, Labor Force, Families, and Housing, Puget Sound Congested Production Area: June, 1944" (Washington, D.C., Government Printing Office, 1944), pp. 7, 9.

12. "Women's War Work Recruiting Campaign," OCWS, RG 215, WARC, Box 7, NA; Letter, Innis to Gill, CCPA, RG 212, Box 95, NA; Baltimore Sun, July 4, 1943, January 30, 1944, May 7, 1944, March 4, 1945; Seattle Times, June 30, 1943.

13. Baltimore News Post, November 30, 1943; Seattle Times, April 5, 1942.

14. "General Comments of Workers, Baltimore, Maryland," WBA, RG 86, Box 1541, NA; "Detroit Post-War Study, 1944," WBA, RG 86, Box 1541, NA; Seattle Times, February 3, 1944; "Comments of Workers on Specified Items—Seattle and Tacoma, Washington," WBA, RG 86, Box 1545, NA.

15. "General Comments of Workers, Baltimore, Maryland," WBA, RG 86, Box 1541, NA; "Detroit Post-War Study, 1944," WBA, RG 86, Box 1541, NA; Navy Yard Salute, March 6, 1943; "Comments of Workers on Specified Items—Seattle and Tacoma, Washington," WBA, RG 86, Box 1545, NA.

16. "General Comments of Workers, Baltimore, Maryland," WBA, RG 86, Box 1541, NA; "Detroit Post-War Study, 1944," WBA, RG 86, Box 1541, NA; Seattle Times, March 27, 1942, September 25, 1942, October 18, 1942; Aero

Mechanic, December 31, 1942, May 6, 1943, January 6, 1944; *Navy Yard Salute,* February 11, 1944; "Comments of Workers on Specified Items—Seattle and Tacoma, Washington," WBA, RG 86, Box 1545, NA.

17. "General Comments of Workers, Baltimore, Maryland," WB, RG 86, Box 1541, NA; "Detroit Post-War Study, 1944," WBA, RG 86, Box 1541, NA; "Comments of Workers on Specified Items—Seattle and Tacoma, Washington," WBA, RG 86, Box 1545, NA; WBB 209, pp. 50, 52.

18. U.S., Department of Commerce, Bureau of the Census, *Current Population Reports; Housing,* Series P-71, No. 28, "Housing Characteristics of the Baltimore, Maryland, Metropolitan District, August 19, 1947; Winifred Bolin, "Past Ideals and Present Pleasures: Women, Work and the Family, 1920–1940" (Ph.D. diss., University of Minnesota, 1976); *Detroit Free Press,* January 14, 1943.

19. "Field Operating Report, Baltimore," June 1945, BES, RG 183, Box 161, NA; "Report on Conference of Women in War Industries," April 1943, WBA, RG 86, Box 1533, NA; "Employee Counseling: A Report," February 25, 1944, WBA, RG 86, Box 1540, NA; "Meeting of the Michigan Federal Coordinating Committee, August 10-11, 1943," CCPA, RG 212, Box 48, NA; "Supplement to Report on Adequacy of Labor Supply, For: Seattle-Bremerton, Washington Area," September 1943, BES, RG 183, Box 415, NA.

20. "Problems of Women War Workers in Detroit," WPB, August 20, 1943, OCWS, RG 215, WARC, Box 10, NA; CCPA, "Narrative Report as of March 31, 1944," CCPA, RG 212, Box 50, NA; "Labor Market Report for Detroit, Michigan," May 1943, BES, RG 183, Box 183, NA; "WMC Monthly Field Operating Report, Detroit Area," February 1944, BES, RG 183, Box 183, NA.

21. WMC, "Labor Demand Supply Supplement, Detroit Labor Market Area," January 1944, BES, RG 183, Box 183, NA; WMC, "Bi-Monthly Labor Demand Supply Supplement to Field Operating Report, November 1, 1944–May 1, 1945, Detroit Labor Market Area," BES, RG 183, Box 183, NA; Memo, Frank M. Landers to William F. Schaub, May 31, 1943, CCPA, RG 212, Box 48, NA; Letter, William J. Cronin to F. M. McLaury, April 12, 1944, CCPA, RG 212, Box 51, NA.

22. "The Washington Labor Market," November 1943, BES, RG 183, Box 413, NA; Labor Market Developments Report, Detroit Labor Market Area, Month ending July 31, 1946," BES, RG 183, Box 184; "Composite Report on the Puget Sound Area," May 14, 1944, OCWS, RG 215, Community Reports, Region XII, Box 17, NA; "Women in the Wartime Labor Market," August 30, 1943, WBA, RG 86, Box 1536, NA.

23. "Labor Market Developments Report, Baltimore," March 1943, BES, RG 183, Box 161, NA; U.S., Department of Labor, Bureau of Labor Statistics, "Labor Conditions in the Aircraft and Shipbuilding Industries in the Tacoma and Seattle-Bremerton Areas," January, 1943–May, 1944, CCPA, RG 212, Box

95, NA; "Women in the Wartime Labor Market," August 30, 1943, WBA, RG 86, Box 1536, NA; "The Washington Labor Market," November 1943, BES, RG 183, Box 413, NA.

24. WBB 209, p. 36; "Composite Report on Puget Sound Area," May 15, 1944, OCWS, Community Reports, RG 215, Box 17, NA.

25. WBB 209, p. 35.

26. WBB 209, pp. 38, 44.

27. WBB 209, pp. 38, 44; *Bremerton Sun*, March 2, 1942.

28. "Reports on Women at Work, Magazine Division, OWI," June 1943, WBA, RG 86, Box 1537, NA; "Labor Market Developments in the Detroit Area," November 5, 1943, BES, RG 183, Box 17, NA; "Labor Market Developments Report, Baltimore," March 1943, July 1943, BES, RG 183, Box 161, NA; *Seattle Times*, February 27, 1942.

29. *Baltimore Afro-American*, December 18, 1943; "Where Can We Get War Workers?" Public Affairs Pamphlet No. 75, 1942, BES, RG 183, Box 162, NA.

30. *Seattle Times*, November 15, 1942, April 17, 1944.

31. *Baltimore Sun*, May 7, 1944; "Annual Report, WMC, Maryland Area," BES, 1943, RG 183, Box 163, NA; *Detroit News*, March 29, 1942, March 31, 1942; *Seattle Times*, June 12, 1942, January 17, 1943; *Aero Mechanic*, September 3, 1942; *Navy Yard Salute*, October 10, 1942, April 3, 1943, April 17, 1943.

32. "Work and Wage Experience of Willow Run Workers," *Monthly Labor Review* (December 1945): 1086; *Life*, July 6, 1942.

33. *Detroit News*, February 7, 1942, February 18, 1942, April 3, 1942; *Baltimore Sun*, September 13, 1943, May 16, 1944, June 4, 1944.

34. WBB 209, pp. 29, 45; U.S., Department of Commerce, Bureau of the Census, "Characteristics of the Puget Sound Congested Production Area," p. 11.

35. WBB 209, p. 46; U.S., Department of Commerce, Bureau of the Census, "Characteristics of the Puget Sound Congested Production Area," pp. 9–15; U.S., Department of Commerce, Bureau of the Census, Population Series CA-3, No. 9, "Characteristics of the Population, Labor Force, Families, and Housing, Detroit-Willow Run Congested Production Area: June, 1944" (Washington, D.C. Government Printing Office, 1944), p. 16; Chafe, pp. 192–93.

36. WBB 209, p. 47; *Baltimore Afro-American*, April 24, 1943, May 1, 1943, May 29, 1943, August 31, 1943; "Employment of Negro Labor at the Glenn L. Martin Aircraft Plant in Baltimore, Md.," June 18, 1941, BES, RG 183, Box 165, NA; "Employee Counseling: A Report," February 25, 1944, WBA, RG 86, Box 1540, NA; "Where Can We Get War Workers?" Public Affairs Pamphlet No. 75, 1942, BES, RG 183, Box 162, NA; Memo, Frank M. Landers to William F. Schaub, May 31, 1943, CCPA, RG 212, Box 48, NA.

37. *Baltimore Afro-American*, July 31, 1943, April 17, 1943; "Supplement to Report on Adequacy of Labor Supply For: Seattle-Bremerton, Washington Area," September 1943, BES, RG 183, Box 415, NA.

38. Clive, p. 439; *Baltimore Afro-American*, July 31, 1943; "Survey of the Detroit Labor Stabilization Program," BES, RG 183, Box 183, NA.

39. *Baltimore Afro-American*, April 17, 1943; "Labor Market Report for Detroit, Michigan," May 1943, BES, RG 183, Box 183, NA; "Summary Report, Baltimore Labor Market Area," May 9, 1942, OCWS, RG 215, WARC, Box 7, NA.

40. *Baltimore Afro-American*, April 17, 1943; "Where Can We Get War Workers?" Public Affairs Pamphlet No. 75, 1942, BES, RB 183, Box 162, NA; "Special Labor Market Survey, Baltimore, Maryland," March 1942, BES, RG 183, Box 165, NA.

41. "Report on Special Field Visits Regarding Need for Day Care of Children of Women Employed in Defense Industries," April 6, 1942, OCWS, RG 215, Children's Division, Box 3, NA; "Labor Market Developments Report, Baltimore," March 1943, July 1943, BES, RG 183, Box 161, NA.

42. "Where Can We Get War Workers?" Public Affairs Pamphlet No. 75, 1942, BES, RG 183, Box 162, NA; "Labor Market Developments Report, Baltimore," July 1943, BES, RG 183, Box 161, NA; *Baltimore Afro-American*, January 2, 1943, May 29, 1943, July 3, 1943.

43. "General Comments of Workers, Baltimore, Maryland," WBA, RG 86, Box 1541, NA; *Baltimore Afro-American*, January 19, 1943, April 24, 1943, July 31, 1943; "Labor Market Developments in the Detroit Area," November 5, 1943, BES, RG 183, Box 17, NA; "Supplement to Report on Adequacy of Labor Supply For: Seattle-Bremerton, Washington Area," September 1943, BES, RG 183, Box 415, NA.

44. U.S., Bureau of the Census, "Characteristics of the Detroit-Willow Run Congested Production Area," p. 16; "Day Care of Children of Working Mothers," March 25, 1942, OCWS, RG 215, Children's Care Division, Box 3, NA.

45. "General Comments of Workers, Baltimore, Maryland," WBA, RG 86, Box 1541, NA; *Baltimore Afro-American*, September 25, 1943.

46. "Employee Counseling: A Report," WBA, RG 86, Box 1540, NA; *Baltimore Afro-American*, January 2, 1943, January 16, 1943, May 29, 1943, July 3, 1943.

47. "General Comments of Workers, Baltimore, Maryland," WBA, RG 86, Box 1541, NA; *Baltimore Afro-American*, April 17, 1943; Clive, p. 482; Robert Weaver, *Negro Labor: A National Problem* (New York: Harcourt, Brace, 1946), p. 294; A. G. Mezerik, "Getting Rid of the Women," *Atlantic* (June 1945); 82.

48. "General Comments of Workers, Baltimore, Maryland," WBA, RG 86, Box 1541, NA.

49. Weaver, pp. 17, 19–20, 25, 285–86.

50. Mezerik, p. 82; "Firm Schedule: Boeing Aircraft Company," January 1943, WBA, RG 86, Box 1413, NA; *Seattle Times*, June 7, 1942; September 24, 1942, November 22, 1942, April 4, 1943; *Aero Mechanic*, May 14, 1942.

51. "Women's War Recruiting Program, Baltimore Area," OCWS, WARC, RG 215, Box 7, NA; "Firm Schedule: Boeing Aircraft Company," January 1943, WBA, RG 86, Box 1413, NA; *Seattle Times*, August 20, 1942; *Aero Mechanic*, July 23, 1942.

52. *Baltimore Evening Sun*, August 18, 1942; Straub, "Government Policy Toward," p. 180; Myer, pp. 46–47.

53. *New York Times*, June 8, 1943; Lowell Carr and James Stermer, *Willow Run: A Study of Industrialization and Cultural Inadequacy* (New York: Harper & Brothers, 1952), pp. 174–75.

54. *Seattle Times*, September 27, 1941, August 12, 1942, May 2, 1943; *Navy Yard Salute*, July 31, 1943.

55. *Seattle Times*, December 24, 1941, April 19, 1942, December 5, 1942; *Washington State CIO News*, November 1942.

56. *Seattle Times*, August 6, 1942; 104 *Reporter*, March 6, 1942, April 17, 1942, August 6, 1942, August 13, 1942.

57. 104 *Reporter*, August 6, 1942, August 13, 1942.

58. *Seattle Times*, August 21, 1942, September 9, 1942, September 11, 1942, September 18, 1942; 104 *Reporter*, August 27, 1942, September 17, 1942, September 24, 1942, November 5, 1942, November 26, 1942.

59. *Seattle Times*, March 4, 1942, March 26, 1942, March 27, 1942.

60. Ibid., March 24, 1942, March 26, 1942, March 27, 1942, April 7, 1942.

61. Ibid., March 28, 1942, October 6, 1942.

62. Ibid., December 6, 1942, February 3, 1943, February 4, 1943.

63. Ibid., October 22, 1942, July 18, 1943, August 8, 1943; *Aero Mechanic*, September 17, 1942, December 24, 1942.

64. *Seattle Times*, October 22, 1942; *Aero Mechanic*, June 18, 1942, December 24, 1942; 104 *Reporter*, July 29, 1943; *International Association of Machinists, Local 79, Bulletin* [hereafter cited as *IAM Bulletin*], November 1942.

65. *Seattle Times*, October 27, 1942.

66. *Seattle Times*, August 8, 1943; *Boeing Magazine*, March 1943; *Baltimore Evening Sun*, September 23, 1942.

67. "Detroit Post-War Study," 1944, WBA, RG 86, Box 1541, NA; *Seattle Times*, October 18, 1942, October 24, 1942, January 10, 1943; *Boeing News*, September 1942; *Aero Mechanic*, December 17, 1942; 104 *Reporter*, November 5, 1942.

68. *CIO News*, August 30, 1943; "General Comments of Workers, Baltimore, Maryland," WBA, RG 86, Box 1541, NA; *Seattle Times*, October 25, 1942,

March 7, 1943; "Seattle—A Boom Comes Back," *Business Week*, June 20, 1942, pp. 26, 28 –32; Letter, Margaret Kay Anderson to Mary Anderson, October 4, 1943, WBA, RG 86, Box 1413, NA.

69. "Labor Turnover in Essential Industries in the Baltimore Labor Market Area," September 1942–December 1943, BES, RG 183, Box 162, NA; "Annual Report, WMC, Maryland Area," 1943, BES, RG 183, Box 163, NA; "Problems of Women War Workers in Detroit," WPB, August 20, 1943, OCWS, WARC, RG 215, Box 10, NA; "Sample Survey of the Experience of Major Firms in the Baltimore Area Under the Maryland Stabilization Plan," August 11, 1943, BES, RG 183, Box 162, NA; *Seattle Times*, October 25, 1942, March 7, 1943, March 26, 1943, March 28, 1943, July 28, 1943; Henry T. Buechel, "Absenteeism in Seattle War Plants," *Northwest Industry* 2 (September 1943): 6.

70. "The Detroit Victory Council, A Suggested Plan for Phase One of the Campaign," November 10, 1943, CCPA, RG 212, Box 51, NA; "Annual Report, WMC, Maryland Area," 1943, BES, RG 183, Box 163, NA; Carr and Stermer, p. 12; Letter, William F. Dorn to Corrington Gill, October 14, 1943, CCPA, RG 212, Box 49, NA; "Composite Report on Health, Welfare and Related Activities in the Detroit, Michigan War Area," December 22, 1943, OCWS, Community Reports, RG 215, Box 5, NA; "Problems of Women War Workers in Detroit," WPB, August 20, 1943, OCWS, WARC, RG 215, Box 10, NA; Letter, Sherwood Gates to Rufus Newman, August 9, 1944, OCWS, General Classified, Michigan (Region V), RG 215, Box 134, NA; *CIO News*, August 30, 1943.

71. "Supplement to Report on Adequacy of Labor Supply for: Seattle-Bremerton, Washington Area," August 1943, BES, RG 183, Box 415, NA; U.S., Bureau of the Census, "Characteristics of the Puget Sound Congested Production Area," p. 12; "Labor Market Developments Report, Baltimore," September 1942, BES, RG 183, Box 161, NA; "Labor Market Developments Report For: Seattle-Bremerton, Washington Area," March 1943, BES, RG 183, Box 415, NA; *Seattle Times*, October 21, 1942.

72. "Labor Market Report for Detroit, Michigan," May 1943, BES, RG 183, Box 183, NA; "Labor Market Developments in the Detroit Area," November 5, 1943, BES, RG 183, Box 17, NA; "Reports on Women at Work," Magazine Division, OWI, June 1943, WBA, RG 86, Box 7, NA.

73. "Employee Counseling: A Report," February 25, 1944, WBA, RG 86, Box 1540, NA; "Progress Report #7, Baltimore Area, WMC" August 8–20, 1943, OCWS, WARC, RG 215, Box 7, NA.

74. *Navy Yard Salute*, September 19, 1942; 104 *Reporter*, November 2, 1944; Letter, Jennie Mohr to Mary Anderson, June 1, 1943, WBA, RG 86, Box 1413, NA; "Report on Womanpower Utilization Meeting," June 9, 1943, WBA, RG 86, Box 1413, NA.

75. "Employee Counseling: A Report," February 25, 1944, WBA, RG 86, Box 1540, NA; "Labor Market Developments Report, For: Seattle-Bremerton, Washington Area," March 1943, BES, RG 183, Box 415, NA; *Ammunition*, August 1944; "Report on Conditions Affecting Production at Willow Run, Local 50, UAW-CIO," February 26, 1943, CCPA, RG 212, Box 50, NA.

76. "Employee Counseling: A Report," February 25, 1944, WBA, RG 86, Box 1540, NA; *Seattle Times*, December 21, 1943; *Boeing News*, September 1942; *Navy Yard Salute*, September 19, 1942, December 5, 1942; 104 *Reporter*, July 29, 1943; "Report on Womanpower Utilization Meeting," June 9, 1943, WBA, RG 86, Box 1413, NA.

77. 104 *Reporter*, July 29, 1943.

78. Memo No. 32, Margaret Kay Anderson to Mary Anderson, June 7, 1943, WBA, RG 86, Box 1413, NA.

79. *Aero Mechanic*, May 14, 1942, March 18, 1943, July 13, 1944; Memo No. 32, Margaret Kay Anderson, June 7, 1943, WBA, RG 86, Box 1413, NA.

80. *Bremerton Sun*, March 11, 1942; *Navy Yard Salute*, May 29, 1943, July 10, 1943, August 28, 1943, October 2, 1943, November 10, 1944, August 3, 1945; "Training, PSNY, Bremerton, Washington," [n.d.], WBA, RG 86, Box 1413, NA.

81. 104 *Reporter*, March 18, 1943, May 11, 1944, June 1, 1944; Memorandum, Caroline Manning to Field Representatives, WBA, RG 86, Box 1404, NA; "Past and Future Outlook on Field Activities in Region 13," Margaret Kay Anderson to Mary Anderson, August 5, 1943, WBA, RG 86, Box 1413, NA.

82. *Seattle Times*, November 20, 1942, February 7, 1943, March 14, 1943; "Firm Schedule: Boeing Aircraft Company," January 1943, WBA, RG 86, Box 1413, NA; "Training, PSNY, Bremerton, Washington," [n.d.], WBA, RG 86, Box 1413, NA; "Ninth Meeting Washington Industrial Area Labor Supply Committee," July 22, 1942, WBA, RG 86, Box 1413, NA; "Labor Market Developments Report, Baltimore," September 1942, BES, RG 183, Box 161, NA; "Composite Report on Health, Welfare and Related Activities in the Detroit, Michigan War Area," December 22, 1943, OCWS, Community Reports, RG 215, Box 5, NA.

83. "Supplementary Trainees and War Production," 1944, WBA, RG 86, Box 1543, NA; "Report for the Baltimore Administrative Area for February, 1944," BES, RG 183, Box 162, NA; "Enrollment in Vocational Courses, Washington," January 31, 1943, Langlie Papers, RG 11–12, Box 12-4, WSA; "Firm Schedule: Boeing Aircraft Company," January 1943, WBA, RG 86, Box 1413, NA; "Training, PSNY, Bremerton, Washington," WBA, RG 86, Box 1413, NA; *Seattle Times*, August 31, 1941.

84. WMC, "Monthly Field Operating Report, Detroit Area," April 1944, BES, RG 183, Box 183, NA; *Seattle Times,* April 2, 1942, April 5, 1942, September 28, 1943; 104 *Reporter,* November 5, 1942; *Washington State CIO News,* December 1942.

85. WMC, "Monthly Field Operating Report, Detroit Area," April 1944, RG 183, Box 183, NA; "Seniority in the Automobile Industry," *Monthly Labor Review* (September 1944): 463-74; *Aero Mechanic,* December 7, 1944; 104 Reporter, May 11, 1944, June 1, 1944; Memo, Jennie Mohr to Mary Anderson, September 1, 1943, WB, RG 86, Box 1413, NA.

86. "Work and Wage Experience of Willow Run Workers," *Monthly Labor Review* (December 1945): 1085; "Women in Trade Unions During the War Period," November 1944, WBA, RG 86, Box 1351, NA; *Ammunition* (August 1944): 12; Memo No. 32, Margaret Kay Anderson to Mary Anderson, June 7, 1943, WBA, RG 86, Box 1413, NA.

87. 104 *Reporter,* February 25, 1943; *Washington State CIO News,* November 1942; *IAM Bulletin,* January 1943.

88. Mezerik, pp. 79-82; *Ammunition* (August 1944); 1, 6-9, 28, 32.

89. Mezerik, p. 79; *Ammunition* (August 1944); 1, 6-9, 28, 32; "Women in Trade Unions During the War Period," November 1944, WBA, RG 86, Box 1351, NA.

90. *Aero Mechanic,* November 26, 1942, December 3, 1942, December 17, 1942, October 28, 1943, December 2, 1943, March 22, 1945.

91. *Aero Mechanic,* May 7, 1942, October 1, 1942, March 4, 1943.

92. *Aero Mechanic,* June 18, 1942, July 2, 1942, July 9, 1942, August 27, 1942.

93. *Seattle Times,* July 26, 1942, November 22, 1942, March 25, 1942; *Navy Yard Salute,* January 19, 1945.

94. *Martin Star,* July 1943; *Aero Mechanic,* June 4, 1942, June 18, 1942, July 1, 1943, July 15, 1943, June 15, 1944, November 9, 1944.

95. *Life,* July 6, 1942; *Baltimore Sun,* March 6, 1945.

96. *Baltimore Sun,* March 4, 1945; *Boeing News,* June 1942; *Seattle Times,* March 15, 1942, January 16, 1944.

97. *Baltimore Sun,* July 4, 1943; *Seattle Times,* June 18, 1942; *Aero Mechanic,* May 28, 1942.

98. Myer, pp. 44-45; *Seattle Times,* July 18, 1943.

99. Carr and Stermer, p. 9; "Boeing's Role in the War—1943 . . . ," *Northwest Industry* 4 (December 1944): 39-40.

100. "General Comments of Workers, Baltimore, Maryland," WBA, RG 86, Box 1541, NA; *Seattle Times,* August 7, 1942; *Navy Yard Salute,* February 27, 1943, June 30, 1944.

101. *Aero Mechanic,* July 29, 1943.

102. Hartmann.

3

THE FAMILY
IN WARTIME

The issue of World War II's effect on family life engaged the attention of many Americans while the war was being waged; wartime changes and the responses to them were important in shaping Americans' values and behavior in the postwar era. For many Americans the war seemed to presage rapid changes that threatened the integrity of conventional family patterns and values. Men were entering the armed forces or migrating to centers of war industry to seek employment, leaving their wives and children behind. Many wives and mothers were taking jobs for the first time, disrupting traditional family role divisions and living patterns. Children were finding themselves more on their own as their opportunities for activities outside of the home increased and parental supervision decreased. The sense of urgency created by wartime conditions accelerated the processes of both family formation and dissolution as marriage, birth, and divorce rates skyrocketed. The housing shortage, child care problems, the tensions of geographic and social mobility, and other adversities of wartime living contributed to the stresses on family life.

Nevertheless, traditional attitudes and behaviors displayed considerable tenacity under the pressures of wartime circumstances. In many ways, the war reinforced and perpetuated existing role divisions and their ideological underpinnings. With its emphasis on the centrality of the male role of warrior and protector, it widened the experiential gap between men and women and reaffirmed the greater cultural value attached to male activities. Traditional roles and responsibilities retained their appeal for many women, who eschewed the work opportunities afforded women during the war and devoted themselves instead to their increasing duties at home. Moreover, the level of anxiety generated by the wartime changes and its accompanying resort to institutions of social control to manage individual conduct served to contain the forces for change.[1]

In no facet of social conduct did this situation hold more true than in the area of sexuality. Because of the altered circumstances governing male-female relations and the disruption of established family and sexual relationships caused by wartime military and economic mobilization, many thought that a reliance on conventional values and controls would be inadequate to sustain the revised double standard of post-Victorian America. As a result, a renewed vigilance regarding women's sexual conduct and an increasing resort to psychological and social welfare authorities to explain and regulate women's behavior characterized the war years. Wartime practices, then, provided a precedent upon which postwar America built.[2]

One indication of the continuing psychological and social importance of family life to Americans was the zeal with which they assumed family obligations, especially in the early months of the war. Faced with the uncertainties and difficulties of wartime, many young couples decided to go ahead and get married or have children rather than wait until the war ended. Nationally, there were 1,118,000 more marriages between 1940 and 1943 than would have been expected at prewar rates. In addition, the nation experienced a 25 percent increase in the population aged five and under. In the areas under study, Seattle experienced the most pronounced acceleration of marriage and birth rates. The proportion of women over the age of fifteen who were married increased from 57.5 percent to 62.5 percent from 1940 to 1944, while the figures for Detroit indicated only a slight increase, from 63.7 percent to 64.6 percent. In the Seattle area the number of children under five grew 77 percent, while the number rose 34.7 percent in the Detroit Willow Run area.[3]

The rush to the altar was a product of several tendencies that were especially important in wartime. As a consequence of the war boom economy, many couples could finally afford to get married. Others with established relationships moved up their wedding dates to give themselves some time before the husband joined the military. For many, including large numbers of young women, however, the prospect of a long war fostered a sense of urgency regarding marital prospects and caused them to push for marriages. Many young women considered "get your man while you can" a good wartime strategy. They worried that it would be difficult to sustain an existent relationship if a long separation was not preceded by marriage and that it would be difficult to make a good match if they waited until they were older.[4]

A particularly pernicious fear felt among the generation coming to maturity was that they would lose out to their younger sisters if they deferred marriage very long, given the cultural tradition dictating that men marry women younger than themselves. Coeds at Wayne University had these apprehensions reinforced when Dr. Paul Popenoe, director of the American Institute of Family Relations, gave a bleak talk on their wartime marital prospects. Most young women, however, did not need an expert explanation of their plight. The shortage of men in their age groups soon became readily apparent as millions of young men left to serve in the armed forces. By 1944, the sex ratio (the number of men per 100 women) in the twenty–twenty-four age group was 47.9 nationally, 29.7 in the Detroit-Willow Run area, and 37.7 in the Seattle area.[5]

The psychological dimensions of the unbalanced sex ratio of the war years have not been fully explored. Clearly, however, for many young women men became a scarce and valued commodity. The growing popularity of going steady among middle-class teenagers, the rise in teenage marriages, and the revision of standards of sexual conduct among some younger women were all cultural expressions of this wartime phenomenon. In a marriage-oriented but male-scarce society, getting and retaining male attention and approval became an even greater preoccupation for many girls and women than it had been before the war.[6]

Seattle offers a good indication of the impact and implications of the male deficit in a war boom community which served as a servicemen's center as well as a center of war industry. Because the large number of military personnel in the area offered a solution to the male shortage in the resident population, the area became a magnet for young girls seeking relationships with servicemen. They often arrived penniless, without a job or a place to live, and with no one in the community to turn to. In Bremerton such girls were taken to the city police station for overnight detention. Some were runaways who were returned to their parents; others stayed in the area and took jobs to support themselves. In some cases they applied to the county welfare department for aid when their relationship with soldiers did not work out. In Tacoma three such girls, all sixteen years old, ended up in the custody of the juvenile authorities after they were stranded by their soldier husbands, whom they had met and married within ten days of their arrival from Idaho. When they were found by police morals squad officers, they had $.21 between them and were ashamed and afraid to tell their parents of their plight.[7]

Marriage thus remained an important focus for women's aspirations during the war years despite the demographic and labor force changes occurring. In the Seattle area especially the number of teenage marriages skyrocketed. The proportion of girls aged fifteen to nineteen who were married rose from 7.0 percent in 1940 to 12.4 percent in 1944. According to Hildegard Stevenson, girls' counselor at Roosevelt High School, many girls were marrying at a younger age than usual for fear of not marrying at all if they deferred doing so. Among single women workers interviewed by the Women's Bureau in Seattle the vast majority reported plans to marry servicemen at some later date. Prewar values and assumptions shaped the response of women to wartime changes; rather than devising a more autonomous and woman-centered lifestyle in response to better job opportunities and a lessened chance for marriage, most seemed to intensify their commitment to conventional family and sex role patterns.[8]

Whether they were war brides or not, many wives faced the prospect of separation from their husbands, often for prolonged periods of time, as military service disrupted family life. Although only 8 percent of American wives were married to servicemen, young wives faced a much greater chance of separation from their husbands. In 1944, over half of the teenaged wives and over one-third of those aged twenty to twenty-four in the Seattle area reported their husbands absent. Despite Selective Service policies that reaffirmed the American commitment to family life by deferring husbands and fathers for as long as possible, many men with family responsibilities eventually faced the draft. Because of the large number of occupational deferments granted to men in war boom communities, married men and fathers faced the draft sooner there than in other areas of the country. In January 1943, Michigan Selective Service officials announced that they would start drafting husbands who did not have children. In Seattle, married men were drafted beginning February 1, 1943, and by the end of the year large numbers of fathers were being called up as well.[9]

Other men with families chose to enlist, many for patriotic reasons; others because they preferred to volunteer rather than to wait for the inevitable draft. Seattle furniture dealer Isadore Rogoway, for example, explained his decision to join the army and leave his wife and three children by stating that he had "more to defend" than a single man. Some joined the service in order to escape marital problems, usually exacerbating an already bad situation. Such dereliction of family duties on the part of men did not provoke the ambivalent or hostile response that decisions by women which ostensibly diminished their commitment to family duties would elicit. In the Ruth Alden advice column in the *Detroit Free Press*, for example, a woman who signed her letter "Embittered" wrote of her grief over the enlistment of her husband, who had left her and their three children alone but financially secure so that he could fight in the war. Alden denied that his first responsibility was to his family at home and advised the woman to stress to her children that their father and other men were making sacrifices to keep their homes and families safe.[10]

Another cause of family separations was the decision by many men to migrate to war centers in order to take jobs in the burgeoning defense industries. Although they intended to send for their families as soon as they had secured employment and found adequate housing, doing so often took considerably longer than they had anticipated because of the critical housing shortages in such places, especially in the early years of the war. In Detroit, for example, the director of the Home Registration Office, W. Joseph Starrs, declared in January 1943 that the housing problem was rapidly going from desperate to hopeless. Landlord discrimination against couples with children only made the situation that much worse for those newcomers who wanted to send for their families.[11]

Decisions by public housing officials frequently worsened the problem for those who wanted to keep their families intact. In an October 1942 meeting of WMC officials and others concerned about the housing shortage in Baltimore, economy with public money and the necessity for a speedy recruitment of workers weighed more heavily with officials than did family integrity. Several, including Captain John Brown, the War Department liaison officer, urged that every possible way of housing male workers without their families be explored. In Willow Run, federal housing projects ultimately provided more than adequate housing space for single men, but those with families considered themselves lucky to find anything.[12]

If the housing shortage was a problem for whites, it was a crisis for blacks. Given the prewar backlog of substandard and overcrowded housing for blacks, they faced an even more difficult and immediate need than did white workers. Yet during the war private home construction was minimal and confined to white neighborhoods, and public housing for nonwhites became embroiled in the politics of prejudice as public officials and private groups argued over the funding and locations of housing projects for blacks. In Detroit in 1942, riots broke out when the Sojourner Truth Housing Project was located in a white area. Because controversy almost always followed a decision to build black housing, such projects were sometimes abandoned and usually delayed. As of June 30, 1944, 60 percent of the planned black housing units in Baltimore were not yet begun or only barely under way. Even when white housing was not filled, blacks were kept out. At the Willow Run dormitory, for example, vacancies were plentiful by 1944, but it was not considered "feasible" to open them to blacks. In Baltimore, officials noted a surplus of white housing by August 1944, while non-white housing remained in short supply.[13]

Whether caused by housing difficulties or by military obligations, the separations experienced by families during wartime produced their share of marital strains. In Seattle, for example, many men, when they could not find a place for their families, pleaded with the Home Registration Office to write to their wives and confirm that housing was not available because their failure to send for their families had caused serious discord. Among the servicemen's wives interviewed by Women's Bureau representatives, a surprising number indicated plans to divorce their husbands after the war, noting that their marriages had been rocky before or that they had met someone else in his absence.[14]

Not surprisingly, no issue generated a greater emotional response than that of marital fidelity on the part of servicemen's wives. As Susan Hartmann has pointed out, wartime separations occasioned a considerable literature condoning infidelity on the part of the warrior husband as natural and inevitable, while urging the importance of the wife's faithfulness to a successful postwar reconciliation. Considerable anxiety on this score was evidenced in a column by Army Chaplain Captain H. A. Robinson in the *Baltimore Afro-American*, in which he warned servicemen's wives that those proved unfaithful could have their allotments stopped or be divorced by their husbands.[15]

Yet many women, especially some who had entered into hasty war marriages at a young age, found adhering to such high standards of conduct very difficult. For many of these young war brides, marital bonds were tenuous, and the desire for companionship, social activities, male approval, and sexual experience which had contributed to their hasty marriages persisted even in their husbands' absence. Some found that the loneliness of wartime separation was exacerbated by conventional mores which limited their social activities and their opportunities for companionship. Given the absence of an ethos of female cameraderie and the strength of the idea that women's sociability and recreation should center around men, the continuation of premarital social patterns by some young married women who found themselves alone should not have been surprising. Advice columnists received countless letters from such women, who found it extremely difficult to stay home while other young women could go out without censure. One such letter to Dorothy Dix pointed out that married servicemen could participate in the same social activities as single men while their wives could not seek the company of men in any way and complained that such a double standard was "unfair, intolerable, and lousy." According to the Kinsey survey, infidelity among very young married women increased to some extent during the 1940s, making them the only group to experience such a change.[16]

Other strains took their toll on marriages as well. Constantly changing shifts at work, incompatible work schedules, the necessity to develop new role divisions in response to the new duties assumed by wives, the lack of privacy in overcrowded war housing, and the new opportunities for social and sexual contacts outside marriage as women and men worked together to a greater extent than they ever had before all contributed to marital discord during the war years. Such conflicts could begin when a wife decided to take a job and her husband objected, either because he thought that it would reflect on his abilities as a breadwinner or because it would detract from family life. Many women went ahead and entered the labor force, despite their husbands' objections. Most were able to work it out somehow. One of the happier cases was that of

Gertrude Anderson, an employee of a Tacoma furniture company, who commented, "When I told my husband . . . that I was coming down here to work, he threatened to leave home. But now he's happy and I am, too."[17]

Not every case had such a happy resolution, however. For Elsie Parson, a Seattle Boeing employee, her decision to take a war job led to divorce court, where Superior Court Judge Roger Meakim refused her petition for a divorce, stating:

> I can't order a reconciliation, but I can deny the divorce with the provision that this woman quit her job and undertake to rear her family properly. . . .
>
> It is not her privilege to work when her husband objects and when her duty is toward her children. It will be too bad for Boeing, but this temporary war expediency is ruining too many families.

He ordered her husband to pay the house payments and give her $100 a month and continued the case for three months "in the hope that the couple reforms its ideas and submerges its personal desires." The final disposition of the case is unknown, but it does indicate that at least the judge tried to use his power to enforce traditional family organization at the expense of the growing independence of women.[18]

Parson was not alone in her willingness to take advantage of wartime work opportunities in order to end an unhappy marriage. A twenty-one-year old rivet bucker told *Aero Mechanic* columnist Gerry Colson, "I love my job. For the first time since I was married—at 17 years old—I'm having some fun and feel free. My husband, who is nice as pie now, has had his way before this, but we're separating and I'm moving into a house with three other Boeing girls." According to Colson, similar situations could be found throughout the plant. King County Clerk Norman Riddell agreed with her observation, commenting, "Women, with children or without, just seem to be getting more independent and rather than keep their families intact are turning to the divorce courts. In most cases they are war working wives and mothers. Otherwise they probably wouldn't choose to go on their own." Orville Robertson, executive secretary of the Seattle Family Society, noted that women who had been unhappily married, some for years, were displaying assertiveness and independence once they could get high-paying jobs.[19]

Whether a product of women's increasing independence or of other sources of marital strain, the war did spawn a rising number of divorces. In Wayne County, the number rose 28 percent between 1938 and 1943. As early as 1941, Baltimore experienced a 38 percent annual increase in the number of petitions for divorce filed. Nationally, the divorce rate for women aged fifteen and older rose from 8.8 per 1,000 in 1940 to 14.4 per 1,000 by 1945.[20]

As in other areas of family relations, the new wartime prosperity had contradictory effects on marital relationships. In some cases, increased economic security eased the stresses caused by inadequate incomes. The improved economic situation of male wage earners allowed some husbands to provide support without relying on other family members' contributions, enabling their wives to withdraw from the labor force and strengthening the economic basis for male authority within the household. In general, however, the opening up of high-paying industrial jobs to women threatened a greater equalization of income levels between working-class men and women than was likely in the middle-class; as a result the economic foundation for female dependence and subordination was correspondingly strained in some working-class households. According to a postwar study on the effects of working wives on family power relationships, the increased influence in family decision making fostered by the wife's employment is more pronounced in working-class than in middle-class households. Moreover, the strict separation of male and female spheres of activity characteristic of working-class social organization and the exaggerated stress on ostensibly sex-specific attributes were threatened by the sexual integration of the previously male blue-collar workplace. The hostility of male workers when women intruded into their work world reflected an attempt not only to protect their prerogatives in the labor force but to preserve the ideological and cultural bases for their family authority as well.[21]

Men of the middle class, by contrast, did not experience a comparable incursion into the jobs traditionally allocated to them because the expansion of white-collar jobs for women occurred in traditional "women's" fields, including teaching, nursing, and clerical categories. As noted above, class barriers inhibited many middle-class women from taking advantage of opportunities for better-paying factory jobs. Although the economic contributions of women in middle-class families increased during the war, such changes did not raise any real possibly of eliminating income differentials or undercutting male prerogatives in the family or general economy. Thus, the subversive potential of wartime changes operated with diminished effects in middle-class marriages.

In response to the potentially disruptive effects of new roles and other wartime changes on family relations, the cultural stress on women's special responsibilities to maintain smooth-running and amicable households despite difficulties was increased. As wartime inconveniences and cramped conditions sparked family conflicts, the homemaker's task of mediating disagreements and enhancing interpersonal relations assumed exaggerated importance, leaving little room for individual assertion and taking an especially high toll on women's emotional resources. Mrs. Edgar C. Thompson, president of the Michigan Congress of Parents and Teachers, told members of her organization that the first duty of wives in wartime was not voluntary work (much less paid employment) but rather keeping family morale high and, especially, providing a happy home for their husbands, who, according to Thompson, were bearing the brunt of the war experience.[22]

Harriet Arnow provided a model of such feminine sacrifice in her perceptive and sensitive fictional account of the life of Gertie Nevels, a mountain woman who followed her husband to wartime Detroit so that he might realize his dreams, even though it meant the denial of her own ambitions and needs. Once ensconced in her tiny, inadequate housing project home, Nevels found that the new imperative of urban wartime living was adjustment and that her role as wife, mother, and neighbor was to facilitate that goal. In conformity with the dictates of educational experts and against her own inclinations, she forced her young daughter to abandon an imaginary playmate, a decision with tragic consequences. Caught in an urban environment she neither liked nor understood, Nevels seemed to spend much of her time explaining, cajoling, and mediating disputes in order to foster a sufficient acceptance of the new life and keep it from destroying her family and whatever community the project residents had managed to generate.[23]

Child care responsibilities increased for many mothers during the war as a result of serious overcrowding in the schools in some war boom communities. The material priorities of the war years, the delays involved in obtaining federal priorities permission and federal aid to expand school facilities, and the speed with which the situation worsened inhibited the satisfactory resolution of the problem. By February 1942, the Detroit area had 30,000 children on half-day sessions. The city of Detroit had three-fourths of its high schools operating with double sessions. In Baltimore school officials put two elementary schools on double sessions and then refused admission to children from the growing trailer parks and housing projects in the fall of 1942. As a result of such actions, many mothers found that their children were home much more than under normal circumstances.[24]

Wartime conditions created other difficulties and responsibilities for the housewife as well. As a result of the housing and other shortages, performing previously routine chores became inconvenient, time-consuming, and difficult. While the performance of her household tasks was made more complex by the need to conserve natural resources and foodstuffs, a whole host of voluntary activities clamored for her time. Many women planted victory gardens and canned the foods they produced, knitted sweaters for soldiers, spent several hours a week as volunteers for various civil defense services, helped in salvage drives, or engaged in a variety of other war-related activities.[25]

For some women the challenges of wartime living were especially difficult. Probably no war boom community in the nation rivalled Willow Run for its overcrowded and squalid living conditions as it attempted to create a community almost overnight in order to accommodate the thousands of workers who came, many with their families, to take jobs at the Ford Bomber Plant. For many of these newcomers, tents, shacks, trailers, housing project apartments and houses, and other makeshift quarters served as home during the war years. A Washtenaw County Health Department report in late 1942 found 3,000 workers housed in basements and garages and 13,000 in trailers, tents, and substandard rooms and houses. Some homes were erected without the benefit of sewer or water systems. Backyard wells and privies situated dangerously close to one another posed a constant health problem and represented a considerable challenge to the homemaker desirous of maintaining any standard of cleanliness.[26]

The diary of Mrs. John Castle in Lowell Carr and James Stermer's study of Willow Run indicates the extent of the difficulties posed. The wife of a bomber plant employee and mother of a school-age son, Castle struggled to make a home of their small trailer but did so against insurmountable odds. She had to get her hot water in a service room 300 feet from the trailer. She did her laundry in a communal laundry room, where hot water was scarce and rarely available after the early morning hours; moreover, the large numbers of people served by the camp utility house made waiting for available machines almost inevitable. Because the grounds had not been planted with grass, dirt and mud were ever present, inside and out, despite continual cleaning.[27]

For those women whose husbands worked evening or night shifts, keeping the children quiet while their husbands slept required constant vigilance and frayed the nerves of all concerned. The absence of play-grounds, recreation facilities, or even yards meant that there were few appropriate places for children to play. Consequently, they crowded into trailer camp restrooms and utility rooms, which were always crowded, dirty, and noisy as a result. Those mothers who kept their children at home faced long hours during which their responsibility to keep the children occupied, quiet, and out of trouble took a great deal of their time and taxed their imagination and patience.[28]

The inadequacy of public transportation and the absence of commer-cial services nearby kept many of these women sequestered in their homes. Moreover, the transient population of their makeshift commun-ities, the inhospitable reception accorded newcomers by the established residents, and the class, religious, and regional differences among in-migrants militated against the development of a strong social network to provide support and companionship. When their husbands worked long hours and their domestic responsibilities kept them tied to their homes, many housewives found that social isolation became the worst aspect of wartime conditions. In his *State of the Nation*, John Dos Passos gave the syndrome a name, noting that Detroit was filled with "trailer-wacky women," who could get no respite from their children or their cramped quarters.[29]

For in-migrant and older resident alike, the wartime rationing and curtailment of consumer goods and services created considerable incon-venience. Shopping and food preparation came to entail the juggling of ration cards and points; changing menus to take into account shortages of meat, sugar, vegetables, and other staples of the American diet; and adjusting shopping schedules in order to get scarce items whenever they happened to be available. The necessity to conserve scarce resources meant more time devoted to the cultivation of victory gardens, to home canning, and to segregating and saving the tin cans, shortening, and other products for the various salvage drives.[30]

Restrictions on the production of clothing, shoes, and household appliances meant considerable time and effort expended in sewing, mending, and repairing as well as in shopping for items that were diffi-cult to procure. Homemakers had to be resourceful in making do and making over in order to compensate for unavailable or inadequately apportioned items, from egg beaters to children's shoes. At the same time, the curtailment of commercial repair services further complicated the homemaker's plight. A Detroit Victory Council survey revealed that inadequate shoe, radio, and electrical appliance repairs and the curtailment of laundry services posed the greatest difficulties for Detroit consumers.[31]

In-migrants faced even greater consumer problems than did established residents. Commercial operations frequently gave priority to regular customers; access to laundry and other services was denied to many newcomers. The scarcity of grocery stores and other retail outlets in the vicinity of housing projects and trailer parks and in other rapidly growing suburban areas meant that in-migrant customers had little recourse but to accept the prices, quality, and terms of the businesses in their areas. Blacks were especially victimized by such circumstances because the development of commercial services for black housing projects lagged behind that of white projects and discrimination and/or racial tension was frequently the rule in private businesses in the area.[32]

Because of the sacrifices expected of wartime homemakers, considerable patriotic reward was conferred on those who performed their work well and with the proper spirit. Jean McBride, director of the *Detroit News* test kitchen, told participants in a Detroit Homemakers' Conference that maintaining a clean house was a patriotic duty because clean fabrics and equipment lasted longer, contributing to the conservation of materials needed for war production. Women who were members of the Baltimore Block Brigade received a letter reminding them that the shortage of health care personnel meant that their responsibilities to maintain family health had assumed greater importance. Emphasizing the different spheres allotted to men and women in the war effort, the *Seattle Times* stressed the importance of the contributions made by housewives as follows: "Men fight the war with bayonets, long hours at defense jobs, 'leisure' hours at air-raid drills. Women fight the war with stewpans, knitting needles, alarm clocks that go off at 4 o' clock in the morning, rudely awakened babies, unelastic budgets, fast-rising prices." It later noted that "the kitchen and the sewing room are the housewife's battleground."[33]

Such patriotic rhetoric, however, could not disguise the fact that women had been delegated a disproportionate share of the burden of coping with civilian deprivation while public officials and private groups did little to alleviate the situation. The women's sections of newspapers offered recipes and advice on coping with wartime short-ages. Various organizations offered courses in nutrition, first aid, home appliance repair, and the like. In Baltimore, the Pratt Library opened a war service center, modeled after British projects, to provide information on victory gardens, rationing, and conservation and a swap shop for scarce items. Although it offered canning classes in 1943 and 1944, the Baltimore Civilian Mobilization Commission rejected a proposal to establish canning centers that would make scarce equipment available to the public on the grounds that they would be too costly. Seattle housewives, however, benefited from the opening of such centers in the schools there.[34]

Given the extent of the need for public and private cooperative efforts to ease the housewife's burden, the degree to which housework remained individualized and privatized during the war years is striking. Because of the cultural priority accorded military and industrial activities, devoting time or resources to reducing the level of effort required to accomplish domestic tasks received little attention. To the extent that they participated in socialized, cooperative work, housewives did so in order to extend their altruistic service from their families to their communities and nation rather than to rationalize their own work.[35]

If she chose not to add paid employment to her other duties, the housewife was expected to participate in a variety of volunteer activities, ranging from war bond drives to Red Cross work. To the extent that the shortage of volunteer workers allowed, voluntary organizations often assigned jobs on the basis of conventional ideas as to appropriate sexual spheres. Male volunteers generally became air raid wardens and auxiliary policemen and firemen while women did clerical work, aided in child care centers, handled housing and rationing chores, and coordinated salvage activities. When the Baltimore Volunteer Office needed workers to remove scrap from the lots where it had been collected, it decided to use high school boys because such work was "not desirable" for women. In the 1942 War Chest fund-raising campaign in Seattle, women work-ers handled the residential areas while the limited number of men available covered the downtown business and industrial areas. Similarly, when Baltimore was organizing its Block Brigade, the Civilian Mobiliza-tion Commission (CMC) refused to refer male volunteers as block captains because men had other more important work to do and the work was deemed best done by women.[36]

Not surprisingly, such stereotyping extended to the designation of leadership positions as well. Local victory committees generally delegated civil defense, war production, and labor supply slots to men, while women were given responsibility for consumer affairs, housing, and child care. In at least one case the arbitrary designation of volunteer responsibilities resulted in many resignations by women leaders. When the Maryland Council of Defense decided in the wake of Pearl Harbor to transfer some of the civil defense duties previously done by the women's division to the main council body on the grounds that these increasingly important responsibilities should then be done by men, women leaders and volunteers left the organization en masse. The flood of resignations included Mrs. John L. Whitehurst, chairwoman of the Baltimore County Women's Committee, and the entire Baltimore County Committee. Although treated as a comic episode in the official state history of the war, the incident marked one of the few serious protests against sex stereotyping during the war years. Significantly, however, the women did not explore the feminist implications of the situation, which thus did not serve as a catalyst for feminist organization or activism. Moreover, for those women who stayed in civil defense work, the sharp sexual division continued as a source of annoyance.[37]

Stereotyping among volunteer workers was not so thoroughgoing elsewhere, however. Because of the shortage of men, some women became air raid wardens, and hundreds participated in the Aircraft Warning Service. In Detroit, for example, women were initiallly discouraged from volunteering as air wardens, but by March 1942, civil defense officials were urging them to sign up as wardens because the number of male volunteers would not be sufficient. Some women occupied important leadership positions in local victory committees and other civic and charitable organizations, developing their administrative and other skills and helping to shape wartime decisions.[38]

Although volunteer work during the war frequently involved participation in activities traditionally undertaken by unpaid workers, the expansion of government and other services at a same time when labor was in short supply also fostered the utilization of volunteers for work that had previously been done primarily by paid employees. Such volunteers were especially important in staffing expanding government agencies, including the Office of Price Administration, Selective Service, and the U.S. Employment Service. In Seattle, 77 percent of the OPA workers in 1944 were volunteers. In Baltimore, more than 300 women were recruited to do clerical work in the OPA fuel oil rationing offices alone. The volunteer office of the Baltimore Civilian Mobilization Commission was selective, however, in referring volunteers to those agencies having trouble getting paid help. It was willing to supply volunteers to the OPA for its rationing programs because the work was sporadic and seemed directly related to the war effort, but it balked at sending women to the USES because they worked side by side with paid clerical help doing routine filing.[39]

Women thus alleviated the labor shortage of the war years not only by taking paid work but also by contributing thousands of hours of labor to government agencies, day-care centers, hospitals, and other services. They were willing to do so because of the patriotic sanction accorded such work and because those employers were willing to be flexible in assigning hours of work, formal "hiring" requirements, and the provision of on-the-job training when the labor they were receiving was free. Moreover, employers were able to delegate responsibility for the recruitment and assignment of workers to the volunteer offices, thus saving on personnel and administrative expenses. With such benefits, it is not surprising that employers had little inclination to offer paid work on a temporary, part-time basis to large numbers of women.

War-related activities thus claimed much of the homemaker's time, both in and out of the home. Despite her various contributions to the war effort and the continuing importance of her traditional responsibilities, the status of the homemaker seemed to decline, at least in a relative sense, during the war years as more attention and honor were conferred on the soldier and the woman employee in a war job. When the Detroit Diary column in the *Detroit Free Press* suggested that housewives riding city busses give up their seats to women war workers, it provoked a heated defense of the importance of the "WIK" (Wife in Kitchen) in wartime. One irate housewife wrote that women took war jobs for money, not patriotic reasons, and asked:

What is all this ado about female war workers? Where do they get the idea that they are to be bowed to just because they wear a defense badge and a pair of slacks? All these workers are actually tired from is mentally computing the amount they've earned for that one day.

She further pointed out that housewives were tired, too, from shopping, "waiting around for service, rushing through crowds trying to buy the necessities in face of all these shortages and making the best of everything." Other writers agreed with her, frequently mentioning the housewife's essential role in maintaining home front morale.[40]

Despite the increasing difficulties and the relative decline in the status of homemaking, it retained its appeal for the vast majority of American women. Although historians usually note the extent to which the war promoted an exodus of wives from the home into war industries and other jobs, only 26 percent of American wives worked for pay during the war. Moreover, those with lessened home responsibilities were the most likely to attempt to combine paid employment and domestic responsibilities. Servicemen's wives were three times more likely to take a job than other wives. By contrast, mothers of young children were less inclined to seek employment than other wives.[41]

Nonetheless, the wartime changes were extensive enough to promote considerably anxiety regarding a perceived abrogation of family responsibilities on the part of women. Dr. Robert Foster, director of Family Life Services of the Merrill-Palmer School in Detroit, told a meeting of employee counselors there that women's entrance into war industries had resulted in "some distortion of values, irregular family routines, promiscuity, lack of respect by men [for women], and a rejection of feminine roles." In an article in *Survey Midmonthly*, Josephine Abbott wrote that women who worked were "repudiating their children in their newly found freedom" and that "many of them are rejecting their feminine roles. They wish to control their own fertility in marriage, and say they never wanted the children they had." Scare stories about "latchkey children" and "eight-hour orphans" filled the newspapers and magazines, even though most surveys showed that the vast majority of working mothers made arrangements for the care of their children before they took jobs. In Seattle, L. L. Hegland, administrator of the King County Welfare Department, reported that some Boeing employees left their children to sleep in locked cars in the parking lot while they worked. Similar stories were told by other social welfare officials.[42]

It is not clear, however, whether child neglect and abuse became more commonplace during the war or merely more visible. In the Willow Run area, long-term residents discussed the possibility of circulating a petition demanding better care of their children on the part of newcomers, whom they perceived to be neglectful and thoughtless in childrearing.

Police and other agencies noted an increase in the number of abandoned and neglected children brought to their attention. According to Seattle police statistics, the number of juvenile girls referred to them because of abuse, neglect, or abandonment increased from 151 in 1940 to a wartime high of 343 in 1944. Social welfare agencies also reported an increase in applications for the placement of small children on the part of their mothers. Some of these cases were the desperate response of parents to the lack of housing for families and/or the lack of adequate day care. At the same time, the war did provide a patriotic rationale for women who found their parental responsibilities too much to cope with and wished to place their children with others in order to go to work.[43]

It is likely, however, that the number of women who actually abandoned their prescribed duties was small. What is significant is the level of anxiety that wartime changes and opportunities generated regarding such a possibility. The fear expressed about women rejecting their children, especially by psychologists and social welfare officials, reflected a surprising anxiety about the presence or strength of the "maternal instinct." Similarly, the apprehension regarding the abandonment of feminine roles belied the conventional wisdom regarding an ostensibly immutable feminine personality. As the postwar period would indicate, war-created uncertainties regarding sex roles could lead just as easily to a retreat into traditionalism as to a full acknowledgment of the implications of new behaviors.

The war affected family roles and relationships in other ways as well. Because of the absence of some fathers who were in the military, the employment of larger numbers of mothers, and the greater importance of other outside activities in the lives of parents, parental supervision over their children was lessened to some extent. Many younger children spent a significant proportion of their time at a day-care center or at the home of a baby-sitter. Many teenagers took jobs and participated in voluntary activities. Some migrated to defense centers to seek employment, leaving their families behind and moving into housing project dormitories or cheap downtown hotels. Older children's growing independence, financial and otherwise, and their increasing outside activities contributed to the disorganization of traditional family structure.[44]

Among the activities that claimed the time of many youngsters were voluntary duties similar to those engaged in by adults. Schools, community organizations, and youth groups organized young people to aid in scrap drives, victory garden projects, Red Cross and civil defense work, and a variety of other war-related endeavors. Many high school students belonged to the national High School Victory Corps; Seattle high schools set aside one class period a day for Victory Corps work. Although some of these activities, including the conservation efforts and victory gardens, enlisted large numbers of both boys and girls, the charitable work of young people also reflected the sexual division of labor found in similar adult activities. Girls knitted sweaters and afghans while boys became messengers for air raid wardens. Classes in child care, home nursing, and first aid sponsored by the Victory Corps, the Red Cross, and the Girl Scouts, enlisted only girls. The Victory Corps itself was divided into five divisions, three of which were concerned with preparing boys for military service. In Seattle, the Junior Volunteer Hostesses, the 12,000 young women aged eighteen to twenty who spent more than 9 million hours dancing with servicemen during the war years, took pride in the "poise, clothes consciousness, and . . . radiant personality" developed by those who participated.[45]

The easy availability of work for teenagers caused concern for parents, educators, and community officials throughout the nation. Among those aged seventeen and under, applications for Social Security cards increased 201.2 percent for girls and 146.9 percent for boys between 1940 and 1942. In Seattle, where the changes were especially pronounced, the proportion of boys aged fourteen to seventeen in the labor force increased from 8.9 percent in 1940 to 46.9 percent in 1944, while the percentage of girls in the same age group jumped from 3.7 percent to 29.5 percent. The comparable figures for Detroit were an increase from 13.4 percent to 27.9 percent for boys and a jump from 7.7 percent to 20.5 percent for girls. A study in Baltimore high schools found that more than half of those aged sixteen and over had jobs, while one-fourth of those under sixteen were employed. Moreover, many of these students were working long hours in addition to their hours spent on school work.[46]

In order to ease the burden on those students who worked and to cut down on the number dropping out of school altogether to take jobs, some local school officials instituted programs allowing students with part-time jobs to attend school for fewer hours and providing for some sort of regulation by the schools. Under the Seattle program, high school juniors and seniors were given academic credits for work outside of school and were limited to a total of forty-eight hours a week at school and work. In addition, employers were required to make regular reports to the schools. Officials at Bremerton High School were especially lenient in granting work permits to their students because they feared idleness was a worse peril for those on double sessions than overwork.[47]

Whether they accommodated the changed pattern of students' lives or not, the schools faced serious problems as a result of the increase in working teenagers. In Detroit the truancy rate increased 24 percent between 1938 and 1943. Many who continued to attend school were in fact only physically present. Journalist Agnes Myer noted that students at Bremerton High School posed no discipline problems because many were asleep in class. Most alarming of all, however, was the high school dropout rate, which accelerated dramatically as students left school for jobs. Nationally, high school enrollment dropped by over 1 million between 1941 and 1944. In Baltimore, the problem was especially acute among black students. Many of those who quit school to take war jobs would never finish their education. According to a Women's Bureau study, a large proportion of the girls under the age of twenty who were employed had not finished high school and did not plan to do so.[48]

In response to the situation, the Children's Bureau and the U.S. Office of Education launched a national back-to-school drive in 1944. Noting that half of the teenagers who took jobs ended up leaving school, they also urged employers to hire older workers. In Maryland, school officials used themes like "invest in yourself" and "you can be better than you are" to encourage students to sacrifice the short-term benefits of war work in order to realize the long-term advantages of further schooling. As a result of such efforts, the dropout rate increased only negligibly in the last year of the war.[49]

Employers' willingness to lower their age requirements for employment and to be less than zealous in ascertaining the ages of young workers and the cooperation of local government officials, who relaxed their standards governing the employment of minors in order to fight the labor shortage, all contributed to the large-scale employment of young people. In 1943 Boeing dropped its age requirement by one year, to sixteen for boys and seventeen for girls. The Washington State Department of Labor and Industries lowered the minimum work age for boys to fifteen, although it issued some work permits for fourteen-year-olds. U.S. Department of Labor investigators found five times as many violations of the Fair Labor Standards Act regarding minors in 1944 than in

1940, a rate which indicated that disregard for the law seriously challenged officials' ability to stem the tide of illegal youth employment.[50]

Of special concern to community officials were those teenaged workers who moved to defense centers in order to seek work, some in direct response to war industry recruitment efforts directed at them. Many were apprehended as runaways even before they could obtain employment or lodging, either because of their age or their inability to handle the problems of getting established in a new community. Lacking family and community ties, some chose to live in cheap hotel districts where taverns and movies provided their recreation and traditional restraints on youthful caprice were almost nonexistent. For those young workers who lived in housing project dormitories, greater opportunities for organized recreational activities existed and the development of a sense of community was possible, although their dormitories often constituted a segregated enclave within the projects and the Federal Public Housing Authority generally made few attempts to regulate the dormitories or to provide adequate recreation programs.[51]

The increased mobility of young people was only one of the more extreme indications that the war was fostering significant changes in the home life and outside activities of children. Many community officials who had previously coped with the threats to child welfare caused by poverty worried that the prosperity of the war years had created its own perils for youngsters. Many expressed concern that the problems of child neglect and juvenile delinquency might have been intensified by the loosening of family ties, the separation of families, the rising divorce rate, the employment of teenagers at high salaries, and, most particularly, the expanded employment of mothers.[52]

Most law enforcement and other officials cited parental neglect as the most important contributor to increased juvenile delinquency and contended that working mothers were a primary cause of such negligence. In a survey of school, court, and law enforcement officials conducted by the Michigan Juvenile Delinquency Study Committee, family breakdown and the consequent lack of supervision of children by their parents was cited as the most important determinant of delinquency. Others echoed this concern; a Seattle woman observed in a letter to the editor of the *Seattle Times*, "statistics show that there is an appalling increase in juvenile delinquency in wartime and I believe lack of proper supervision at this critical time in their lives contributes largely to the cause."[53]

Because the problem of juvenile delinquency receives more attention in wartime, popular perceptions as to the extent of such behavior are often exaggerated. In the Seattle area this was especially true as a result of a few highly publicized incidents which gave the impression of greater juvenile wrongdoing than actually occurred. Moreover, the increased concern about juvenile misconduct could have resulted in stricter enforcement and more arrests, giving the impression that delinquency was increasing at a greater rate than it actually was. It seems likely that this was especially true with regard to sexual delinquencies by adolescent girls, who were often incarcerated to be tested under the stepped-up wartime program for venereal disease control although they had broken no laws.

Nationally, juvenile crime statistics indicated a trend of decreased incidents of misconduct by minor boys, primarily because they were either working or in the armed forces, and significantly increased complaints about juvenile girls, primarily for running away or sexual offenses. Wayne County, Michigan, experienced a 33 percent increase in juvenile delinquency among boys and an 89 percent increase among girls between 1938 and 1943. In Seattle, the number of complaints about juvenile boys declined from a high of 1,647 in 1941 to 1,185 in 1945, while complaints about girls rose from 614 in 1940 to 1,308 in 1943 and then declined to 1,182 by 1945. Overall, the figures indicate a 32 percent increase in the number of juvenile cases between 1940 and 1943, followed by a 12 percent decline between 1943 and 1945. Although the problem was serious, it was not as bad as many alarmists in the community perceived it to be.[54]

Every city experienced some problems with so-called commando gangs of boys, who imitated military organization and violence. In Detroit, they invaded night clubs and terrorized the patrons. The Motor City also had its share of zoot suiters, whose nonconformity in dress and conduct sometimes led to conflicts with the law. One of the most sensational episodes involving juvenile misconduct during the war occurred in the Seattle suburb of Renton in the spring of 1944. Described as "the worst mess in the history of Renton" by the *Seattle Times* and the "juvenile-delinquency shocker of the year" by *Newsweek*, it generated a heated controversy in the community fed by grossly inaccurate statements given by local law enforcement officials and even more exaggerated accounts in the media. As is true in such situations, the initial sensationalism had more impact than later, more accurate, reports.

The dispute centered on the causes and extent of juvenile delinquency in the area and the appropriate community response to the situation.[55]

The whole episode began when seventeen-year-old Eva Pettie told King County sheriff's officers of the existence of a gang called the "Wolf Pack," which had access to liquor and threw promiscuous parties in the dormitories of local housing projects. According to the girl, the gang would admit girls to membership only if they first had intercourse with the entire male membership. In response to the charges, authorities at the Renton Housing Project evicted over 100 teenaged boys and girls, imposed a 10 P.M. curfew on all residents, and banned liquor from the project. According to King County Sheriff Harlan Callahan, those evicted included several children under sixteen years of age whose parents had altered their birth certificates so that the children could obtain war jobs. Renton Police Chief Vincent Stewart stated that those evicted also included five ex-convicts, all of whom had their paroles revoked for participating in the dormitory parties with minors. Sheriff's Captain Jack Best stated that cabdrivers had been selling liquor to the youths, most of whom were facing imminent induction into the armed forces, and added, "They were having one last fling and with no regard for law and order."[56]

Sheriff Callahan promised a complete investigation of the problem and predicted wholesale arrests. Fifteen young people and three adults were immediately taken into custody, and Callahan estimated that between seventy-five and one hundred persons were involved, including the children, parents, and the bartenders and cabdrivers who had provided liquor to the minors. The Washington State Liquor Control Board began an investigation of the taverns that it suspected of selling to youths. In addition, the county health department decided to check the young people for venereal disease.[57]

Law enforcement officials were quick to blame the situation on the influx of war workers from the Midwest. Police Chief Stewart commented:

It's a case of big money and little supervision. The area is flooded with war working families who have come here from the Midwest. Parents are busy working and the kids run wild. The young fellows are making too much money. They buy cars and run around all hours of the day and night.

Callahan asserted that the juvenile delinquency was caused by "New Dealism," stating:

> They shipped hundreds of them out here to the Pacific Northwest, unaccompanied by relatives, chaperoned only by New Dealist appointees, and dumped them down in the housing projects here, at Renton, Port Townsend, and elsewhere, as they are now about to do at Bremerton—boys and girls together to shape their own moral destinies. Sprinkled amongst them were a lot of experienced criminals, degenerates and others, secretly released from prisons before the expiration of their sentences because the New Dealists insisted these convicts were needed in the war effort.[58]

The story attracted nationwide attention and was seriously distorted in the retelling. According to *Newsweek*, one of the girls in the "Wolf Gang" admitted to having intimate relations with thirteen boys and another claimed ninety such encounters. Most of the original accounts left the impression that the gang had large numbers of boys and girls in its membership and echoed the Callahan assertion that most were young people recruited for jobs in area war plants who were "brought in largely from the Middle West minus parental care, supervisors, or welfare workers."[59]

Once the final arrests were made in the case and court proceedings begun, it became clear that the claims of Callahan and others regarding the scope of the problem and its cause were quite inaccurate. In contrast to published reports of its membership, King County Welfare Department records indicate that the "Wolf Gang" itself had only six members, including only one girl. Moreover, none of the young people involved had been specifically recruited by area war industries, although several worked in them. Most were the children of migrant war workers residing in housing projects or trailer camps. All of the juveniles taken into custody lived with their parents, not in unsupervised housing project dormitories.[60]

The number brought to trial turned out to be considerably less than the seventy-five to one hundred predicted by Callahan. Charges were brought against eleven young men, including one juvenile with a prior record who was tried as an adult, for contributing to the delinquency of a minor or for morals offenses. The three convicted on the latter charge were guilty only of attempting to entice five Renton High School girls into their car and were given suspended sentences. Four youths aged nineteen to twenty-five were found guilty of contributing to the delinquency of a minor by having sexual relations with a minor girl. Three of them were sentenced to six months in jail with the last three months suspended and the fourth was given a three-month suspended sentence. Judge William Hoar told one of the defendants:

> The girl was well on her way to becoming a prostitute. You are one of those who helped her along the route. This trend toward loose conduct and breaking down of moral fibers is due to the war, I presume. Too many young people are losing sight of their sense of decency and respect for young girls and marriage.

Charges were dropped against one nineteen-year-old for lack of evidence and against three others who were allowed to join the armed forces.[61]

In other cases brought before juvenile authorities, two girls guilty of sexual misconduct were sent to the Martha Washington School for Girls, a seventeen-year-old boy who admitted to having a drinking problem was given a suspended sentence to the State Training School, and a seventeen-year-old Kent boy who had never been in trouble before becoming involved with this group of juveniles was released to his parents. In addition to the young people charged in this episode, three adults, including two mothers and a bartender, were convicted of contributing to the delinquency of a minor and/or serving liquor to minors. The bartender, J. M. Trueman of Renton, was also accused of attempting to molest a fifteen-year-old girl; he was fined $150 and given a sixty-day suspended sentence on the condition that he leave the area.[62]

An examination of the background of six of the juveniles involved in the Renton affair shows that the factors contributing to their unfavorable development were present to some extent before the war began. All three of the girls for whom information is available were from broken homes, two had an alcoholic parent, and in all cases relationships between parents and child were severely strained. The most extreme case of family instability was that of fifteen-year-old Delores Hoefs, whose parents, although only recently separated, had a long history of strife in their marriage. The mother, Pearl Hoefs, who was among those convicted of contributing to the delinquency of a minor, was accused of being a prostitute and an alcoholic by her estranged husband. According to a King County Welfare Department report on the episode, Delores "had had extensive sex experience and had not lived by any accepted standards for some time." The information that is available on the three boys provides little insight into their family situations but does indicate that one of them had been in trouble before and was characterized by "serious sex aberrations" in the opinion of the psychologist at the State Training School.[63]

On the other hand, conditions unique to the wartime situation contributed to the delinquent behavior of the young people. The easy availability of war jobs caused at least three of the five young people old enough to work to quit school and seek employment. As a result they had money to spend and greater freedom from parental control. Moreover, five of the six youths had migrated to the Seattle area with their families since the war began. In at least three of the cases the mother worked. Thus, lessened parental supervision, a lack of roots in the community, and an increasingly important peer group added to the causes of the Renton situation.[64]

Many community officials were outraged at the distorted publicity given the Renton incident, claiming that the name "Wolf Gang" had attracted undue attention to a juvenile delinquency problem that was in fact no worse than in many other war boom communities in the nation. U.S. District Court Judge Lloyd L. Black, who headed the Seattle Juvenile Protection Committee, noted that the numbers involved were quite small and stated that statistics showed that juvenile delinquency in Renton was no worse than in the nation as a whole. Renton Mayor Ed Burrows agreed, adding, "The situation needs corrective measures, but certainly is not alarming." Residents of the Renton Housing Project held a protest meeting and adopted a resolution demanding that Sheriff Callahan retract his statement that all of the youthful offenders were project residents. They contended that they had been smeared by the publicity attendant to the incident and objected to the curfew and ban on liquor in the project.[65]

Others expressed concern that the publicity would hamper labor recruitment for area war industries. According to Judge Black, local employers would require an additional 5,000 youths sixteen to seventeen years of age to meet production quotas and that the prospects of obtaining them had been hurt by recent events. Mrs. Don Pirie, the Girl Scout leader in the Renton Housing Project, predicted that mothers who were employed would quit their jobs out of concern for the safety and well-being of their children unless the juvenile delinquency situation was cleared up. In fact, however, no such mass exodus took place.[66]

Local officials reacted to the perceived rise in juvenile offenses in a variety of ways. In Baltimore, they responded much as they did to other war-created difficulties—by doing as little as possible. Mayor Theodore McKeldin named a Youth Committee, which included both black and white young people. In January 1944, the Baltimore Police Department established a Juvenile Protective Bureau to serve as a referral agency so that juveniles accused of minor offenses could receive casework services rather than being reported to the Juvenile Court. The development of recreation programs for young people so characteristic of most cities concerned with juvenile delinquency was retarded in Baltimore by the determination on the part of local officials to minimize spending and resist federal initiatives. As a result, only a small number of new playgrounds and recreation centers were established in wartime Baltimore, and most of them were located in federal housing projects.[67]

Detroit, by contrast, benefited from the organization and financial support of programs developed to curb delinquency by the State of Michigan. In September 1943, the Governor's Youth Guidance Committee was formed to recommend and implement these programs. As a result of its efforts, the number of full-time county agents and assistants to juvenile courts rose from eight to fifty-one during the war. By the summer of 1944, the governor's committee had 164 local committees focusing on youth recreation, law enforcement, and child welfare problems. Under a 1945 state law, these local groups were assisted by four field representatives funded by the state.[68]

Officials from public and private agencies in Detroit also supported various youth programs. In 1943, the city of Detroit established seventy-five centers for young people aged fourteen to seventeen, encouraging the members to develop their own programs and providing trained recreation leaders for guidance. The Lutheran Churches of Detroit established youth clubs in 100 churches to be open in the afternoons and evenings. In order to overcome the class bias in their operations so that they might reach more people, the settlement houses and other private organizations added juke boxes and coke bars to their youth centers and tried to ensure that their patrons could enjoy themselves in a place where they were free from improvement efforts.[69]

Local schools also provided various programs and services in order to prepare their students for wartime responsibilities, foster a sense of participation in the war effort, aid students with problems, and encourage constructive activities so that juvenile delinquency might be curbed. School officials in Detroit hired additional personnel to increase the attendance staff and placed one or more persons in each school to deal full time with troubled children. In addition to expanding their extra-curricular activities for students, schools also altered their course offerings to meet wartime requirements. Math and science courses were more heavily emphasized and courses in aeronautics, drafting, automobile mechanics, electricity, industrial arts, and other fields designed to develop skills useful in war industries or the armed forces were added. School systems in Baltimore and elsewhere in the nation developed "pre-induction" courses of a technical nature with the advice and guidance of the U.S. Army and Navy.[70]

In some cases the curricular changes of the war years contributed to a decrease in sex role stereotyping in the schools as girls were encouraged to enroll in many courses previously considered more appropriate for boys, including math, physics, aeronautics, and drafting. The "Miss Teen" columnist for the *Seattle Times* articulated the new attitude as follows:

When it comes to school days, many an "about 17" will be working part-time and digging into . . . of all things . . . math and science. During wartime, it's "the thing" to be wise about such matters, and who wants to be left out anyway? Moping about home-work and avoiding once-termed "tough" subjects has grown "stale" among those in the know.

Moreover, some schools offered home economics training for boys to enable them to shoulder their increased household responsibilities better. In Baltimore, an experimental program offering home economics to boys and shop to girls in some junior high schools was so successful that it was adopted in most of the city's junior highs by 1944.[71]

At the same time, however, the persistence of conventional attitudes and the emphasis on preparing boys for military service tended to limit the amount of change created by the alterations in the curriculum. Of the 2,000 high school students in the state of Washington enrolled in aeronautics courses in 1942, only 150 were girls. In Baltimore, the persistence of single-sex high schools and the conservatism of the school board minimized the amount of curricular change as most technical courses were added only in the boys' high schools. School officials in Maryland tried to ensure that girls in secretarial courses would not opt for nontraditional work by discouraging them from transferring into technical courses. The vast majority of home economics classes, including the special wartime child care courses, were still taken only by girls.[72]

In addition to changes in academic courses, some schools authorized the establishment of special "hardening" classes in physical education for high school boys to prepare them for military service. Although Detroit school officials claimed that the purpose of their new program was to develop good health and not "husky gun fodder," the curriculum included military track, which utilized obstacle courses, and weaponless defense and offense. In Seattle the program added wall scaling, simulated battlefield exercises, and obstacle courses. Cal Johnson, a participating high school student, commented on the attitude of the boys toward the increased emphasis on physical fitness: "The boys have finally found something 'to get tough about' and are doing it, too, on the football field, basketball floor, and in their commando gym classes." The war thus strengthened male socialization for aggressiveness, violence, and physical strength. Maryland officials, however, cut back on their commando classes on the grounds that they were too strenuous.[73]

Although the primary focus of wartime youth programs was on positive programs rather than coercive efforts to induce conformity to laws and mores, some communities modified law enforcement practices in order to cope with so-called teenage troubles. Many experimented with youth curfews and laws mandating parental responsibility for the actions of their children. The Seattle statute set a mandatory curfew of 10 P.M. for children under fifteen and required that those between the ages of fifteen and eighteen be able to give acceptable reasons for being out after 10 P.M. Parents were made responsible for their children's whereabouts and could be fined if found negligent. Many law enforcement officials were less than enthusiastic about such laws because they were so difficult to enforce consistently.[74]

The most extensive reliance on coercive measures occurred in response to perceived sexual misconduct on the part of young girls and women. Dubbed "victory girls," "khacky-wackies," and "free girls" by the wartime media, girls and women who seemed to be flaunting conventional morality received a great deal of attention from public officials and private groups intent on preventing female "sex delinquency" and on safeguarding public morals and health. Although she eluded precise definition, the "victory girl" was usually assumed to be a woman who pursued sexual relations with servicemen out of a misplaced patriotism or a desire for excitement. She could also, however, be a girl or woman who, without actually engaging in sexual relations, was testing the perimeters of social freedom in wartime America in ways that suggested sexual misconduct or a vulnerability to new temptations.[75]

The most important official effort to limit women's social and sexual freedoms during the war came in the guise of the wartime social protection program. Although designed to protect public health and increase military efficiency by preventing and treating venereal disease, the social protection campaign encompassed a broader effort to isolate women whose conduct indicated that they might be sexually active outside of the institution of marriage and to provide them with medical treatment, if necessary, and with punishment and/or rehabilitative counseling so that they might lead more upright lives. Responsibility for the coordination of this effort came within the purview of the Social Protection Division of the Office of Community War Services, an agency which expanded a health program into a purity campaign dedicated to the search for "incipient and confirmed sex delinquents" who, not coincidentally, happened always to be women.[76]

Under the guidance of the SPD, which suggested the necessary changes in the laws, state and local governments devised the legal context within which the police operated. The essential requirement was that all women arrested or held for investigation on various morals charges also be detained for mandatory testing for VD. In order to accomplish the purposes of the program, morals laws had to be changed so that they would be sufficiently broad and vague to allow the apprehension of women whose conduct was regarded as "suspect." Thus, prostitution came to be defined not only as intercourse for hire but also as indiscriminate or promiscuous intercourse. SPD literature constantly noted that the commercial aspect was not the critical element, that a prostitute was, in effect, any woman who was sexually active despite the lack of "sincere emotional content" in the relationship. Other statutes were also broadened so that disorderly conduct became conduct "endangering morals, safety, or health" and vagrancy could include lewd, wanton, or lascivious speech or behavior. Laws against loitering, frequenting bars, or falsely registering in a hotel as married were also used to further the program.[77]

Devising the necessary legal framework for juvenile girls was less crucial since the police and courts already had considerable discretion in handling cases involving minors. As a result, young girls found by police in places or at hours they deemed inappropriate were questioned, turned over to juvenile court or social welfare authorities, or brought home to their parents, who were informed as to their whereabouts and actions. In Baltimore, local police informally enforced a curfew for girls by questioning those found in public places unescorted after hours. Detroit police routinely subjected runaway girls to VD testing, although they exempted runaway boys from that requirement.[78]

Of the three communities studied only Baltimore deviated from the general pattern of accelerated anti-vice campaigns directed primarily at women. As with other federal programs, Baltimore officials viewed the SPD with suspicion. Marie Duffin, the SPD representative in Baltimore charged with organizing a local social protection committee, complained to her chief, Eliot Ness, that Baltimore was "traditionally individualistic, reactionary and antagonistic to Federal participation" and would not cooperate with the SPD. Although such a local group was finally formed, it resisted SPD advice with regularity. Moreover, the Maryland State Health Department was reluctant to force anyone, even those named in VD contact reports, to take mandatory health tests, and the state legislature refused to pass SPD-inspired laws increasing health department authority to require tests and quarantines and broadening the definition of prostitution to include sexual intercourse without hire. On a few occasions the Baltimore police used a law against "leading a dissolute and disorderly course of life" when two or more instances of illegal intercourse without fee could be proved, but they generally lacked the legal framework or the will to conduct the massive dragnet employed by other cities.[79]

Federal officials did succeed, however, in persuading Baltimore officials to reorganize the judicial procedures in prostitution cases and in encouraging local judges to increase the severity of their sentences in morals cases. As a result, women charged in such cases were more frequently referred to the Criminal Court for trial, and those convicted were usually given stiff jail sentences. Such intervention in the affairs of local judiciaries typified SPD policies. In Seattle, Judge James Hodson received a letter of praise for his cooperation from Arthur Fink of the SPD. That such actions on the part of a federal agency tended to compromise the independence of the judiciary did not seem to concern the federal zealots.[80]

Baltimore was not typical of war boom communities in its caution in morals enforcement. In Detroit women who were suspected of "immoral" activities were detained under a disorderly person investigation. They could be held for investigation, tested for VD, held until the results were in, and then released without any court action or legal recourse. One of the most despicable war practices involved the abuse of ostensibly private VD contact reports provided by the military or by public health authorities. In Seattle the names of women reported as contacts were turned over to local police for investigation; in Baltimore, they were given to the casework service as prospective recipients of rehabilitative counseling.[81]

It is impossible to determine exactly how many women were affected by this program. FBI statistics, which seriously undercount the number of women detained by local police departments because many local departments did not send in crime reports for misdemeanors and many of the women taken in during the war were never formally charged, do indicate a 95 percent increase in women officially charged with morals violations between 1940 and 1944. Totals for prostitution only went up 17.6 percent, while those for disorderly conduct jumped 183.8 percent, vagrancy, 121.1 percent, and other sex offenses, 134.6 percent. In Seattle, which was particularly zealous, various reports indicate that as many as 300 women a month were detained. Although they were ostensibly brought in as part of a public health campaign, a study of 2,063 women held by the Seattle police in 1944 found that only 366 (17.3 percent) actually had venereal disease. Yet all of them had to spend four or five days in the county jail awaiting the results of the health examination.[82]

Seattle officials devised a particularly elaborate program for female "sex delinquents," one which was frequently cited by the SPD as a model for other cities. Once they had been tested for venereal disease, the women and girls taken into custody by the police were handled in a variety of ways. All found to be infected were treated and could be forced to participate in various rehabilitation programs. Younger girls without prior records were usually sent to the Rapid Treatment Center, which offered vocational training and individual counseling in order to make them self-supporting and to equip them to lead more conventional lives. Prostitutes, repeaters, and others deemed less likely to be amenable to rehabilitation were kept in the county jail until treated. All minor girls apprehended, whether they had venereal disease or not and even if they had broken no laws, were remanded to the Juvenile Court. Although they were generally referred to one of several social welfare agencies, women who were tested and did not have VD were free to reject the proffered counseling services.[83]

Women detained for testing who had also been charged with criminal offenses were, of course, in the hands of the courts. The vast majority of these women were accused of violating statutes regulating moral conduct, including those prohibiting promiscuous behavior, drunkenness, or patronizing bars too frequently or without escort. In 1944 Judge James Hodson of the Seattle Municipal Court devised a parole system for the large numbers of women first offenders held on these morals charges. Under his program the women were required to work, live a clean and temperate life, keep good company, and stay away from undesirable places. If a woman followed the rules, the case against her would be dropped. The system ensured a high level of cooperation from the women, even though they had not been convicted of anything, because it enabled them to escape the possibility of further embarrassment.[84]

The reliance on counseling programs to foster a more satisfactory adjustment to society's expectations on the part of the "victory girl" characterized the social protection effort late in the war. Because the use of detention and the threat of criminal proceedings did not seem to constitute a sufficient deterrent, federal officials urged local agencies to establish some form of rehabilitation program for female offenders. These programs varied in their levels of sophistication, the numbers of women they served, and the degree of compulsion they utilized. In Detroit, all young and first offenders were interviewed by a policewoman for possible referral to a social agency for casework services. The Baltimore protective service provided counseling for those referred to it by clinics, agencies, police, or the courts but could only require cooperation from those on probation.[85]

The lack of compulsion in the programs caused some officials to request legal and other changes so that women would be less free to reject their services. Mazie Rappaport, a social worker who directed the Baltimore program, asked SPD officials how counseling could be made mandatory for those who had broken no laws and expressed anxiety regarding the level of control available when she wondered, "Is the policeman watching these girls or are they watching the policeman?" Seattle officials also expressed a desire for a casework service in a "somewhat authoritarian setting" so that more control could be obtained. In 1943 the SPD discussed the possibility of a program of "modified supervision" for women who had been released upon completion of their jail sentences; it was suggested that it be operated by the Children's Bureau (!) so that the element of detention would not be "obvious on the surface." The plan, which involved an unconstitutional interference by federal agencies in local law enforcement and a total disregard for the civil liberties of the women it was supposed to aid, was never pursued.[86]

In their zeal to "protect" women from themselves, some communities went to rather ridiculous lengths to prevent unsanctioned sexual conduct. In Detroit, military officials blamed the State Liquor Control Commission for not stopping contacts in bars and urged the enforcement of restrictions on women patronizing taverns. Lieutenant John I. Ward suggested that unescorted women be segregated from other patrons and that "chaperone conditions" be established in bars. After they were advised that it was illegal to refuse admission to unescorted women, Detroit officials resorted to a prohibition against serving unescorted women at a bar after 8 P.M. and a proviso that those served in dining areas had to remain unescorted. Tavern owners who were unwilling to risk their liquor licenses reluctantly enforced the strictures. One of them wondered, however, "If the ladies are allowed in the Army, Navy and Marines, will some one, any one, please tell me how you're gonna keep them outta the bars?"[87]

Detroit officials also decided to enforce selectively the local ordinance prohibiting cohabitation by persons not married to one another in order to promote fidelity on the part of servicemen's wives. Frank C. Schemancke, chief assistant county prosecutor, instituted legal proceedings in 1945 against Mary Sue Jones, a woman whose husband was serving overseas, and Arthur Reeves, the man with whom she lived. Schemancke promised to prosecute such cases relentlessly in order to "protect servicemen."[88]

In most cases, the male partners of the women who were charged or detained for health testing were neither arrested not held in quarantine for a mandatory health examination. Military personnel picked up by the police were usually turned over to military authorities, while civilian men were sometimes required to report to the local health department for testing. None were ever referred for social welfare counseling. Some social protection officials conceded the inefficacy and unfairness of such a discriminatory system but did little to correct it. Seattle authorities planned in 1944 to expand the program to include men as soon as the facilities were available to do so but never followed up on the decision.[89]

Despite the large numbers of women involved and the widespread disregard for their rights, there was little protest against the program. Roger Baldwin of the American Civil Liberties Union circulated a memo to all local branches of the organization urging them to deal sympathetically with the police on this matter. UAW officials in Detroit complained that the police were unnecessarily zealous in detaining juvenile girls for minor transgressions and protested against actions which needlessly labeled the girls as immoral. In Seattle and other places some of the women caught in the police dragnet because of "suspicious" but lawful behavior protested their incarcerations as violations of their rights to privacy and lawful treatment. Several brought suit for false arrest, and others filed writs of habeas corpus demanding that they be charged with specific crimes or be released from jail. Although a few cases were thrown out because the arresting officers did not have a warrant, the courts generally upheld the right of law enforcement agencies to jail women without charges on the grounds that such measures were necessary to protect the public health. The means of determining which women posed potential threats to public health and the sex discrimination implicit in the enforcement of the law were not questioned.[90]

The extent to which the "victory girl" represented a new mode of sexual behavior is not clear. It is likely that wartime circumstances promoted some change in sexual conduct, especially on the part of younger women. According to Army and Navy venereal disease contact reports, 26.6 percent of the contacts named by their personnel were under twenty years of age. In Detroit, teenagers accounted for an increasing proportion of VD cases during the war years. Although much of the literature on "victory girls" reflected the assumption that they were single, a surprising number were young married women. In Seattle, for example, a study of 210 women detained on morals charges revealed that only sixty-nine were single, eight were widows, and the rest were or had been married. Moreover, 71 percent of the married women had husbands in the military. Kinsey statistics, which indicate an increase of extramarital relationships on the part of very young wives in the 1940s, support the possibility of an increase in marital infidelity occasioned by wartime separations.[91]

Despite the temporary changes of the war period, the war did not promote a long-term revision of sexual values or conduct. The revised double standard of post-Victorian America persisted despite superficial strains caused by war-created circumstances. The premises on which social protection officials based their actions indicated the continuing strength of the idea that men had a stronger sex drive than women and of the norms which urged that women had a special moral responsibility to curb male lust. An official of the American Social Hygiene Association contended that educational material asking soldiers to avoid exposure to venereal disease was "working up against a very powerful urge." By contrast, the ASHA publication, "Boy Meets Girl in Wartime," asserted that women were less easily aroused than men and should consequently assume responsibility for controlling sexual conduct. Social protection authorities explained female "sex delinquency" in terms of a need for love, attention, and excitement rather than for sexual gratification, and as a manifestation of emotional maladjustment. Moreover, they viewed freedom of sexual expression for women as a hazard to the institution of the family and to society as a whole. Ray Lyman Wilbur, president of the ASHA, declared that "fewer taboos for our women and girls all add up to a major threat to the family." Thus, while men were assumed to be acting solely on the basis of immutable biological urges, women were believed to be responding to cultural and emotional promptings subject to modification through informed public policy, including rehabilitative counseling programs.[92]

Analysis of changes in wartime conduct must also take into account the extent to which behavior defined as deviant for women was actually congruent with feminine sex role prescriptions. In many cases, the girls and women arrested during the war were only seeking male approval, companionship, and possibly marriage, goals encouraged by society's sex role injunctions. Having been urged by their culture to focus their aspirations on marriage and to give the appearance of sexuality in order to attract men, they found it increasingly difficult to heed the warnings about proscribed sexual behavior when many men made continued attention contingent on sexual cooperation. That it was frequently the desire for male companionship that motivated many labeled as "victory girls" is indicated by their high unemployment rates, their frequent unwillingness to accept referral to high-paying war jobs, and their concentration in service jobs, especially those which would enable them to meet servicemen.[93]

The wartime concern over the "free girl" in some ways represented a counteroffensive against the new modes of behavior characteristic of post-Victorian America and an attempt to reconcile the contradictions in sexual mores for women by reaffirming more traditional values. By contrast with the 1920s, when popular misconceptions regarding new psychological theories were used to justify a freer sexual expression for women and men, the actions of social welfare and other agencies in the 1940s showed the extent to which psychology was beginning to serve the interests of those seeking to inhibit sexual and social freedom for women. At a time when the culture was giving women conflicting signals regarding their sexuality, psychologists and social workers were being delegated the primary responsibility for adjusting women to more repressive standards.[94]

The wartime reaction to the possibility of increased social and sexual freedom for women mirrored the response to all changes in women's roles and circumstances fostered by the war. Women's conduct received constant scrutiny, which reflected considerable anxiety over the continuation of a marriage and family system predicated on the willingness of women to subordinate their needs and aspirations to those of others. Although the war offered women new opportunities for independence and role flexibility and challenged conventional stereotypes regarding women's physical and emotional makeup, it also promoted considerable apprehension about family stability and a strong desire to return to more traditional family forms once the war was over. Rather than providing clear-cut alternatives to previous sex role definitions, the war years generated contradictory tendencies, confusion, insecurity, and anxiety. Given this ambivalence, the continuation of contradictory behavior in the postwar years should not have been surprising; neither should the attempt to reconcile conflicting values and behaviors with the strident certitudes of the postwar "feminine mystique."

Notes

1. Susan Hartmann, "Prescriptions for Penelope," *Women's Studies*, 5 (1978); D'Ann Campbell, "The Unorganized Housewife" (Paper presented at the convention of the Organization of American Historians, April 1978); Sanday; Gladys Gaylord, "Marriage Counseling in Wartime," *Annals of the American Academy of Political and Social Science* 229 (September 1943): 41.

2. Karen Anderson, "The Victory Girl in Wartime America" (paper presented at the conference of the Southeastern Women Studies Association, Johnson City, Tennessee, February 1979.)

3. U.S., Bureau of the Census, Series PM-1, No. 3, "The Wartime Marriage Surplus," November 12, 1944, p. 1; U.S., Bureau of the Census, Series P-46, No. 2, "Estimated Population of the United States By Age, Color, and Sex: 1945 and 1944," January 27, 1946, p. 1; U.S., Department of Commerce, Bureau of the Census, "Characteristics of the Detroit-Willow Run Congested Production Area," pp. 2, 10; U.S., Department of Commerce, Bureau of the Census, "Characteristics of the Puget Sound Congested Production Area;" pp. 7, 9; Precise statistics are not available for Baltimore, but it also experienced rising marriage and birth rates. *Baltimore Sun*, December 25, 1941, January 1, 1942; Memo, Myrtle Cohan to Irving Posner, September 11, 1944, OCWS, WARC, RG 215, Box 7.

4. *Detroit News*, April 16, 1942; *Baltimore Afro-American*, November 13, 1943; Anderson, "Victory Girl."

5. *Detroit News*, February 26, 1942; U.S., Bureau of the Census, Series P-46, No. 2, p. 1; U.S., Bureau of the Census, Series CA-3, No. 9, p. 7; U.S., Bureau of the Census, Series CA-3, No. 8, p. 7.

6. Anderson.

7. *Seattle Times*, November 1, 1942; *Tacoma News-Tribune*, January 22, 1942; "Field Report, Margaret Barnett," February 19–20, 1943, Records of the Washington State Department of Social Security [hereafter cited as DSS], RG 75, Washington State Archives, [hereafter cited as WSA]; Letter, Edwin Cooley to Eliot Ness, August 14, 1943, OCWS, RG 215, Box 228, NA; Memo, Mary Roberts to Mona Callister, February 7, 1942, DSS, RG 75, WSA.

8. U.S., Department of Commerce, Bureau of the Census, "Characteristics of the Puget Sound Congested Production Area," p. 9; "Comments of Workers on Specified Items—Seattle and Tacoma, Washington," WBA, RG 86, Box 1545, NA; *Seattle Times*, July 9, 1944.

9. *Detroit Free Press*, January 14, 1943; *Seattle Times*, September 11, 1942, January 7, 1943, November 20, 1943, January 8, 1944; Polenberg, p. 145; U.S., Department of Commerce, Bureau of the Census, "Characteristics of the Puget Sound Congested Production Area," p. 9.

10. Campbell; *Detroit Free Press*, January 7, 1943; Marie C. Smith, "Public Agency Examines Impact of War on Child Care," in Child Welfare League of America, *The Impact of War on Children's Services*, OCWS, RG 215, Children's Care Division, Box 2, NA; *Seattle Times*, August 27, 1942.

11. *Detroit Free Press*, January 14, 1943; "Preliminary Report, Baltimore Area," OCWS, Community Reports, RG 215, Box 4, NA; Clive, p. 208; Campbell.

12. "Summary of Minutes of October 29, 1942 Conference—Office for Emergency Management," WMC, Baltimore Area, OCWS, Community Reports, RG 215, Box 4, NA.

13. "Preliminary Report, Baltimore Area,"OCWS, Community Reports, RG 215, Box 4, NA; Memo, I. Posner to Lavinia Engle, August 29, 1944, OCWS, WARC, RG 215, Box 7, NA; "Minutes, Federal Coordinating Committee for Michigan," October 14, 1943, OCWS, WARC, RG 215, Box 10, NA.

14. "General Comments of Workers, Baltimore, Maryland," WBA, RG 86, Box 1541, NA; "Detroit Post-War Study, 1944," WBA, RG 86, Box 1541, NA; "Comments of Workers on Specified Items—Seattle and Tacoma, Washington," WBA, RG 86, Box 1545, NA; Letter, L. L. Hegland to Ruth FitzSimons, September 19, 1942, DSS, RG 75, WSA.

15. Hartmann, "Prescriptions," p. 231; *Baltimore Afro-American*, November 27, 1943; Clive, p. 545; John F. Cuber, "The Adjustment of College Men to Military Life: Case Data," *Sociology and Social Research* 27 (March-April 1943): 269.

16. Anderson; Alfred C. Kinsey, *Sexual Behavior in the Human Female* (Philadelphia: Saunders, 1953), pp. 423, 442; *Baltimore Sun*, January 16, 1945; *Detroit News*, January 3, 1945, January 30, 1945, February 7, 1945.

17. "General Comments of Workers, Baltimore, Maryland," WBA, RG 86, Box 1541, NA; "Detroit Post-War Study," WBA, RG 86, Box 1541, NA; "Comments of Workers on Specified Items—Seattle and Tacoma, Washington," WBA, RG 86, Box 1545, NA; Clive, pp. 545-46; Myer, pp. 36-37; *Seattle Times*, December 5, 1942.

18. *Seattle Times*, February 14, 1945.

19. *Aero Mechanic*, December 31, 1942; *Seattle Times*, April 8, 1943, July 2, 1944, October 29, 1944.

20. "Needed? Family Case Work Services for Detroit," February 21, 1944, CCPA, RG 212, Box 48, NA; *Baltimore Sun*, January 3, 1942; Abbott L. Ferriss, *Indicators of Change in the American Family* (New York: Russell Sage Foundation, 1970), p. 123.

21. Mirra Komarovsky, *Blue-Collar Marriage* (New York: Random House, 1964), pp. 28, 33, 153; David M. Schneider and Raymond T. Smith, *Class Differences in American Kinship* (Ann Arbor: University of Michigan Press,

1978), pp. 106–7; David M. Heer, "Dominance and the Working Wife" in *The Employed Mother in America*, ed. F. Ivan Nye and Lois W. Hoffman (Chicago: Rand McNally, 1963), pp. 258, 261; Theodore Caplow, *The Sociology of Work* (Minneapolis: University of Minnesota Press, 1964), pp. 238–46.

22. Florian Znaniecki, "The Impact of War on Personality Organization," *Sociology and Social Research* 27 (January-February 1943); *Detroit News*, February 15, 1942.

23. Harriet Arnow, *The Dollmaker* (New York: Avon, 1954).

24. "Composite Report, Detroit," December 22, 1943, OCWS, Community Reports, RG 215, Box 5, NA; "Supplementary Report on War Area, Baltimore, Maryland," July 10, 1943, FSA, OCWS, Community Reports, RG 215, Box 4, NA; Memo, Joseph Louchheim to Charles Taft, August 14, 1942, OCWS, General Classified, Maryland (Region IV), RG 215, Box 124, NA.

25. "Minutes of Committee on Volunteer Office," WRC, RG 2010, Box 70, MHS.

26. Myer, p. 34; Memo, James W. Greater to Helen Rowe, December 26, 1942, OCWS, General Classified Files, Michigan (Region V), RG 215, Box 134, NA; "A Description of Health Problems in the Area of the Willow Run Plant of the Ford Motor Company, Washtenaw County, Michigan, As Of February 27, 1943," Washtenaw County Health Department, CCPA, RG 212, Box 49, NA.

27. Carr and Stermer, pp. 98–101.

28. Carr and Stermer, pp. 95, 117.

29. John Dos Passos, *State of the Nation* (Boston: Houghton-Mifflin, 1944) p. 55; *Detroit News*, March 7, 1942; Louise Olson and Ruth Schrader, "The Trailer Population in a Defense Area," *Sociology and Social Research* 27 (March-April 1943): 301-2.

30. Campbell; *Seattle Times*, March 15, 1942, March 26, 1942.

31. Campbell; "An Inventory of Goods and Services Shortages in Metropolitan Detroit," August 1944, Detroit Victory Council, CCPA, RG 212, Box 50, NA.

32. Memo, Dr. Otto K. Engelke to Frank Mc Laury, March 28, 1944, CCPA, RG 212, Box 48, NA.

33. *Detroit News*, April 8, 1942; Letter, Helen P. Hartz to Members of the Block Brigade, September 27, 1943, WRC, RG 2010, Box 72, MHS; Straub, "Government Policy Toward," pp. 6–8; *Seattle Times*, March 15, 1942, May 3, 1942; Rupp, pp. 139–40.

34. *Washington Star*, May 2, 1943; *Baltimore Evening Sun*, May 4, 1944; *Baltimore Sun*, December 15, 1942; *Baltimore American*, May 30, 1943; *Detroit News*, April 7-8, 1942; "Minutes, Baltimore Nutrition Committee," WRC, RG 2010, Box 71, MHS; *Seattle Times*, June 15, 1943.

35. Znaniecki, p. 176

36. "Minutes, Committee on Volunteer Office," September 9, 1942, October 22, 1942, WRC, RG 2010, Box 70, MHS; *Seattle Times*, June 14, 1942, August 1, 1942, October 25, 1942.

37. *Baltimore Sun*, January 15, 1942; "Minutes, Committee on Volunteer Office," March 1, 1943, WRC, RG 2010, Box 70, MHS; City of Seattle, Civlian War Commission, *Final Report: Seattle Went to War*, p. 91; Maryland Historical Society, War Records Division, *Maryland in World War II*, Vol. 3 (Baltimore: Maryland Historical Society, 1958), p. 182.

38. *Detroit News*, March 11, 1942; *Seattle Times*, September 28, 1942; March 22, 1942, May 29, 1942.

39. *Baltimore Evening Sun*, November 2, 1942; "Minutes, Committee on Volunteer Office," August 28, 1942; WRC, RG 2010, Box 70, MHS; *Seattle Went to War*, p. 65.

40. Campbell; *Detroit Free Press*, January 11, 1943, January 19, 1943.

41. U.S., Department of Labor, Women's Bureau, Special Bulletin No. 20, "Changes in Women's Employment During the War (Washington, D.C.: GPO, 1944), p. 29; U.S., Department of Commerce, Bureau of the Census, "Characteristics of the Puget Sound Congested Production Area," p. 11.

42. "Employee Counseling: A Report," February 25, 1944, WBA, RG 86, Box 1540, NA; Josephine Abbott, "What of Youth in Wartime?", *Survey Midmonthly* 79 (October 1943): 265; "8-Hour Orphans," *Saturday Evening Post*, October 10, 1942; Henry L. Zucker, "Working Parents and Latchkey Children," *Annals of the American Academy of Political and Social Science* 236 (November 1944): 43-48; Polenberg, pp. 147-48; Letter, L. L. Hegland to Ruth FitzSimons, September 19, 1942, DSS, RG 75, WSA.

43. Carr and Stermer, p. 245; Charlotte L. Hanson, "The Effect of the War Upon the Life of Children in Institutions," in Child Welfare League of America, *Bulletin*, June 1943, OCWS, Children's Care Division, RG 215, Box 2, NA; City of Seattle, *Annual Reports*, Police Department, 1939–45.

44. *Seattle Went to War*, p. 29.

45. "Progress Report for Children's Bureau Commission on Children in Wartime," January 1, 1943, OCWS, Director's Subject File, RG 215, Box 3, NA; *Seattle Went to War*, p. 52; *Seattle Times*, March 9, 1942, September 6, 1942, May 23, 1943.

46. "Increases in the Number of Child Workers," *Monthly Labor Review* (November 1943): 942; Elizabeth S. Magee, "Impact of War on Child Labor," *Annals of the American Academy of Political and Social Science* 236 (November 1944): 104; U.S., Department of Commerce, Bureau of the Census, "Characteristics of the Puget Sound Congested Production Area," p. 10; U.S., Department of Commerce, Bureau of the Census, "Characteristics of the Detroit-Willow Run Congested Production Area," p. 14.

47. *Seattle Times*, May 16, 1942, April 4, 1943; "Seattle-Bremerton Congested Area," [n.d.], OCWS, RG 215, Box 32, NA; Washington at War I (August 26, 1942) no. 3; "Accomplishments in Maryland Schools," 1940–45, Maryland Department of Education, WRC, RG 2010, Box 82, MHS.

48. "Employee Counseling: A Report," February 25, 1944, WBA, RG 86, Box 1540, NA; Memo, Myrtle Cohan to Irving Posner, September 11, 1944, OCWS, WARC, RG 215, Box 7, NA; "Needed? Family Case Work Services for Detroit," February 21, 1944, CCPA, RG 212, Box 48, NA; Myer, p. 107; Magee, p. 104; "National Back-To-School Drive," Children's Bureau and U.S. Office of Education, August 7, 1945, OCWS, Director's Subject File, RG 215, Box 2, NA.

49. "National Back-To-School Drive," Children's Bureau and U.S. Office of Education, August 7, 1945, OCWS, Director's Subject File, RG-215, Box 2, NA; "Annual Report of the Board of School Commissioners of Baltimore City," Year Ending June 30, 1945, p. 131, and Year Ending June 30, 1941, p. 143, WRC, RG 2010, Box 84, MHS.

50. Magee, p. 105; Caroline Legg, "Student Wage Earners in Wartime," U.S. Department of Labor, Children's Bureau, December, 1943, WRC, RG 2010, Box 116, MHS; "Firm Schedule: Boeing Aircraft Company," January 1943, WBA, RG 86, Box 1413, NA; State of Washington, Department of Labor and Industries, *Tenth Annual Report*, p. 20.

51. Ralph Carr Fletcher, "Runaway Youth to Detroit During the War," *Social Service Review* 22 (September 1948); 350–51; Memo, Frederick Brunton to V. M. Graham, May 9, 1944, DSS, RG 75, WSA; "Seattle-Bremerton Congested Area," [n.d.], OCWS, RG 215, Box 32, NA; "Composite Report on Puget Sound Area," May 15, 1944, pp. 193–94, OCWS, RG 215, Box 17, NA.

52. "Employee Counseling: A Report," February 25, 1944, WBA, RG 86, Box 1540, NA; "Michigan Juvenile Delinquency Report," Juvenile Delinquency Study Committee, September, 1943, OCWS, Director's Files, RG 215, Box 28, NA; *Seattle Went to War*, p. 29; *Seattle Post-Intelligencer*, April 25, 1944; *Catholic Northwest Progress*, March 5, 1943; *Seattle Times*, May 2, 1943, May 21, 1944.

53. "Michigan Juvenile Delinquency Report," Juvenile Delinquency Study Committee, September 1943, OCWS, Director's Files, RG 215, Box 28, NA; *Seattle Times*, November 15, 1942.

54. "Conference on Juvenile Delinquency," Federal Security Agency, August 3, 1943, OCWS, Director's Subject File, RG 215, Box 3, NA; City of Seattle, *Annual Reports*, Police Department, 1939–1945; Letter, Herbert Ward to Katharine Lenroot, January 15, 1943, Records of the Children's Bureau [hereafter cited as CB], RG 102, Federal Records Center, Suitland, Maryland [hereafter cited as FRC].

55. Fritz Redl, "Zoot Suits: An Interpretation," *Survey Midmonthly* 79 (October 1943): 259-62; OWI, "Report on Juvenile Delinquency," October 10, 1943, OCWS, Director's Subject File, RG 215, Box 3, NA; *Seattle Times*, April 26, 1944; *Newsweek*, May 8, 1944.

56. *Seattle Times*, April 26, 1944, April 27, 1944, May 4, 1944; King County Welfare Department, Summary, June 5, 1944, Juvenile Court "Wolf Pack" Cases [hereafter cited as "Wolf Pack"], DSS, RG 75, WSA.

57. *Seattle Times*, April 26, 1944, April 27, 1944, May 1, 1944.

58. Ibid., April 27, 1944, May 1, 1944.

59. Ibid., May 1, 1944; *Seattle Post-Intelligencer*, April 29, 1944, April 30, 1944; *Newsweek*, May 8, 1944.

60. *Seattle Times*, May 14, 1944; "Wolf Pack," DSS, RG 75, WSA; City of Seattle, Civilian War Commission, *Minutes*, Vol. 2, May 19, 1944.

61. *Seattle Times*, May 2, 1944, May 9, 1944, June 2, 1944; "Wolf Pack," DSS, RG 75, WSA.

62. *Seattle Times*, April 27, 1944, May 2, 1944, May 18, 1944; "Wolf Pack," DSS, RG 75, WSA.

63. "Wolf Pack," DSS, RG 75, WSA.

64. Ibid.

65. *Seattle Times*, May 4, 1944, May 7, 1944; City of Seattle, Civilian War Commission, *Minutes*, Vol. 2, May 19, 1944; Letter, T. O. Hoagland to Sherwood Gates, May 8, 1944, OCWS, RG 215, Box 228, NA.

66. *Seattle Times*, May 4, 1944, May 14, 1944.

67. *War Program News*, Region IV, May 1944, and August 1944, OCWS, General Classified, Region IV, RG 215, Boxes 9 and 10, NA; Memo, P. N. Binford to John Neasmith, June 15, 1943, and "Baltimore, Maryland" (Report), December 10, 1943, OCWS, General Classified, Maryland, (Region IV), RG 215, Box 124, NA.

68. "The Michigan Youth Guidance Commission," July 1, 1945–April 1, 1946, OCWS, Director's Files, Social Protection, RG 215, Box 112, NA.

69. Memo, Downing Procter to Mark McCloskey, October 27, 1943, OCWS, General Classified, Michigan (Region V), RG 215, Box 134, NA; Council of Social Agencies, Metropolitan Detroit, *Council Clippings*, March 1, 1944, OCWS, General Classified, Michigan (Region V), RG 215, Box 134, NA; "Composite Report on the Detroit Area," OCWS, Community Reports, RG 215, Box 5, NA.

70. Memo, Downing Procter to Mark McCloskey, October 27, 1943, OCWS, General Classified, Michigan (Region V), RG 215, Box 134, NA; "Accomplishments in Maryland Schools," 1940–45, Maryland Department of Education, WRC, RG 2010, Box 82, MHS; "Suggestive Policies for Pre-Induction Training Courses," Maryland Department of Education, WRC, RG 2010, Box 82, MHS.

71. "Annual Report of the Board of School Commissioners of Baltimore City," Year Ending June 30, 1945, p. 93, WRC, RG 2010, Box 84, MHS; *Baltimore Sun*, September 3, 1942, December 9, 1942; *Seattle Times*, April 29, 1942, September 27, 1942, April 16, 1944, November 26, 1944; *Bremerton Sun*, January 23, 1942; "Family Life Education in the Curriculum," *Marriage and Family Living* 5 (August 1943): 62.

72. "Annual Report of the Board of School Commissioners of Baltimore City," Year Ending June 30, 1945, pp. 75, 82, WRC, RG 2010, Box 84, MHS; "Suggestive Policies for Pre-Induction Training Courses," Maryland Department of Education, WRC, RG 2010, Box 82, MHS; *Seattle Times*, September 27, 1942, February 7, 1943, April 23, 1944; City of Seattle Biennial Report, Education Board, *Annual Report*, Year Ending June 30, 1943, p. 2; State of Washington, Superintendent of Public Instruction, June 20, 1940–June 20, 1942, p. 25.

73. *Detroit Free Press*, January 3, 1943; *Baltimore Evening Sun*, September 4, 1943; *Seattle Times*, September 13, 1942; September 20, 1942, April 16, 1944; City of Seattle, Education Board, *Annual Report*, Year Ending June 30, 1942, p. 6.

74. "Composite Report on the Detroit Area," December 22, 1943, OCWS, Community Reports, RG 215, Box 5, NA; Memo, Downing Proctor to Mark McCloskey, October 27, 1943, OCWS, General Classified, Michigan (Region V), RG 215, Box 134, NA; *Seattle Times*, February 17, 1943, August 20, 1943, September 13, 1943.

75. "Why? What? How? Social Treatment of the Sex Delinquent," OCWS, Social Protection Division, RG 215, Box 149, NA; *Seattle Times*, April 2, 1944.

76. Raymond F. Clapp, "Social Treatment of Prostitutes and Promiscuous Women," *Federal Probation* 7 (April-June 1943): 23-27; Memo, Charles Livermore to Thomas Devine, May 15, 1945, OCWS, Social Protection Division, RG 215, Box 1, NA.

77. Leo Wilson, "Sex Delinquency Versus Human Resources," November 1, 1945, OCWS, Social Protection Division, RG 215, Box 142, NA; "Teamwork in VD Prevention," 1943 Report of the American Social Hygiene Association, OCWS, Social Protection Division, RG 215, Box 1, NA; Memo, John F. Williams to Thomas Devine, May 29,.1945, OCWS, Social Protection Division, RG 215, Box 14, NA.

78. *Baltimore Evening Sun*, February 20, 1943; Fletcher, p. 353; "Composite Report, Detroit," December 22, 1943, OCWS, Community Reports, RG 215, Box 5, NA; Elsa Castendyck, "The Impact of the War on Children and Youth—and Resources for Treatment," Proceedings of Meeting of Children's Bureau Commission on Children in Wartime, February 4, 1943, OCWS, Director's Subject File, RG 215, Box 3, NA.

79. Memo, Marie Duffin to Eliot Ness, November 2, 1942, OCWS, General Classified, Maryland (Region IV), RG 215, Box 124, NA; Memo, James S. Owens to Acting Director, Director of Social Protection, January 31, 1945, OCWS, Social Protection Division, RG 215, Box 12, NA; Memo, James S. Owens to Thomas Devine, May 10, 1945, OCWS, Social Protection Division, RG 215, Box 12, NA; "Supplementary Report on War Area, Baltimore," OCWS, Community Reports, RG 215, Box 4, NA.

80. Memo, Marie Duffin to Eliot Ness, November 2, 1942, OCWS, General Classified, Maryland (Region IV), RG 215, Box 124, NA; Memo, James S. Owens to Eliot Ness, February 17, 1943, OCWS, General Classified, Maryland (Region IV), RG 215, Box 124, NA; Owens to Thomas Devine, May 14, 1945, OCWS, Social Protection Division, RG 215, Box 12, NA; Letter, Arthur E. Fink to Judge James Hodson, April 28, 1944, OCWS, Social Protection Division, RG 215, Box 15, NA.

81. "Composite Report on Health, Welfare, and Related Activities in the Detroit, Michigan War Area," December 22, 1943, OCWS, Community Reports, RG 215, Box 4, NA; Memo, Edwin J. Cooley to T. Devine, February 5, 1946, OCWS, Social Protection Division, RG 215, Box 117, NA; Mazie Rappaport, "A Protective Service for Promiscuous Girls," *Federal Probation* 9 (January-March 1945): 33.

82. "FBI Fingerprint Records," OCWS, Social Protection Division, RG 215, Box 130, NA; "A Study of 210 'Disorderly' Girls, Seattle, Washington, Council of Social Agencies," in Letter, Edwin Cooley to Eliot Ness, July 27, 1943, OCWS, General Classified, RG 215, Box 228, NA.

83. "Composite Report on Puget Sound Area," May 15, 1944, OCWS, RG 215, Box 17, NA; Memo, B. Burhans to Mark McCloskey, December 15, 1944, OCWS, RG 215, Box 227, NA; Memo, Arthur Fink to Eliot Ness, May 9, 1944, OCWS, RG 215, Box 227, NA; "Services Offered Arrested Girls, Seattle, Washington," OCWS, RG 215, Box 32, NA; Letter, Pearce Davies to Richard Neustadt, January 30, 1945, OCWS, RG 215, Box 32, NA.

84. *Seattle Times*, April 2, 1944; "A Study of 210 'Disorderly' Girls, Seattle, Washington, Council of Social Agencies," in Letter, Edwin Cooley to Eliot Ness, July 27, 1943, OCWS, General Classified, RG 215, Box 228, NA.

85. "Composite Report on Health, Welfare, and Related Activities in the Detroit, Michigan War Area," December 22, 1943, OCWS, Community Reports, RG 215, Box 4, NA; "A Preliminary Analysis of Certain Statistics Relating to Prostitutes and Promiscuous Women," January 26, 1944, OCWS, Social Protection Division, RG 215, Box 131, NA; Rappaport, pp. 33-34; "Paper Read by Miss Rappaport at the Maryland State Conference of Social Work," in Memo, James S. Owens to Director, Division of Social Protection,

August 17, 1944, OCWS, Social Protection Division, RG 215, Box 12, NA; "Monthly General Report on Region XII," December 15, 1944–February 15, 1945, OCWS, Director's Files, Social Protection, RG 215, Box 158, NA.

86. Rappaport, p. 34; "War Program News, Region IV," September-October 1944, OCWS, General Classified, Region IV, RG 215, Box 9, NA; "Paper Read by Miss Rappaport at the Maryland State Conference of Social Work," in Memo, James S. Owens to Director, Division of Social Protection, August 17, 1944, OCWS, Social Protection Division, RG 215, Box 12, NA; "Monthly General Report on Region XII," December 15, 1944–February 15, 1945, OCWS, Director's Files, Social Protection, RG 215, Box 158, NA; "Conference on Juvenile Delinquency," FSA, August 3, 1943, OCWS, Director's Subject File, RG 215, Box 3, NA.

87. *Detroit Free Press*, March 28, 1945, March 30, 1945, April 3, 1945; Memo, Walter A. Hixenbaugh to Thomas Devine, June 11, 1945, OCWS, Social Protection Division, RG 215, Box 12, NA; Memo, John F. Williams to Michael Morrissey, November 9, 1944, OCWS, Social Protection Division, RG 215, Box 12, NA.

88. *Detroit News*, February 10–11, 1945.

89. Memo, Edwin Cooley to Eliot Ness, May 24, 1944, OCWS, General Classified, RG 215, Box 228, NA; "Monthly VD Index of Seattle, Washington," April 1944, OCWS, General Classified, RG 215, Box 228, NA; Memo, James S. Owens to Eliot Ness, September 28, 1943, OCWS, General Classified, Region IV, RG 215, Box 9, NA.

90. Memo, Edwin Cooley to Eliot Ness, August 23, 1944, OCWS, General Classified, RG 215, Box 228, NA; Ragnar T. Westman to Surgeon General, U.S. Public Health Service, September 24, 1943, OCWS, General Classified, RG 215, Box 228, NA.

91. "The Age of Promiscuous Women and Girls Spreading Venereal Disease," OCWS, Social Protection Division, RG 215, Box 130, NA; "Annual Report, Social Hygiene Division (Detroit)," 1943, CCPA, RG 212, Box 52, NA; "A Study of 210 'Disorderly' Girls, Seattle, Washington, Council of Social Agencies," in Letter, Edwin Cooley to Eliot Ness, July 27, 1943, OCWS, General Classified, RG 215, Box 228, NA; Kinsey, pp. 423, 442.

92. "Conference on VD Control, Headquarters, Second Services Command," September 18, 1944, OCWS, Social Protection Division, RG 215, Box 114, NA; American Social Hygiene Association, "Boy Meets Girl in Wartime," p. 15, OCWS, Social Protection Division, RG 215, Box 137, NA; *New York Times*, February 2, 1943; "Social Protection," OCWS, Social Protection Division, RG 215, Box 147, NA; "A Study of 210 'Disorderly' Girls, Seattle, Washington, Council of Social Agencies," in Letter, Edwin Cooley to Eliot Ness, July 27, 1943, OCWS, General Classified, RG 215, Box 228, NA.

93. From Files of Mrs. Luce, ASHA, OCWS, General Classified, Maryland (Region IV), RG 215, Box 124, NA; "Case Summary of 30 Female Prisoners, Dayton, Ohio, Workhouse," February 1943, OCWS, Social Protection Division, RG 215, Box 130, NA; "Conference on Juvenile Delinquency," FSA, August 3, 1943, OCWS, Director's Subject File, RG 215, Box 3, NA; Memo, Thomas Devine to John Williams, February 19, 1945, OCWS, Social Protection Division, RG 215, Box 6, NA; *Tacoma Health Bulletin*, Vol. 1, No. 4, April 1944, OCWS, Social Protection Division, RG 215, Box 131, NA.

94. Gilman M. Ostrander, "The Revolution in Morals," in *The Twenties: The Critical Issues*, Joan Hoff Wilson, ed., (Boston: Little, Brown, 1972), pp. 131–132.

4
CHILD CARE
IN WARTIME

In order to accommodate and promote the increased employment of
mothers, the federal government and local authorities collaborated on a
wartime day-care program unprecedented in its scope and level of commitment to public child care. Because it involved the recognition and
countenancing of vast changes in the social role of women, no service
generated more controversy than the wartime child care effort. If successful, it could challenge deeply held beliefs regarding the importance of
the mother-child bond and the role of the family in child nurture. The
day-care program taxed the imagination and resources of federal and
local officials alike as they faced the challenge of organizing, financing,
and creating day-care facilities and attendant services to reach hundreds
of thousands of people in a very short period of time.

Because of the bureaucratic nightmare created by the federal day-care
program and the inadequacy of federal funding, local variables proved
crucial in determining the kind of system provided to working women
in a war boom community. Some communities lacked the leadership,
resources, or will to implement even the minimal program made possible
by federal grants; others were overwhelmed by the impact of the war
and its consequent strain on community facilities, personnel, and budgets. Those communities with a strong tradition of civic activism, a
structure of facilities and services capable of supporting a program, an
educational establishment committed to the possibilities of public child
care, and the willingness to take the initiative when federal aid proved

belated, insufficient, or completely unavailable managed to come the closest to the goal of a low-cost, high-quality program meeting the needs of an appreciable number of those it sought to serve.[1]

The haphazard way in which the federal program developed resulted in the dispersion of authority throughout a variety of federal agencies. This dispersion and the legal obstacles contained in some state and local statutes served to delay the planning and implementation of local programs. Moreover, the attempt to create one program to work efficiently within the welter of state and local agencies assigned responsibility for implementing it fostered bureaucratic in-fighting and militated against the development of uniform standards as to the quality of care provided. At all levels of government, agencies quarreled over jurisdiction in the area of child care. The result was, in the words of one observer, "an all-pervading confusion."[2]

Funding for the federal day-care program was provided under the Lanham Act, a law passed in early 1942 to give emergency assistance to communities hit hardest by the transition to a wartime economy. It made no specific provision regarding funds for child care, but administration officials finally decided that they could be included among the special services necessitated by the disruptions of war. When Senator Elbert D. Thomas of Oklahoma introduced a bill in 1943 authorizing funding specifically for child care, it was defeated, a victim of agency in-fighting and administration preference for a temporary program stressing institutional, custodial care rather than a long-term system designed to create an educational program that would meet wartime needs as well as build a foundation for high-quality care in the postwar period.[3]

Once a community had decided to apply for federal funds, it was confronted with a bureaucratic tangle which served to delay the granting of funds and inhibit the creation of programs. Local school boards or welfare agencies had to submit their requests for child care appropriations to the appropriate state agencies, which then had to approve and forward them to the regional representative of the U.S. Office of Education and to the state and federal FWA offices. Once they had certified the requests, the money was granted and the state agency involved, generally the state board of eduction, became responsible for program supervision, although the local school boards usually assumed control of the day-to-day operation of the centers.[4]

In order to qualify for federal funds, the community had to prove that the problem of child care was caused or increased by war programs, that large numbers of women were being employed, that their labor was essential to war production, and that local financing could not meet the community's needs. Moreover, the community had to assume responsibility for 50 percent of the cost of operating the centers. Money from presidential emergency funds was allocated by the Office of Defense Health and Welfare Services for the limited purpose of documenting the community's requirements in regard to child care. Needless to say, receipt of such funds was predicated on successfully negotiating yet another fund application process.[5]

As a result of the obstacles created by the federal program, local initiative was especially important in the establishment of day-care programs in the early stages of the war. In some cases, however, hostility to the idea of mothers working and to the concept of public child care worked to impede the development of day-care programs as private individuals and public officials urged job discrimination against mothers as a better means of dealing with the situation. The executive council of the National Parent-Teacher Association took a position opposing the employment of young mothers as detrimental to child welfare, prompting similar resolutions from local parent-teacher groups. After the Children's Wartime Committee of the Washington State Defense Council recommended that mothers of children under the age of fourteen not work, the Seattle Times advised employers not to hire such women. The War Manpower Commission took the official position that all other sources of labor be exhausted before mothers of young children were hired. As late as November 1943, the governor and superintendent of public instruction in Michigan contended that child neglect by working mothers posed a major social problem and advocated limiting war jobs to women without child care responsibilities.[6]

Despite such recommendations and the pressures of an adverse public opinion, many women responsible for the care of young children did choose to work. In the Seattle area, day-care needs were outstripping available facilities even prior to America's official entry into the global conflict in December 1941. Not surprisingly, among the first mothers to seek employment were low-income women who were divorced, widowed, or separated from their husbands. Greater opportunities for well-paid jobs and a war-induced inflation, which resulted especially in higher costs for lower-rent housing, combined to impel such women to seek work. In the fall of 1941 the Pierce County Welfare Department reported that although its Aid to Dependent Children rolls were decreasing, requests for child care were being received faster than they could be filled. By December 1941, parents were even attempting to place their children in foster homes because they could not find adequate day care.[7]

As the wartime economic expansion gained momentum in defense centers, the child care situation worsened faster than community resources could be mobilized to meet it. The lure of high-paying war jobs brought more women into the labor force, increasing the demand for child care services and eroding the numbers of persons, usually women, who could provide them. Many who constituted the traditional sources of informal care, such as friends, neighbors, relatives, and even teenaged siblings, were taking jobs too. Moreover, many in-migrant women lacked the extended family support network on which working mothers historically had relied.[8]

Prior to the establishment of centers under the Lanham Act, the only federally financed centers in operation were those created during the Depression to care for the children of women working for the WPA. In most communities they had been supplemented by a limited number of private nurseries, which could not easily accommodate greater numbers of children. In areas that required the regulation and licensing of private child care establishments, the opening of new approved centers was seriously impeded by the lengthy and cumbersome administrative procedures involved. Regardless of local legal requirements, a reliance on private centers would have made it difficult to place them where they were needed or to assure control over the quality of the services and facilities offered.[9]

By the time the formal programs under the Lanham Act were launched, the need for them had become acute. According to federal guidelines, day-care facilities would be required for one child for every ten working women in a defense center. By late 1942, when Seattle opened its first centers in anticipation of Lanham funding, 75,000 women were employed. At the time, the city had seven WPA nurseries and three private operations serving a total of 350 children; the Seattle Civilian War Commission reported a backlog of 1,500 applications for child care. In Tacoma, where 20,000 women were employed, only one day-care center was open. Baltimore, with 145,000 women in the labor force by late 1942, relied on sixteen WPA centers and a few private nurseries run by charities.[10]

In Detroit, where the extended reconversion period delayed the mobilization of women, the development of an effective public day-care program was correspondingly delayed. Unlike many defense centers, Detroit had an extensive prewar system of private nurseries inspired in part by the Merrill-Palmer School, a pioneer in providing nursery school services and training for their personnel. The private facilities, however, proved to be of limited utility in meeting the wartime crisis because most were open only six hours a day and only about half of their enrollees were the children of working women. Moreover, many were unwilling to alter their policies or expand their services in order to accommodate the needs of mothers working in defense industries. As a result, by the spring of 1943, when Lanham funds enabled the city to take over the WPA nurseries threatened with closure because of the ending of WPA funding, those seventeen centers were supposed to serve a population of 350,000 working women.[11]

Preschool nurseries represented only a part of the child care need generated by the war. Mothers of school-age youngsters, especially those whose children were in the lower grades, had a particularly difficult time finding caretakers to supervise their children in the hours before and after school, and no group facilities were available to them. The situation was worsened by the double-sessioning of elementary schools in many overcrowded areas. Rural Wayne County, for example, had thousands of children on half-day schedules. In Bremerton, school officials eliminated the kindergarten program in all schools and limited first grade classes to only two elementary schools so that 700 children aged five and six were not in school in the spring of 1942.[12]

The lack of public child care services spawned makeshift, informal group care arrangements which were almost impossible to regulate or eliminate. In some cases these arrangements evolved almost spontaneously. Baltimore recreation officials had to struggle with the problem of "stowaways," children too young to care for themselves who were left on playgrounds surreptitiously by their parents as they went to work. Recreation center leaders also reported that they were assuming day-care responsibilities as children of working parents made the centers a second home. In Seattle, the manager of the toy loan center for the

Rotary Youth Foundation found herself running a day-care center when children would stay there because they had nowhere else to go.[13]

A more serious problem, however, was caused by the growing number of commercial nurseries, which appeared to fill the child care void. Often overcrowded, unclean, and poorly supervised, these centers remained a persistent dilemma for the authorities throughout the war years. Yet for many mothers these centers represented the only alternative to no care at all for their children. They also offered flexibility in hours and admission policies so that women could leave their children while they looked for work, shopped, or went out. In Bremerton, one such private nursery cared for over 300 different children, many on an hourly basis, in a period of less than three months in the spring of 1942.[14]

The licensing laws for such centers varied from state to state. In Washington a 1933 state law specified that all such child care facilities were to be licensed by the county welfare department or private child placement agencies authorized by the Division for Children of the State Department of Social Security. In Detroit, the Board of Health licensed day care and boarding homes, while the Wayne County Welfare Department, formed in 1943, did so outside of the city. Baltimore, by contrast, did not regulate such facilities despite the recommendation of federal authorities that it change its laws in this regard. Regardless of the legal requirements, unapproved centers played an important role in wartime child care arrangements.[15]

Some employers complained that the lack of adequate child care facilities hampered them in their efforts to recruit women workers, especially in the early stages of the war. The Hudson plants in Detroit, for example, told the USES that the lack of day care was impeding the expansion of their work force. According to the USES office in Seattle, the lack of day care was the reason most cited in the refusal of women applicants to accept referral to Boeing. Surveys of Baltimore women taken to determine why more were not taking war jobs revealed that many could not make adequate child care arrangments.[16]

As the situation worsened, community organization to meet the problem improved. Although their reasons for supporting public day care varied, employers, unions, and community civic organizations worked together to try to create a workable program. Some advocated day care as a long overdue community service which should become permanent;

many others reluctantly supported it as a temporary expedient to provide the only alternative to widespread child neglect with its consequent social problems. Some professional educators saw the wartime program as a precedent for a peacetime system in which parents, children, and community could benefit from the expertise of the child guidance authority. Others, however, agreed with John Reid of the Seattle School Board, who accepted the necessity of public day care during the war but believed that once the war was over "we must start running our community so that mothers can stay home and look after their own children."[17]

Most viewed public child care as crucial to providing the womanpower needed to increase the production of vital war materials. For them, the issue of child welfare was secondary. According to Pearce Davies, assistant regional director of the Seattle Office of Defense Health and Welfare Services, "Unless the program does make women available for work, there is no merit in it." Whether they advocated day care in order to release women for paid employment or primarily out of concern for the well-being of the affected children, few in the day-care coalition at the local level supported it in order to revolutionize family relations and give women the opportunity for greater independence and choice in their lives. Despite the differences in their perspectives on the issue, the various proponents of public child care were united at least temporarily in their purposes and efforts during the war years.[18]

The level of community support generated for the programs varied considerably, dramatically affecting the quality and scope of the services provided. In the Baltimore area the reluctance of local authorities to take on new responsibilities or to spend public funds on anything so controversial as day care seriously hampered efforts to create a local system. As late as October 1942, manpower officials and the Baltimore Council of Social Agencies agreed that the area should not consider providing day care until the pool of women workers was more fully mobilized. Federal officials worried that state and local day-care planning was inadequate and that as late as July 1943 the community still had little precise information regarding the child care needs of women workers. By that time, however, the city had taken over the sixteen WPA nurseries, expanded their enrollments, and added two more preschool centers, all with the aid of Lanham grants.[19]

In Baltimore County, day-care advocates encountered considerably more difficulty with local officials. The county superintendent of schools and the school board were unwilling to assume responsibility for a child care program. As a result, supporters of such a system had to search for an official local sponsor and had to incorporate as the Pre-School Centers of Baltimore County, a group unique in the wartime child care program. Christian Kahl, president of the Baltimore County Commissioners, agreed to sponsor the group's applications for federal funds, but his role was the only one played by a local official. The county program was administered instead by Professor Esther Crane of Goucher College; Mrs. James Swartz, who headed a private nursery in the area; and other volunteer assistants.[20]

Officials in Detroit and Seattle, by contrast, organized relatively early to submit applications for federal funds and to begin the operation of local centers in anticipation of federal support. Both had effective local day-care groups by the spring of 1942, and had begun conducting surveys to determine day-care needs and seeking funds to open the centers. Almost as soon as the auto industry had begun hiring women workers, child care representatives in Detroit were urging federal officials to authorize the use of Lanham funds for an extensive day-care program. Like other cities that acted early on the day-care situation, Seattle and Detroit found that federal inertia cost them much precious time.[21]

Officials in the State of Washington faced special difficulties in opening centers prior to the receipt of federal aid because of legal restraints on spending by public schools. A 1933 state law prohibited the use of school revenues for programs for preschool-age children. Moreover, the State Department of Education could not use its emergency funds for nurseries and could not legally guarantee the replacement of money advanced by school districts in anticipation of the receipt of federal funds if such funds were denied. There was no immediate legislative recourse as the state legislature was not to meet again until 1943.[22]

By contrast with Baltimore and some other defense centers, where official timidity regarding the assumption of any risk in day-care funding delayed the development of a program, Seattle school officials sought support from other community agencies in order to begin operation of preschool nurseries before the approval of its application for Lanham Act funds, citing the probability that federal money would ultimately

be received and noting the immediacy of the problem. As School Superintendent Worth McClure stated, "The problem is right on our doorstep. You might say the babies are on our doorstep. And their mothers
are going into war work in greater numbers every day." The school
board thus authorized an expenditure of $10,000 to be used to equip the
centers, and the Seattle-King County War Chest agreed to underwrite
the appropriation. In accordance with the wartime arrangement worked
out for the already existent WPA nurseries, the school board was to
choose the teachers for the new nurseries and the WPA to pay their
salaries. Before agreeing to the school board's role, Director John B.
Shorett insisted that the program be undertaken only as an emergency
measure and only for the duration.[23]

Once a community found adequate financing to begin a program, it
was confronted with the necessity of providing suitable sites, equipment,
and personnel for the nurseries. Not surprisingly, those areas where the
need for child care facilities was greatest were those least able to meet it.
The countless other problems created by the war, especially those
attendant to rapid population growth, claimed much of the revenues
and attention of local government. Local charities, especially those
which already offered some sort of child care, found their physical and
monetary resources strained to the breaking point early in the war.
Wartime shortages of personnel and materials posed special difficulties
for the rapid implementation of an extensive new public program.[24]

Finding sites for the centers that would be appropriately located and
suitable for use as nurseries created the greatest difficulties for local
authorities throughout the war. School buildings often offered the best
recourse for day-care centers, but the schools were generally short of
space and their facilities frequently not designed for the use of preschool
children. Reliance on churches, community buildings, and other such
facilities was limited by the difficulties in securing permission for their
use and because many were either structurally unsuitable or poorly
located. Despite these disadvantages, day-care officials relied on whatever was available in the initial stages of the program, awaiting the
funding and materials allocations that would enable them to build or
renovate more suitable quarters. As the program evolved, wartime
housing projects provided a growing proportion of the preschool
centers.[25]

In Baltimore County the lack of cooperation from the county school board meant that the day-care group had to be especially resourceful in seeking out buildings for use as centers. More so than most systems, they relied on the aid and cooperation of local war industries and businesses. Bethlehem Steel, for example, provided them with two buildings for centers (one of which was designated for blacks), a lot for a playground, and crews of workmen to do the necessary alterations work. Others donated money and buildings. Even with such cooperation, the search for buildings was almost incessant. When the center located at the Maryland State Teacher's College in Towson proved to be too far from the plants it was supposed to serve, every member of the Pre-School Centers association participated in a five-month search for a reasonable alternative. All the while, Martin Aircraft, Bendix, and Black and Decker complained that the lack of day-care centers near their plants was costing them women workers.[26]

Whether housed in churches, housing projects, or other buildings, wartime nursery centers were often overcrowded, ill-equipped, and poorly located. The efforts to provide quarters for the Middle River Center near Baltimore typified the difficulties encountered regarding the establishment of adequate facilities. Originally housed in two trailers that had to be abandoned because they failed to meet health code standards, the Middle River facility was then transferred to the Federal Public Housing Authority (FPHA) administration building at the Victory Villa Housing Project. The center accommodated up to eighty preschoolers in one room at the rear of the building. Meals were prepared with the aid of two hotplates and a small oven. The children shared the one bathroom in the building with the FPHA employees who worked there. In order to reach the outdoor play space the children had to be taken across a heavily traveled highway. A federal observer commented, "I should think they would all have developed claustrophobia from the crowding, the confusion and the noise."[27]

The obstacles encountered by day-care officials in the Puget Sound community of Bremerton indicated the kinds of problems created by the competing claims of other services and agencies. Because the Army had taken over public playgrounds and school yards for its encampments and because the school buildings in the district were extremely overcrowded, these areas could not be used for nursery school or recreation projects. Makeshift facilities in the housing projects thus housed the community's nurseries. These were often small, poorly located, and substandard in lighting and ventilation. The East Park Nursery School, for example, was located in an old house left at one end of the project site and had no outdoor play space, even though it served some kindergarten and early elementary-age children in addition to the preschoolers. The center at the all-black Sinclair Housing Project did not have adequate play space, was in poor condition, and was not readily accessible from the houses in the project. By May 1944, five nurseries were operating in the projects, all at or over capacity. Because of the lack of other facilities, working mothers who lived outside of the projects had no centers available for their children.[28]

Staffing the nurseries meant finding persons with professional qualifications in teaching or child guidance to supervise the program, hiring cooks and custodial personnel, and enlisting volunteers to aid in various ways. Because of the shortage of professionally trained personnel and the competition from war industries, recruiting and training personnel became an acute problem. As a result, officials frequently had to hire persons who had not completed their college degrees as teachers for the nurseries and encourage them to take specially devised courses from local colleges or the public schools. The attempt by public officials to set high standards for nursery teachers in order to maintain quality and ensure public confidence in the program sometimes impeded the hiring or retention of sufficient numbers of teachers. In Detroit, for example, officials had to delay the opening of six completed centers in late 1943 because of a lack of qualified personnel to staff them.[29]

Although the requirements for volunteers in the child care program were usually less definite than those for supervisors, local schools, colleges, and community organizations made available various training options for volunteer day-care workers. Young girls, who formed an important part of the child care volunteers, could receive training as aides from the Girl Scouts, the High School Victory Corps, and the Red Cross. Within the Seattle system, which stressed professionalism more than most, volunteers had to take courses offered by the University of Washington, the Seattle schools, or the Red Cross in order to acquire a certificate for emergency volunteer service in child care. Ironically, Baltimore, which had no formal requirements for volunteers, also had the greatest dificulty recruiting persons to help in the program. In

January 1943, the Baltimore Civilian Mobilization Commission issued a call for volunteers, warning that several nursery schools would have to close unless more workers gave their time to the program.[30]

The initial inadequacies of the wartime day-care system hampered officials in their attempts to conquer yet another serious problem—the hostility of many working parents toward the idea of public day care for their preschoolers. For many of them institutional group care seemed like bad public policy and harmful to children. They feared that it would mean the warehousing of their children, who would receive inadequate and impersonal attention in a regimented setting. War worker Mary Salvus commented that she received much criticism because of her decision to take a job and leave her children in a day-care center. She observed that many people were offended by the concept of public child care, adding that to them "it sounds like the Spartans binding their children over to the state." Officials in both Baltimore and Detroit noted that working mothers from rural areas, where supervision of children was more casual than in an urban setting, were especially reluctant to entrust their children to public centers.[31]

In order to eliminate such distrust, the provision of high-quality care for the children and convenience for the working mothers were essential. Yet many wartime centers fell far short of meeting such requirements. In Tacoma, for example, two of the first three centers were located in church basements, which lacked the space, equipment, and play areas necessary for their purposes. Because they were not satisfactory arrangements, parents were reluctant to leave their children in them. Failure to consider the transportation problems of working parents also discouraged the utilization of the centers. Busy, harried working women were understandably reluctant to add to the claims on their time or to take their small children on buses already crowded with war workers. Federal officials reported that locations requiring time-consuming special travel accounted for a large number of poorly attended centers.[32]

With the cooperation of unions, some employers, and local groups, various expedients were devised to provide information on day-care facilities and to encourage their use. As a part of their womanpower broadcasts, Baltimore officials participated in radio programs devoted to day care, stressing the quality of care provided in the Lanham centers and the educational and health benefits for the children who attended. In a typical example of employer promotional efforts, the *Bendix Beam* in Baltimore reassured mothers that they could place their children in group care with confidence as the centers offered "safe and careful supervision . . . good educational experiences, teachers skilled at guidance in living and playing together in peace and good will." In Detroit the Automotive Council for War Production devised an illustrated folder on the advantages of day care and sent it to all plants.[33]

Some potentially beneficial means of promoting the public acceptance of day care were suggested but never implemented. Baltimore social welfare officials considered various means of familiarizing mothers with the care offered by the centers, including scheduling of social events that would encourage them to visit centers and subsidizing an initial period of free care, but did not follow through on the ideas. When Mrs. Edsel Ford suggested that films on day care be shown in the women's restrooms at the Ford plants, Henry Ford rejected the idea. Although Ford was willing to provide jobs for thousands of mothers, he, like many others during the war, was unwilling to face the full implications of the changes set in motion by his own policies.[34]

Early in the war, Seattle and Detroit created day-care information and referral services so that working parents would have access to current information regarding available facilities and so that community officials could better plan to meet public needs. Detroit began with a decentralized system of twenty-three referral centers provided by various social agencies but found that the cooperating groups frequently had other priorities and did not keep day-care information current. As a result, the Detroit day-care committee created the Children's War Service in May 1943, a child care referral service funded by state, federal, and local contributions. Despite their importance, the information services frequently failed to reach many who needed their help and alienated some of their potential constituents from the day-care program. Those services which refused to give day-care information without a personal interview by a social worker, as was the case in Detroit, needlessly inconvenienced working mothers and reinforced the popular misperception that public child care was an arm of welfare. Moreover, it forced women to go through potentially intrusive and judgmental questioning regarding their decisions to work and their provisions for the care of their children. Nevertheless, an imperfect service was greatly preferable to the system in Baltimore, which had no central source for day-care planning and information.[35]

The difficulties in establishing and promoting public nursery schools were dwarfed by those faced by officials who sought to ensure adequate public care for school-age children. It proved very difficult to convince parents of the need for supervisory care for older children, especially when it involved fees to the parents. The quality of program offerings assumed even greater importance than in the nursery school program because the children to be served by it had to be convinced that it was interesting and worthwhile for them. The level of supervision had to be kept minimal as children resented spending any more time in "school" than was already required of them. At the same time, finding sites with the proper space and equipment and hiring supervisory personnel proved even more troublesome than in the nursery school system.[36]

Moreover, overcrowding in the grade schools and federal policies regarding their expansion tended to exacerbate the problem. Before a school district could obtain federal grants or materials allocations to build more school space, it had to be operating facilities at 200 percent of capacity. This meant that many overcrowded districts had large numbers of school-age children, including many very young ones, attending school on half-day sessions. Because many of these children had working mothers, the 200 percent requirements automatically created a day-care problem. Moreover, schools on double sessions had neither the space nor the personnel to operate extended school day-care centers, but the Federal Works Agency stood by its policy. As a result, many children had to defer their schooling or suffer from a lack of educational opportunity or even good custodial care. Meanwhile, local officials struggled to launch a school-age child care system to offer a partial remedy for the situation.[37]

Officials in Detroit and Seattle tried to tackle the problem early, encountering similar difficulties. In October 1942, well before Lanham Act funds for such projects could be assured, Seattle School Superintendent Worth McClure announced a plan to open three centers to serve elementary school children, not including kindergarteners, from 2:30 to 6:00 P.M. Parents wanting their children enrolled in the program were to contact their school principal and the children would be placed under the jurisdiction of the school after school as well as during regular school hours. A fee of $.50 a day was charged, although it could be adjusted on the recommendation of a Family Society social worker.[38]

Despite the demonstrable need for the service and the efforts of school officials to encourage its use, the first centers soon closed because of a lack of enrollment. Although the Civilian War Commission had received 672 requests for care for school-age children, the John Hay School center never opened because it had no enrollment, and the other two centers attracted only four children. Baffled by the failure of parents to enroll their children and convinced that many children were being left unsupervised, school officials continued the project for another week and instructed school principals to continue their neighborhood publicity campaigns. The *Seattle Times* aided by urging working parents to use the centers, pointing out that they would be closed if not used. Such exhortations proved ineffective, however, and the centers quietly folded.[39]

Among the reasons advanced for the failure of the program, the most convincing were that parents were still leary of the idea of public group care, especially for older children, and that they found the charge of $2.50 a week per child too high because they were not sufficiently convinced of the necessity for organized recreational and supervisory programs for school-age children to pay the price. The success of after-school programs offered without charge by churches, housing projects, and community organizations corroborates the latter conclusion. The Fremont Baptist Church program, which had been in existence for four years, found that its enrollment increased from a prewar average of thirty children a week to 100 by November 1942. The housing projects, whose residents included large numbers of war workers and their children, organized extensive recreation programs for school-age children. The Yesler Housing Project program, for example, was open 2 to 9 P.M. and served over 700 children. It was aided by the Seattle Rotary Youth Foundation, which provided equipment for sports and handicrafts. In addition, the YMCA and YWCA operated successful after-school programs, charging a maximum of $.15 a day on weekdays and $.25 on Saturdays.[40]

As early as the summer of 1942, the Detroit Board of Education tried to introduce the concept of organized care for children aged six to sixteen, but it failed to generate sufficient interest in the system and consequently had to abandon it in the planning stage. As originally devised, the program was to involve the expansion of summer school to include recreation and food services to be available fifteen hours a day, six days a week. A lack of publicity regarding the program, the reluctance of parents to provide care for school-age children, and the fact that the mobilization of women workers was only just beginning in Detroit killed this initial attempt at a program for older children. In addition, the proposed link between the day-care system and summer school probably ensured a lessened enthusiasm among the youthful beneficiaries of the system.[41]

The initial difficulties experienced in Detroit and Seattle with the programs for older children were not unusual. By December 1943, an OCWS report by Mary Keeley indicated that such programs had not yet become successfully established. According to the report, the number of such programs was minimal, and most of them served only six to ten year olds. Moreover, most of the school-age canteens were operating much below capacity; fully 70 percent of them were running at less than 60 percent of capacity. Keeley cited a lack of public acceptance as the main reason for the failure of the system, noting that children refused to participate if they did not enjoy the activities made available in the centers.[42]

Keeley's conclusions notwithstanding, such dismal results were not inevitable, as the Seattle program would demonstrate in the coming months. Undeterred by their initial failure, Seattle school authorities tried again in the spring of 1943, when they benefited from a growing public awareness and acceptance of group child care. In order to encourage this trend and to ensure the success of their program, they launched a campaign of public education to apprise parents of the necessity for supervised recreation for school-age children. In addition, they offered a variety of services to meet the disparate needs of older children. By June 1945, thirty extended school centers in Seattle served 1,200 children. A system of activity centers for children aged five to fourteen was begun in March 1944 to provide recreation without the structured organization and food service of the after-school centers and to include junior high school students, who had been left out of all other programs. An immediate success, it was attracting 1,000 regular participants by the summer of 1945. A $60,000 grant from the State Department of Education to cover 50 percent of the instructional costs enabled the school district to run the activity centers at no cost to those using them.[43]

Most other communities, however, did not experience the success that Seattle did in meeting the day-care needs of older children. Some local authorities shared the conviction that recreational and supervisory programs for older children were an expensive strain on overburdened local budgets. Baltimore Mayor Theodore McKeldin, for example, cut back on proposed recreation program expansions in 1943, citing city budget deficits as the reason. As late as 1944, the city had only five extended school centers for school-age children. Fast-growing suburban communities were hard pressed to provide other urgently needed services and lacked the available facilities, the organized social welfare tradition, and the public revenues to provide an adequate system of school-age canteens and recreation activities. In rapidly suburbanizing areas of rural Wayne County, many small school districts found it difficult to secure Lanham funds for extended care programs because the number of school children needing such facilities fell short of the federal minimum required. Overcrowding in the schools, the lack of funds, and the conservatism of school officials in the rural areas inhibited the development of locally supported programs.[44]

If the provision of public care for school-age children was only partially accomplished during the war years, the need for child care services for children under two was hardly met at all. Because public opinion and the vast majority of officials in charge of day care at all levels agreed that group care could not provide the physical needs of infants or nurture desirable emotional development, few public facilities for the care of children under two were established. Instead, state and local officials decided to rely on a closely regulated program of individual care in private homes. Such an approach was hampered by the limited number of persons available to give such care, the need to supervise them closely, and bureaucratic inefficiency and delay in a situation requiring prompt action.[45]

Almost inevitably, the demand for infant care services far outstripped the ability of local agencies to inspect and license individual homes. The delays inherent in the situation were exacerbated by the fact that local agencies were assuming increased responsibilities while they were also experiencing the labor shortages and high personnel turnover that plagued all employers at the time. Consequently they were often understaffed and many of the caseworkers were inexperienced. The rapid turnover in day-care homes added further to the inefficiencies of the system. Between November 1942 and October 1943, the King County office licensed 135 homes, but only eighty-nine were still operating at the end of the year.[46]

When Detroit publicized the existence of the foster care program in early 1943, it received such a volume of requests for the service and applications from potential foster day mothers that its licensing work was seriously impeded. Of the 120 women who volunteered to provide infant care in their homes, only fourteen had had their applications approved within the first month. Moreover, the standards for a license in Wayne County were so stringent that only 9 percent were being approved by 1943. Because officials in the outlying areas around Detroit had to rely on individual home care for many older children as well, the burden on the licensers was even greater than in the city. The reliance on individual care arrangements proved so inadequate that Detroit officials were considering a group approach by 1944, although they never managed to initiate such a program.[47]

One obstacle to such a solution was the staunch opposition of the Children's Bureau, the Child Welfare League, and others to the funding of such programs by the federal government. The Children's Bureau subscribed unwaveringly to the proposition that any infant care arrangement other than one based on a one-to-one relationship between the child and a "mother-person" was detrimental to the healthy development of the child. When the FWA funded an experimental infant care center in San Diego in late 1944 over the opposition of the Children's Bureau, the aggrieved agency sent representative Betsy Trout to investigate. Her report, a classic example of predetermined conclusions, purportedly documented troubling signs of developmental difficulties in infants only recently enrolled in the group care unit. According to Pearce Davies of the OCWS, other agencies received the Trout report with the "governmental equivalent of catcalls and rotten tomatoes." Nevertheless, the San Diego experiment was abandoned, and no others received any federal assistance.[48]

Despite the insistence of the Children's Bureau and other groups that foster home day care was the only workable solution to the infant care problem, the reality of the situation fell far short of the original ideal of closely supervised, individualized care in private homes. In some cities, including Baltimore, no form of regulation was required or attempted. In those areas which mandated licensing for day-care homes, local authorities faced formidable difficulties in trying to force unlicensed facilities to conform to the law and in reinspecting approved homes periodically to ensure continued compliance with the specified standards. Because of the agencies' heavy case load, follow-up inspections of licensed homes were infrequent and inadequate. In order to cope with the problem of unlicensed facilities, agencies had to enforce the law selectively. In Seattle, the welfare department sent a routine letter to the operators of unlicensed centers that had been brought to its attention. These warnings were frequently ignored, however. When that happened, the welfare department had no choice but to ignore the situation unless it had reports of flagrant violations of its standards, in which case it would force the closure of the offending operation.[49]

The programs for the care of children under the age of two were thus beset with many problems. Throughout the war, the provision of day care for their babies remained an expensive and difficult problem for working parents. The shortage of licensed day-care homes and their high cost relative to group care for older children caused many women to leave the labor force entirely or to resort to unlicensed group care or the use of older children to care for their infants. Whether assessed in terms of increasing the female labor force or of providing high-quality, low-cost child care, the services provided for children too young for nursery schools fell far short of their goals.[50]

Once local authorities had defined the scope of their day-care program and had opened the first centers, they faced a continuing problem of refining the system, relocating, and sometimes expanding facilities to improve the quality of the services provided and to meet more fully the exact needs of those served by the system. Documenting those needs in order to ensure maximum use of the centers remained a particularly nettlesome challenge throughout the war. In Detroit, the board of education would not approve the opening of a center until twenty children were signed up to use it. Because there was a six-week delay after the approval, however, the parents of those children would frequently have made other plans by the time the center opened. Moreover, the Detroit system suffered because many centers did not open until 7 A.M., too late to accommodate many women working in defense industries. Detroit officials found that it usually took several months for a center to attain capacity after its opening. Even once that was accomplished, maintaining attendance figures remained difficult as women workers entered and left the labor force rapidly and experienced frequent changes in shift assignment, which entailed equally frequent adjustments in their child care arrangements. The wartime systems thus experienced difficulties with vacancies at the same time that they had waiting lists. As a result, although some centers remained overcrowded throughout the war years, especially those located in housing projects, many others operated considerably below capacity.[51]

The extent of nursery school underutilization varied from community to community and tended to decrease as the programs improved in the quality and convenience of their services. Meanwhile, a fully enrolled program was not necessarily an indication of a successful operation. In the Baltimore area, for example, most facilities operated at or above capacity, but only because the number of centers made available was so minimal in comparison with the demand as a result of the lack of official support for an extensive program. The eight centers in Baltimore County, which received no assistance from local government, served 500 children aged two to ten by the spring of 1945. Detroit, by contrast, had established fifty-three nursery schools with an enrollment of 2,237 by early 1945. The Detroit system, which experienced encouraging growth in enrollment, had serious difficulties in keeping up the daily attendance figures. In Seattle, the centers were functioning at only 80 percent of capacity by the spring of 1945.[52]

Nationally, the problem of underutilization created several difficulties. Sometimes, the difficulties of building enrollment fostered a willingness on the part of officials to abandon faltering centers prematurely or to retard the growth of the program on the grounds of a lack of public acceptance of the need for day care. Those communities with a commitment to the idea of public child care sufficient to make them willing to risk initial shortfalls in parent fee contributions frequently found that their patience was rewarded when a growing public confidence in the program resulted in increasing patronage. Nevertheless, the question of whether to allocate scarce resources and personnel to a controversial new social service with such great initial problems persisted as many officials continued to perceive the costs and obstacles to improvement as more significant than the benefits provided.[53]

An important early disincentive for continued community support for Lanham centers experiencing initial below-capacity enrollments was the FWA stipulation that local sponsors assume the responsibility for 50 percent of the operating expenses for the centers. Because state and local aid for day care was minimal, parent fees had to be relied upon for almost all of the local contribution. Center operating costs were so high, largely because of expenses for personnel and because attendance frequently fell short of capacity, that raising the local share proved extremely difficult for many communities. Moreover, the threat that the FWA would withhold Lanham funds from communities that failed to raise the 50 percent share created uncertainty and delay in implementing planned expansions at the local level.[54]

The debate spawned by the FWA's rejection in August 1943 of Seattle's application for funds to operate the existing forty-two units and to open thirty-eight more in the coming year typified the dilemma posed by the FWA policy. At the time, income from parent fees equalled only 28 percent of the operating costs. Once the FWA had ruled against Seattle's proposal, local officials had to decide whether to meet the contribution requirement by cutting operating costs or by raising more revenue, which would almost inevitably mean raising the fee charged to parents. About the only ways to cut expenses would be to close those centers having the least enrollment and to increase the pupil-teacher ratio, which would result in lessened convenience for parents and poorer-quality care for the children.[55]

The alternative solution was to raise the daily fee from $.50 to $.75, which would be enough to meet the community's obligations. FWA representative Mary Isham supported the increase, noting that $.75 was standard on the West Coast and had not proven a hardship to working mothers or a hindrance to the employment of women. Despite these assurances, Seattle officials were reluctant to raise the fees. Mrs. Robert M. Jones, chairperson of the King County Day Care Committee, expressed concern that the proposed increase would inhibit the employment of women and would cause parents to seek alternative forms of child care that might not be those best for the child. Officials charged with meeting the labor shortage were as reluctant to raise the child care costs of working parents as were those primarily concerned about child welfare. At a meeting held in August to discuss the situation, representatives of the WMC, the USES, and others agreed that higher fees would discourage women from working.[56]

In order to avoid raising fees or curtailing service, local authorities explored alternative sources of funding, but to no avail. A suggestion by Seattle City Councilman David Levine and others that local employers make up the deficit proved impossible to put into practice. Legal restraints on the use of state funds eliminated the possibility of aid from that source. Even the $500,000 appropriated by the state legislature in

1943 for child care centers was unavailable because the law specified that it was to be used only as a revolving fund to underwrite nursery school programs started before federal funds were received. In September, local officials decided to go ahead and raise the fees, only to find in November that the FWA had reversed itself and agreed to meet all costs above those met by the $.50 fee. The whole controversy had underscored the community's dependence on federal funds for a low-cost child care system, demonstrating again the paucity of local resources and the inability and unwillingness of the state government to provide significant aid for such purposes.[57]

Inadequate as it was, the provision of any support for day care by the State of Washington made it unusual in the wartime child care effort and enabled it to continue funding local centers despite the uncertainties created by federal policies. The State of Michigan considered a child care appropriations measure in 1943, but rejected it, despite the fact that the state treasury had a surplus during the war years. As a result, much of the expansion of the system in Detroit and other Michigan communities had to await the resolution of the local contribution issue. Although the Wayne County Day Care Committee had decided that state or local funds were necessary to supplement Lanham grants, the Detroit School Board voted in September 1943 not to ask the Detroit City Council for such support because it feared that the money might come out of school funds. Only California, Connecticut, New York, and New Jersey joined Washington in providing state funds for day care. Many other states, including Maryland, failed even to consider such measures. The day-care situation thus illustrated the extent to which the responsibility for devising and supporting innovative social programs fell to the federal government during the war years, at least in part because of the default of local and state governments.[58]

At the local level, the degree of activism in support of day care varied dramatically. Some local organizations, including those in Seattle and Detroit, worked actively to secure funding, expedite the application process, respond to client needs, and increase public acceptance of the service. Officials in Baltimore, by contrast, organized late and were reluctant to provide funding for anything but a very minimal program. By 1944 a representative of the Maryland Board of Education was questioning whether the benefits of the day-care system justified the expense. In many regards the Seattle system came closest to the goal of a high-quality program that offered a variety of services for all age groups at a moderate cost. Educators within the community were committed to the concept of professional care for children of working mothers and enthusiastically promoted it to prevent the use of haphazard methods of care. Moreover, population growth was slower within the city than in the outlying areas, enabling the Seattle School District to use many of its facilities in the day-care program. Such a situation was typical of the wartime experience; more successful services were provided in the cities, while the need was frequently greatest in the suburban areas to which industries and population were moving.[59]

Despite the inadequacies of several of the systems, the parents who did have public centers available to them seemed happy with the care their children received. When Detroit officials surveyed the parents of children using their centers in 1945, they found that 86 percent of the parents reported that their children benefited physically, and 94 percent thought they benefited socially from the program. When asked about the strengths of the system, mothers using the program in the Seattle area mentioned the supervision by professionally trained teachers, the provision of nutritious meals, and the companionship of other children most frequently. Citing the instruction that the children received in the nurseries, several commented that they thought their children were learning concepts and skills that would help them later in school. Edith Brown, a chauffeur at the Navy Yard, described the View Ridge Play Center as a "marvelous place" and observed that "it would be impossible for me to teach them all the things they're learning at the play center."[60]

Even in communities where officials gave their best efforts to create an extensive child care system, the public programs managed to provide only a small proportion of the child care arrangments utilized by working mothers. Among working mothers surveyed by the Women's Bureau, only 9 percent of those in Seattle, 5 percent of those in Baltimore, and 2 percent of those in Detroit relied on nursery schools to care for their children. According to the study, over half of such mothers relied on their husbands, older school children, or, most often, another relative to care for their children while they worked. The bureau's findings also indicated that a large proportion of mothers in the Seattle area left their children unattended while they worked; 25 percent of those questioned indicated that they made no arrangements for the care of their children. The comparable figures for Baltimore and Detroit were 15 percent and

6 percent. The high figures for the Seattle area could reflect the exceptionally large proportion of women in the area labor force who were in-migrants and would have had fewer relatives or friends in the area to rely on for child care.[61]

Throughout the nation, working mothers turned more often to time-honored methods of child care than to the public system. Many did so because they had no alternatives. Dolly Judkins, for example, left her two daughters with a neighbor while she worked at the Navy Yard because there was no nursery school she could enroll them in. She observed, "I have heard many women on the job mention the scarcity of nursery schools and how hard it is to find adequate care." Others, especially those in low-paying work or with more than one child needing care, could not afford the public system. A black woman employed as a cleaning woman in a Baltimore hotel told the Women's Bureau interviewer that she had relied on her eight-year-old niece to watch her children until school officials intervened; her salary of $14 a week left no surplus to meet the $3 weekly fee per child in a public center.[62]

Others eschewed the public system because they found the idea of group care impersonal or otherwise less satisfactory than the more individual attention given by neighbors or relatives. Christina Hamilton, a helper boatmaker at the Navy Yard, left her two sons in the care of her husband, who worked a different shift, even though the arrangement meant that the boys were left alone for forty-five minutes a day during the shift change. She commented, "I wouldn't care to send them to a play center when their dad makes such a good 'mother'." A Baltimore saleswoman reported to the Women's Bureau that she preferred having her children cared for by their father to sending them to a nursery school because "of the class of people they must mingle with" in the public centers. Others turned to relatives or friends because such arrangements were cheaper, more convenient, or better for their children. Many parents declined to send their children to public centers when they found that the facilities were overcrowded, poorly equipped, or otherwise substandard.[63]

The legacy of the wartime child care system was thus ambivalent. For Wilma Thatcher, a welder whose husband was overseas, it was "the best thing that could happen for working mothers." For many other women the difficulties involving in combining work and family responsibilities during the war years were exacerbated by the problem of making satisfactory arrangements for the care of their children. The failure of local and national authorities to provide a convenient and workable system of day care impeded women's abilities to take advantage of wartime work opportunities, handicapping them for the coming reconversion period. The inadequacies of the wartime program contributed to absenteeism by women workers, prejudicing some employers against them, and promoted employment discontinuity, making it difficult for many to accumulate essential job seniority.[64]

Although it had only served a minority of those it had hoped to, the wartime effort represented the largest commitment to public child care in the nation's history. The federal government spent $51,922,977 on 3,102 centers serving 600,000 children. The end of the war raised the question of whether the program had been merely a temporary and not very satisfactory expedient for an abnormal situation or a good beginning for a permanent, efficient operation. By that time officials had just begun responding to the needs of working mothers, expanding some of the programs that required it and replacing some of the inadequate, overcrowded sites with newer, larger, better-equipped institutions. Moreover, the concept of public care was beginning to gain acceptance among those who would be using it. With the end of the war, however, the unanimity of purpose among supporters of public child care was lost, as was the wartime rationale for day care as an aid to labor recruitment. The fate of the child care program in the postwar period would become enmeshed in the larger question of the place of women in American society, a question given little real consideration by wartime advocates of publicly supported day care.[65]

Notes

1. "Some Observations on the Federal Program for Care of Children of Employed Mothers," Mary Keeley, December 29, 1943, OCWS, Director's Subject File, RG 215, Box 2, NA.

2. Ibid.; "Current Status of Child Care Facilities," FSA, December 9, 1943, OCWS, Director's Subject File, RG 215, Box 2, NA; Howard Dratch, "The Politics of Child Care in the 1940's," *Science and Society* (Summer 1974): 169; Letter, Fred K. Hoehler to Paul McNutt, December 29, 1942, OCWS, Director's Subject File, RG 215, Box 2, NA.

3. Chafe, pp. 166–70; Dratch, p. 180.

4. Ibid.; "General Outline of Proposed State Program for Services to Children of Working Mothers, Washington State Department of Education," OCWS, Children's Care Division, RG 215, Box 9, NA.

5. Ibid.

6. U.S., Department of Labor, *Employment Security Review* 9 (October 1942): 1; *Seattle Times*, January 7, 1942, August 20, 1943; *Detroit Free Press*, January 6, 1943; "Employee Counseling: A Report," February 25, 1944, WBA, RG 86, Box 1540, NA; *Detroit News*, November 11, 1943.

7. "Report on Effects of National Defense Activities," Pierce County Welfare Department (hereafter cited as PCWD) memo, September 30, 1941, DSS, RG; 75, WSA; Kitsap County Welfare Department [hereafter cited as KCWD] memo, Frederick Brunton to Ruth FitzSimons, December 5, 1941, DSS, RG 75, WSA.

8. "Report Regarding Facilities Needed for the 'Day Care' of Children of Working Mothers in the Seattle Defense Area," KCWD, July 22, 1942, DSS, RG 75, WSA.

9. Virginia Kerr, "One Step Forward—Two Steps Back: Child Care's Long American History," in *Child Care—Who Cares?*, ed., Pamela Roby (New York: Basic Books, 1973), p. 162; Memo, Katherine Lenroot to James Brunot, April 21, 1943, OCWS, Children's Care Division, RG 215, Box 6, NA; *Day Care News*, March 1943, OCWS, WARC, RG 215, Box 10, NA.

10. "General Outline of Proposed State Program for Services to Children of Working Mothers in Washington," Washington State Day Care Committee, November 12, 1942, DSS, RG 75, WSA; Memo, Katherine Lenroot to James Brunot, April 21, 1943, OCWS, Children's Care Division, RG 215, Box 6, NA.

11. "Employee Counseling: A Report," February 25, 1944, WBA, RG 86, Box 1540, NA; "Report on Special Field Visits Regarding Need for Day Care of Children Employed in Defense Industries," April 6, 1942, OCWS, Children's Care Division, RG 215, Box 3, NA; "Composite Report, Detroit," December 22, 1943, OCWS, Community Reports, RG 215, Box 5, NA.

12. "Day Care of Children of Working Mothers," March 25, 1942, OCWS, Children's Care Division, RG 215, Box 3, NA; "Progress Report on Foster Day Care," KCWD, July 15, 1942, DSS, RG 75, WSA; "Some Observations on the Federal Program for Care of Children of Employed Mothers," Mary Keeley, December 29, 1943, OCWS, Director's Subject File, RG 215, Box 2, NA.

13. "Summary of Minutes of October 22, [1942] Conference, WMC, Baltimore Area," OCWS, Community Reports, RG 215, Box 4, NA; *Seattle Times*, July 12, 1942.

14. "Progress Report on Foster Day Care Study," KCWD, July 15, 1942, DSS, RG 75, WSA; Memo, Brunton to FitzSimons, February 6, 1942, KCWD, DSS, RG 75, WSA; Memo, L. L. Hegland to FitzSimons, September 11, 1942,

KCWD, DSS, RG 75, WSA; "Report on Special Field Visits Regarding Need for Day Care of Children of Women Employed in Defense Industries," April 6, 1942, OCWS, Children's Care Division, RG 215, Box 3, NA; Clive, pp. 527, 533.

15. Memo, Katherine Lenroot to James Brunot, April 21, 1943, OCWS, Children's Care Division, RG 215, Box 6, NA; *Day Care News*, March 1943, OCWS, WARC, RG 215, Box 10, NA; "Standards for Foster Day Care Homes," June 22, 1942, DSS, RG 75, WSA.

16. "Digest of Discussion, Regional Advisory Council," OCWS, Region IV, June 2–3, 1944, OCWS, General Classified, Region IV, RG 215, Box 9, NA; Memo, William Dorn to Mary Woods, March 31, 1943, OCWS, WARC, RG 215, Box 10, NA; "General Outline," Washington State Day Care Committee, November 12, 1942, DSS, RG 75, WSA.

17. *Seattle Times*, July 13, 1942, September 30, 1942, November 29, 1942, January 15, 1944; *Seattle Business*, November 12, 1942; *Aero Mechanic*, October 15, 1942, December 10, 1942; *Baltimore Sun*, June 9, 1942; *Goucher College Weekly*, November 30, 1943, WRC, RG 2010, Box 32, MHS; Irene E. Murphy, "Detroit's Experience with the Wartime Care of Children," *Proceedings of the National Conference of Social Work* (New York: Columbia University Press, 1943), pp. 136–137; "Composite Report, Detroit," December 22, 1943, OCWS, Community Reports, RG 215, Box 5, NA.

18. *Seattle Times*, December 2, 1942; *Seattle Business*, December 24, 1942.

19. "Summary of Minutes of October 22 [1942] Conference, WMC, Baltimore Area, OCWS, Community Reports, RG 215, Box 4, NA; "Supplementary Report on War Area, Baltimore, Maryland," July 10, 1943, OCWS, Community Reports, RG 215, Box 4, NA; "Reports and Recommendations of Region IV, Office of Defense Health and Welfare Services on Facilities and Services for Industrial Workers in the Baltimore Area," OCWS, WARC, RG 215, Box 7, NA; *Baltimore Evening Sun*, March 16, 1943.

20. "Baltimore County Association for Pre-School Education, Field Reports, Pre-School Centers," March 19, 1946, WRC, RG 2010, Box 32, MHS; Letter, Esther Crane to Esther Monke, June 5, 1946, WRC, RG 2010, Box 32, MHS.

21. "Plans for Services to Children of Working Mothers," January 28, 1943, OCWS, Children's Care Division, RG 215, Box 1, NA; "Employee Counseling: A Report," February 25, 1944, WBA, RG 86, Box 1540, NA; Letter, George F. Emery to FSA, June 15, 1942, OCWS, General Classified, Michigan (Region V), RG 215, Box 134, NA; Letter, Charles Schottland to George F. Emery, July 2, 1942, OCWS, General Classified, Michigan (Region V), RG 215, Box 134, NA; "Composite Report on Health, Welfare, and Related Activities in the Detroit, Michigan War Area," December 22, 1943, OCWS, Community Reports, RG 215, Box 5, NA.

22. Memo, FitzSimons to KCWD, October 20, 1942, DSS, RG 75, WSA; City of Seattle, Education Board, Report of the Public Schools, Year Ending June 30, 1942, p. 3.

23. Dratch, p. 180; "Minutes, Fourth Meeting, Regional Family Security Committee," July 14–15, 1943, OCWS, General Classified, Region IV, RG 215, Box 9, NA; *Seattle Times*, October 4, 1942, November 21, 1942; "General Outline," Washington State Day Care Commitee, November 12, 1942, DSS, RG 75, WSA; City of Seattle, Education Board, Report of the Public Schools, Year Ending June 30, 1943, p. 5.

24. "Labor Market Developments in the Detroit Area," November 5, 1943, BES, RG 183, Box 17, NA; "Composite Report on Health, Welfare, and Related Activities in the Detroit, Michigan, War Area," December 22, 1943, OCWS, Community Reports, RG 215, Box 5, NA; Letter, Agnes Park to Rose Alschuler, OCWS, Children's Care Division, RG 215, Box 3, NA.

25. "Employee Counseling: A Report," February 25, 1944, WBA, RG 86, Box 1540, NA; "Current Status of Child Care Facilities," December 9, 1943, OCWS, Director's Subject File, RG 215, Box 2, NA; Letter, Agnes Park to Rose Alschuler, OCWS, Children's Care Division, RG 215, Box 3, NA; "Report of Day Care Sub-Committee to the Detroit Victory Council," November 24, 1943, CCPA, RG 212, Box 51, NA; Letter, Pearl Wanamaker to Rear Admiral S. A. Taffinder, November 30, 1942, Langlie Papers, RG 11–12, Box 12–4, WSA.

26. Letter, Esther Crane to Esther Monke, June 5, 1946, WRC, RG 2010, Box 32, MHS; Baltimore County Association for Pre-School Education, "Field Reports," March 19, 1946, WRC, RG 2010, Box 32, MHS; "Facts About the Proposed Nursery School to be Built as an Addition to Epsom Chapel," WRC, RG 2010, Box 32, MHS.

27. Memo, E. C. Miliken to McCloskey, August 2, 1944, OCWS, Director's Subject File, RG 215, Box 2, NA; *PM*, July 29, 1943; Baltimore County Association for Pre-School Education, "Field Reports," March 19, 1946, WRC, RG 2010, Box 32, MHS.

28. *Navy Yard Salute*, May 15, 1943, June 26, 1943, March 10, 1944; Memo, Brunton to Scroggie, May 17, 1943, DSS, RG 75, WSA; "Composite Report on Puget Sound Area," May 15, 1944, OCWS, Community Reports, RG 215, Box 17, NA.

29. "Employee Counseling: A Report," February 25, 1944, WBA, RG 86, Box 1540, NA; *Day Care News*, March 1943, OCWS, WARC, RG 215, Box 10, NA; "Labor Market Developments in the Detroit Area," November 5, 1943, BES, RG 183, Box 17, NA; *Baltimore Evening Sun*, April 20, 1943, December 8, 1943; City of Seattle, Education Board, "Report of the Public Schools," Year Ending June 30, 1943, pp. 6, 7.

30. "Labor Market Development Report, Detroit Labor Market Area," November, 1943, BES, RG 183, Box 183, NA; Memo, P. N. Binford to Mark McCloskey, November 12, 1943, OCWS, General Classified, Maryland (Region IV), RG 215, Box 124, NA; *Baltimore Evening Sun*, January 3, 1945; *Seattle Times*, September 19, 1942, November 9, 1942, February 7, 1943, August 5, 1943; "A Few Examples of Child Care Programs Carried on by Girl Scout Groups," OCWS, Children's Care Division, RG 215, Box 2, NA; *Detroit News*, September 19, 1943, November 14, 1943.

31. "Employee Counseling: A Report," February 25, 1944, WBA, RG 86, Box 1540, NA; Carr and Stermer, p. 253; *Washington State CIO News*, November 1942; Baltimore County Association for Pre-School Education, "Field Reports," March 19, 1946, WRC, RG 2010, Box 32, MHS.

32. "Employee Counseling: A Report," February 25, 1944, WBA, RG 86, Box 1540, NA; "Current Status of Child Care Facilities," FSA, December 9, 1943, OCWS, Director's Subject File, RG 215, Box 2, NA; "Composite Report on Puget Sound Area," May 15, 1944, OCWS, Community Reports, RG 215, Box 17, NA.

33. Baltimore Nursery Schools, "Radio Scripts," May 15, 1943, September 18, 1943, WRC, RG 2010, Box 83, MHS; *Bendix Beam*, January 1945; *Martin Star*, April 1943; "Composite Report on Health, Welfare, and Related Activities in the Detroit, Michigan, Area," December 22, 1943, OCWS, Community Reports, RG 215, Box 5, NA.

34. "Minutes, Fourth Meeting, Regional Family Security Committee," July 14–15, 1943, OCWS, General Classified, Region IV, RG 215, Box 9, NA; Carr and Stermer, p. 254.

35. "Composite Report, Detroit," December 22, 1943, OCWS, Community Reports, RG 215, Box 5, NA; Murphy, p. 137; *Day Care News*, April 1943, OCWS, WARC, RG 215, Box 10, NA; *Seattle Went to War*, p. 22; "Employee Counseling: A Report," February 25, 1944, WBA, RG 86, Box 1540, NA; "Day Care of Children of Working Mothers," March 25, 1942, OCWS, Children's Care Division, RG 215, Box 3, NA.

36. "Composite Report, Detroit," December 22, 1943, OCWS, Community Reports, RG 215, Box 5, NA; "Some Observations on the Federal Program for Care of Children of Employed Mothers," Mary Keeley, December 29, 1943, OCWS, Director's Subject File, RG 215, Box 2, NA.

37. Ibid.

38. "Composite Report, Detroit," December 22, 1943, OCWS, Community Reports, RG 215, Box 5, NA; *Seattle Times*, October 17, 1942; Letter, Worth McClure to Board of Directors, Seattle School District No. 1, October 16, 1942, Dietrich Schmitz Papers, Box 11, University of Washington Archives, [hereafter cited as UWA].

39. *Seattle Times*, November 13, 1942, November 22, 1942, February 9, 1943; Letter, Worth McClure to Board of Directors, Seattle School District No. 1, October 30, 1942, Schmitz Papers, Box 11, UWA.

40. *Seattle Times*, November 22, 1942, February 9, 1943.

41. "Composite Report, Detroit," December 22, 1943, OCWS, Community Reports, RG 215, Box 5, NA.

42. "Some Observations on the Federal Program for Care of Children of Employed Mothers," Mary Keeley, December 29, 1943, OCWS, Director's Subject File, RG 215, Box 2, NA.

43. *Seattle Times*, April 6, 1944, April 15, 1944; Letters, Worth McClure to Board of Directors, Seattle School District No. 1, June 25, 1943 and September 17, 1943, Schmitz Papers, Box 11, UWA; City of Seattle, Education Board, "Report of the Public Schools," Year Ending June 30, 1944, pp. 2, 3, 6, and Year Ending June 30, 1945, pp. 51, 52; "Composite Report on Puget Sound Area," May 15, 1944, OCWS, Community Reports, RG 215, Box 17, NA.

44. *Day Care News*, March 1943, OCWS, WARC, RG 215, Box 10, NA; *Baltimore Evening Sun*, July 9, 1943; Letter, H. S. Callowhill to Sherwood Gates, January 13, 1944, OCWS, General Classified, Maryland (Region IV), RG 215, Box 124, NA.

45. Dratch, p. 179; "DSS Field Report," Elizabeth McBroom, July 20, 1944, DSS, RG 75, WSA; "Conclusions Regarding Facilities Needed for 'Day Care' of Children in the Seattle Area," July 22, 1942, DSS, RG 75, WSA.

46. "Field Review of the Children's Division," KCWD, November 1943, DSS, RG 75, WSA; Letter, Bernice Scroggie to Aleta Brownlee, March 12, 1943, OCWS, Children's Care Division, RG 215, Box 9, NA; *Day Care News*, March 1943, OCWS, WARC, RG 215, Box 10, NA.

47. "Composite Report, Detroit," December 22, 1943, OCWS, Community Reports, RG 215, Box 5, NA; "Employee Counseling: A Report," February 25, 1944, WBA, RG 86, Box 1540, NA; *Day Care News*, March 1943, April 1943, OCWS, WARC, RG 215, Box 10, NA.

48. Dratch, p. 179; Kerr, p. 166; Memo, Pearce Davies to Dean Snyder, January 6, 1945, OCWS, Director's Subject File, RG 215, Box 2, NA; Memo, Dean Snyder to Pearce Davies, September 27, 1944, OCWS, Director's Subject File, RG 215, Box 2, NA; "Report of the Conference of the Labor-Union Women with the Children's Bureau on Problems of Youth in the Transition Period," April 18–20, 1945, OCWS, Director's Subject File, RG 215, Box 2, NA.

49. Memo, Katherine Lenroot to James Brunot, April 21, 1943, OCWS, Children's Care Division, RG 215, Box 6, NA; "Field Review of the Children's Division," KCWD, November 1943, DSS, RG 75, WSA; "DSS Field Trip to Seattle," January 26, 1944, DSS, RG 75, WSA.

50. Letter, Mark McCloskey to Judge Samuel Rosenman, November 11, 1943, OCWS, Director's Subject File, RG 215, Box 2, NA; "Field Review of the Children's Division," KCWD, November 1943, DSS, RG 75, WSA; "Employee Counseling: A Report," February 25, 1944, WBA, RG 86, Box 1540, NA.

51. Murphy, pp. 137-38; "Problems of Women War Workers in Detroit," WPB, August 20, 1943, OCWS, WARC, RG 215, Box 10, NA; Zucker, p. 47; *Day Care News*, March 1943, OCWS, WARC, RG 215, Box 10, NA; Memo, E. C. Milliken to McCloskey, August 2, 1944, OCWS, Director's Subject File, RG 215, Box 2, NA; *Detroit News*, September 29, 1943.

52. "Baltimore County Association for Pre-School Education, Field Trip," March 4, 1946, WRC, RG 2010, Box 32, MHS; *Aero Mechanic*, April 19, 1945; City of Detroit, Board of Education, "Report of Survey in All Centers Regarding Nursery and Canteen Service," March 1, 1945, OCWS, WARC, RG 215, Box 10, NA.

53. "Minutes, Fourth Meeting, Regional Family Security Committee," July 14-15, 1943, OCWS, General Classified, Region IV, RG 215, Box 9, NA; "Wartime Child Care Facilities Financed in Part with Lanham Act Funds," OCWS, Director's Subject File, RG 215, Box 2, NA; Letter, James Brunot to E. C. Wine, October 28, 1943, OCWS, Director's Subject File, RG 215, Box 2, NA; Zucker, p. 47; Report, April 17–22, 1944, WRC, RG 2010, Box 32, NA.

54. Murphy, p. 137; "Brief Summary of Conference of Senior Liason Officers," May 3-4, 1943, OCWS, Community Reports, RG 215, Box 4, NA; "Minutes of the Detroit Victory Council Meeting," May 3, 1944, CCPA, RG 212, Box 51, NA; "Employee Counseling: A Report," February 25, 1944, WBA, RG 86, Box 1540, NA.

55. *Seattle Times*, August 13, 1943; Letter, Worth McClure to Board of Directors, Seattle School District No. 1, March 26, 1943, Schmitz Papers, Box 12, UWA; Memo, V. M. Graham to Arthur Langlie, Langlie Papers, RG 11–12, Box 12–19, WSA.

56. Memo, V. M. Graham to Arthur Langlie, August 13, 1943, Langlie Papers, RG 11–12, Box 12–19, WSA; Letters, Worth McClure to Mrs. Robert Jones, September 10, 1943, and Jones to McClure, September 17, 1943, Schmitz Papers, Box 12, UWA.

57. *Seattle Times*, August 13, 1943; Memo, Graham to Langlie, August 13, 1943, Langlie Papers, RG 11–12, Box 12–19, WSA; Letter, Jones to McClure, September 17, 1943, Schmitz Papers, Box 12, UWA; "Minutes of the Washington State Board of Education," June 21, 1943, Papers of the Superintendent of Public Instruction [hereafter cited as SPI], RG 8, Reel #1, Washington State Archives.

58. Clive, pp. 532–33; Dratch, p. 174; "The Michigan Youth Guidance Committee," July 1, 1945–April 1, 1946, OCWS, Director's Files, Social Protec-

tion, RG 215, Box 112, NA; "Education for Victory," September 15, 1943, OCWS, Children's Care Division, RG 215, Box 2, NA; "Employee Counseling: A Report," February 25, 1944, WBA, RG 86, Box 1540, NA; "Labor Market Developments in the Detroit Area," November 5, 1943, BES, RG 183, Box 17, NA.

59. "Labor Market Developments in the Detroit Area," November 5, 1943, BES, RG 183, Box 17, NA; "The Willow Run Area: A Report for the Willow Run Community Council," June, 1943, CCPA, RG 212, Box 48, NA; "Composite Report on Puget Sound Area," May 15, 1944, OCWS, Community Reports, RG 215, Box 17, NA.

60. City of Detroit, Board of Education, "Report of Survey in All Centers Regarding Nursery and Canteen Services," March 1, 1945, OCWS, WARC, RG 215, Box 10, NA; *Washington State CIO News*, November 1942; *Navy Yard Salute*, January 30, 1943, August 25, 1944, February 23, 1945.

61. WBB 209, p. 56.

62. *Day Care News*, April 1943, OCWS, WARC, RG 215, Box 10, NA; "General Comments of Workers, Baltimore, Maryland," WBA, RG 86, Box 1541, NA; *Navy Yard Salute*, August 25, 1944.

63. "General Comments of Workers, Baltimore, Maryland," WBA, RG 86, Box 1541, NA; Clive, p. 536; *Navy Yard Salute*, August 25, 1944.

64. *Navy Yard Salute*, April 15, 1944; "Report of the Conference of Labor-Union Women with the Children's Bureau on Problems of Youth in the Transition Period," April 18-20, 1945, OCWD, Director's Subject File, RG 215, Box 2, NA.

65. Kerr, p. 163; Zucker, p. 47.

5

POSTWAR AND POSTSCRIPT: THE LONG-TERM CONSEQUENCES OF THE WAR

When the long-awaited American victory was suddenly accomplished in August 1945, Americans took to the streets to celebrate the end of the protracted conflict. But for all the relief and happiness occasioned by the ending of the war, the return to peacetime living was fraught with insecurity. The imperatives of wartime had created vast changes in American society, including a return to an economy sufficiently prosperous to create unprecedented economic mobility for millions of Americans. With the dismantling of the war machine came the very real possibility of limited job opportunities and a substantial decline in the standard of living of those same Americans.

The postwar period was to be especially important for women, who had experienced vast changes in their daily lives as a consequence of the war. Because these changes had affected the allocation of functions within the family and the status of women in the labor force, they struck at the roots of the fundamental divisions between the social roles of women and men. By making available to women a variety of jobs at high wages the wartime economy had provided them with an unprecedented degree of choice with regard to their economic roles within the family and the society at large and had thus encouraged greater independence and individual self-expression than traditional sexually defined spheres had allowed. Although limited by the strength of conventional attitudes regarding a woman's appropriate role and behavior, by the tenacity of some discriminatory practices in the face of the wartime labor scarcity, and by the special burdens imposed on working women whose household responsibilities were not significantly lightened by either the family or the community during the war years, the amount of change accomplished in the economic realm in a short period of time was substantial.

Whether the gains of the war period would be reversed or maintained in the long run would depend to a great extent on the special circumstances of the early postwar years. The fundamental determinant would be the general condition of the economy. If jobs proved scarce after the war, women would find their economic choices severely limited. Even if the postwar period generally offered expanded job opportunities, the structure of the economy could make it difficult for women to find work outside of the traditionally low-paying "female" job categories. The most important advances of the war years had come as a result of a growth in jobs traditionally defined as "male" that was sufficiently great to accommodate large numbers of women for the first time, giving women an alternative to poorly paid jobs and thus causing a general increase in the prevailing wage level for women.

Although the state of the postwar economy would be important in determining the long-term social consequences of the war for women, other factors would also have considerable impact. With the return of servicemen from overseas many women would have the chance to plan war-deferred marriages and childbearing. Whether women would find these increased domestic responsibilities incompatible with continued employment would depend on articulated community attitudes toward working wives and mothers and the availability of social services for working women, especially low-cost child care facilities. Women's personal reactions to their wartime work experience would be especially significant in shaping the postwar decisions of women. They would be weighing the personal rewards of doing a job well, the social contacts made possible by working, and the financial independence available to working women against the difficulties caused by the long hours at often physically demanding work, the inconveniences imposed by wartime conditions, and the problems involved in shouldering the double burden of housework and paid employment. If most of them decided that the benefits overshadowed the liabilities, then the entrance of women into the work force, including those with families, would continue in the postwar period.

Although the economic expansion experienced by defense centers during the war had been spectacular, the outlook for the postwar period depended on the size and nature of the wartime growth. All war boom communities had common problems, however. The economic growth of the war years had distorted local economies by greatly expanding the manufacturing sector, increased their dependence on federal spending while increasing federal authority over economic development, and stimulated population growth, especially in the age groups most likely to be in the labor force. In addition, the labor shortage of the war years had accustomed workers to job security, high wages, and considerable choice regarding their work. With the cancellation of war contracts and the beginnings of military demobilization came the prospect of high unemployment, declining wages, and labor unrest. Moreover, the abandonment of price controls at the end of the war raised the specter of spiraling inflation fueled by pent-up consumer demand. The growing reluctance of the federal government to subsidize or regulate economic expansion in the postwar period meant that the problems and possibilities of reconversion became primarily the responsibility of local business and political leaders.[1]

The gloomy economic picture was mitigated, however, by some more propitious circumstances. The backlog of demand for consumer goods and services and the accumulation of liquid assets in the form of bank accounts and government bonds would ease the transition to a peacetime economy. This demand would create jobs in the heretofore labor-starved service sector of the economy. Moreover, the construction and other related industries would benefit from the resumption of the housing construction and public projects deferred during the war years. Even the categories facing the greatest curtailments, including the aircraft and shipbuilding industries, would probably resume peacetime activities at levels considerably above those of the prewar years, primarily because postwar defense spending would be much greater than ever before and the shipyards would be kept busy with repair work for quite some time.[2]

The difficulty of predicting accurately the probable size of the labor force in the postwar period further clouded the economic picture. Wartime opportunities had drawn many people into the labor force, including large numbers of women, older persons, and teenagers, and had prompted many workers to migrate to defense areas. Although some surveys were taken to determine how many new workers planned to stay in defense communities and remain in the work force, their conclusions varied greatly, making precise estimates impossible. In addition, many individual decisions with regard to residential and job permanency would depend as much on the character of the postwar economic structure and the opportunities it would provide as on individual preferences.[3]

In order to facilitate the transition to a peacetime economy, several local and state agencies and organizations established postwar planning committees. The Michigan Council of Defense established its advisory committee as early as June 1941. The Washington State Planning Commission also created a Post Victory Employment Committee, which set up local committees in each county to aid in its work. These and other such groups generally spent their time conducting surveys of various industries to determine their probable employment needs for the postwar period. When it came to establishing programs to increase the size of the postwar labor market, they were generally at a loss for ideas and relied heavily on deferred civic projects to provide economic stimulus. Such projects, however, would be of substantial benefit only to the construction industry and would offer little help for unemployed women workers. This oversight was not surprising, given that women were not usually named to postwar planning groups.[4]

Among the areas under study, Seattle and Detroit faced the greatest challenges in reconverting to civilian production. As early as May 1945, Detroit was experiencing production cutbacks heavier than in any other city. By that time the area labor force had declined from a wartime high of 1,302,000 to 1,078,000. Despite its early curtailment of defense production, the Detroit area faced special difficulties because of the failure of the civilian sector, especially the auto industry, to resume production so that it could provide alternative employment. The War Production Board waited until May 25, 1945, to give the automakers permission to begin making cars on a limited basis. Although the relaxation of federal restraints enabled the industry to begin retooling for civilian production, scarcities of the necessary materials hampered the reconversion process.[5]

Once the war had ended, the government canceled $1.5 billion in Detroit-area contracts, and the auto companies and other war industries released thousands of workers. Within a short period of time, Michigan led the nation in unemployment with almost 200,000 out of work in the Detroit area alone. Moreover, the area economy had 230,000 residents in the military, most of whom would have to be reintegrated into the work force in the next year. By the end of August, however, the auto companies had already begun recalling workers and officials were fore-casting a short reconversion period. Their sanguine outlook was predi-cated on the maintenance of smooth labor relations and an increasing availability of supplies, conditions which were undermined by strikes in the steel, rubber, and glass industries and, especially, by the lengthy strike at General Motors, which began in November 1945. As a result of the strikes and shortages, economic expansion was retarded and Michigan's unemployment rate was still at 12.7 percent by March 1946. Thereafter, however, the pace of recovery accelerated, and by summer the automakers were once again hiring in large numbers.[6]

In contrast to Detroit and other Eastern cities, where the wartime mobilization had involved the conversion of many industries from the production of civilian goods to war materials, Seattle and other Western defense centers had responded to wartime demands by greatly expanding already existing enterprises, notably the aircraft and shipbuilding industries. As a result, the East could convert back to the production of civilian goods and still maintain production levels considerably above prewar levels, whereas the Puget Sound area and other Western war production centers would face much greater difficulties in sustaining the wartime level of economic activity and employment in an essentially civilian economy.[7]

Although the Seattle area did begin its reconversion to peacetime pursuits before the actual ending of hostilities with personnel cutbacks at Fort Lewis and in the shipyards, where layoffs began in early 1945, it was not until V-J Day that the area felt the full impact of the decline in federal spending. At the Puget Sound Navy Yard the number of civilian employees was cut from 33,000 to 20,874 in less than two months, despite the efforts of Congressman Hugh DeLacy to persuade the navy to delay its cutbacks because federal employees were not eligible for unemployment compensation. The private shipyards also faced contract cancellations and large reductions in their work forces after the war ended.[8]

The most drastic effects, however, were experienced by Boeing, which had maintained its high employment levels until V-J Day. Even then company officials remained naively optimistic that production levels and employment could be reduced gradually so that voluntary withdrawals and attrition would account for most of the cutbacks. That prediction remained true for a short while as the number of "quits" significantly exceeded the number of layoffs, the latter limited to those who had been employed by the company for less than ninety days. But on September 5, 1945, the federal government notified the company that its contracts were being canceled, leaving company and union officials, workers, and the community stunned and unprepared. As a result, the eight Boeing branch plants in western Washington were immediately closed, and the Seattle and Renton plants cut their personnel from 29,000 to 21,000. In response the Aeromechanics' Union advised all its members with less than four years' seniority to seek other employment.[9]

Although the unemployment level in the area continued to climb until April 1946, other economic indicators showed little postwar decline. A postwar boom in retail sales, fueled by the resumption of spending for civilian goods and services, created jobs in the service and sales sector. The Puget Sound-area composite index of business activity had almost reattained its August 1945 level by January 1946, declining only moderately in the interim. Employment began to catch up with the general economic upswing in the spring of 1946, aided by the settlement of a strike in the lumber industry and the availability of seasonal jobs in agriculture, construction, and fishing. By July 1947, unemployment had decreased to 4.9 percent of the civilian labor force in King County and 7.1 percent in Pierce County, and the Puget Sound-area composite index had climbed close to its wartime peak. Thus, although unemployment levels remained somewhat high, the transition to a prosperous peacetime economy had been accomplished by mid-1947 without the prolonged and deep recession feared by some observers.[10]

As in Seattle, the transition to a peacetime economy began abruptly in Baltimore. Although some of its smaller industries had been forced to cut back as early as 1944, the major industries were unaffected until the summer of 1945. Within one month of V-J Day, nearly two-thirds of its aircraft workers and one-third of its shipbuilding employees had lost their jobs. Baltimore's diversified manufacturing structure, however, tended to cushion the blow of reconversion. Although aircraft and shipbuilding constituted the largest sources of industrial employment during the war, they did not dominate in the Baltimore economy to the extent that they did in other defense centers. The strength of the electrical and other machine industries, iron and steel, food processing, and textiles provided Baltimore with a strong basis for peacetime factory work.[11]

Outside of aircraft and shipbuilding, many major industries in Baltimore experienced little or no decline after the end of the war. Establishments in the iron and steel category, for example, maintained their wartime employment levels and began hiring more workers by November 1945. The machine industries, which had experienced substantial growth as a result of war contracts, also had good postwar prospects as the predicted market for radios, televisions, and other such products was substantial. Thus, although they faced some reductions in their levels of employment after the war, their postwar labor forces were still more than double that of the prewar period.[12]

Hampered by the strikes at General Motors and in the steel industry and by shortages of important materials, reconversion in Baltimore came more slowly than some had anticipated. Yet by the summer of 1946 the unemployment rate had begun to decline, reaching 6 percent of the labor force by the following October. Buoyed by its postwar commercial and military contracts, Glenn Martin Aircraft, which had cut its labor force to 10,000 by March 1946, had expanded to over 17,000 workers by July and was anticipating further growth. Other employers in all sectors of the economy were experiencing a similar recovery.[13]

In the long run the war did not significantly alter the economic structure of the areas under study. Although employment in the manufacturing sector in the Seattle Metropolitan District grew by 53 percent between 1940 and 1947, the trade and service areas experienced comparable growth, leaving their relative positions the same. As a result, the predominance of white-collar work in the area economy persisted after the postwar readjustment shifted workers from the war-exaggerated manufacturing sector to the traditionally more important commerical and service activities. In Baltimore, where the industrial distribution was also similar to that of 1940, the proportion of workers engaged in clerical and manufacturing work increased slightly, while domestic service declined somewhat. With the recovery of the auto industry by late 1946, the Detroit economy also reverted to its prewar pattern of domination by the manufacturing sector, although the proportion of workers employed in clerical and sales increased slightly.[14]

The changing labor market demands of the postwar period, the nature of the reconversion process, the preferential treatment accorded veterans, and the reimposition of discriminatory policies on the part of employers, unions, and government agencies all contributed to the problems of women workers in the postwar period. Because much of the wartime labor force expansion had occurred before women were hired for production work in large numbers and because women suffered disproportionately from job discontinuity, many of them lacked the requisite seniority to retain their jobs at a time of drastic cutbacks. To make matters worse, the heaviest layoffs occurred in those industries in which large numbers of women were employed, especially aircraft and munitions. Moreover, the subtle discrimination against women practiced by unions and management during the war years had prevented even those women with greater job experience from advancing into the more skilled positions that would provide them with greater job security. Once they were fired, women workers faced overt discrimination as employers and unions alike ignored the seniority and skills they had developed during the war so that young white males could recover their privileged position in industrial work.[15]

The position of women in the postwar economy was further undermined by the widespread conviction that working women would quietly and willingly withdraw from the labor force to make way for male job seekers. As Irene Murphy, secretary of the Detroit Day Care Committee, noted, Americans continued to "cling to the fantasy that women can always be dispossessed of their jobs—that they don't need to work." For many Americans the analogy of Cincinnatus applied as well to the homemaker turned factory worker as to the soldier, as each was expected to return voluntarily to their accustomed activities. Claiming that "women will always be women," Betty Allie, Michigan state workman's compensation chairwoman, predicted in 1943 that working women would return to their homes after the war since that was their first interest. Similarly, the *Detroit News* concluded that "for many [women], no doubt, nature will provide the answer when peace comes." A *Seattle Times* survey in 1944 concluded that most women workers thought a woman's place was in the home and would willingly give up their jobs. Nora DeWitt, an employee of the American Can Company, said, "I think most of the girls plan to stay home and raise families, at least that's what they are saying—and that's about all they talk about. Most of them will be happy to hand their jobs over to their husbands."[16]

Officials at both the Martin Aircraft Company and Boeing remained convinced that employment problems in the postwar period would be largely averted by the voluntary withdrawal of women from the labor market. Despite a poll by the UAW, which showed that 98 percent of the women at the Martin plant wanted to keep their factory jobs after the war, Martin officials continued to rely on a mass exodus of women to render Glenn Martin's promise of equal treatment for women in the postwar world an unimportant issue. When he called for voluntary resignations in August 1945, he was surprised at the low response he got. Speaking for Boeing, Ida DuMars, the general supervisor of women at the Renton plant, claimed that the women employed there were not sorry to lose their jobs. She contended, "They will go back to their homes, and to their beauty parlors and banks and they love the idea. They've done a grand job and learned a lot, but they are glad it is over," adding, "Those who intend to keep on working know their wages will be smaller, but they expect it and don't mind."[17]

In fact, however, the women who had taken war jobs in the years since Pearl Harbor were not of one mind regarding their postwar plans. Some had entered the work force for patriotic reasons and had always planned to quit once the war ended. Genevieve Trofanowski, a Detroit worker discharged from her war job, commented, "I think a woman's place is in the home—except when there's a war on." Others decided to leave the work force because their husbands believed that wives should not work. Mrs. Frank Neff, a wartime employee of the Naval Advance Depot in Tacoma, commented, "My husband wants a wife, not a career woman." For Ruth Rand, a Boeing employee, the end of the war meant an opportunity to give more attention to her children. Some others chose to forgo war jobs because they found the work too demanding. Louise Kanouse, a Tacoma bus driver, claimed, "It is too hard a job for a woman to stick with over a long period of time." In addition, some women workers who had migrated to defense centers to take advantage of wartime work opportunities would be returning to their homes.[18]

Large numbers of women, however, were not so eager to return to domestic responsibilities or prewar conditions. Speaking for herself and three other women employed at Boeing, Anna Juris of Auburn stated, "We aren't quitting until they put us out. We will work as long as they need us, and when we're through we will go back to our meals and dishes and children." Vi Moses, a parts saleswoman for a Ford distributing company in Tacoma, enthusiastically expressed her preference, asserting, "I want to hold onto my job as long as I possibly can." Peggy Wolf, a chauffeur at the Navy Yard, noted that many of the women with whom she worked faced postwar cutbacks with regret, observing, "Many women in here are plenty unhappy, though. The taste of independence has spoiled 'em." They were not alone—a cafeteria worker at Martin Aircraft reported that many of the women there came into the cafeteria and cried after receiving their discharges.[19]

Many women, including most who were not married, had no choice as to whether they would remain in the work force. Jean Andresinr, a former shipbuilder for Bethlehem-Fairfields in Baltimore, spoke for many in her position when she commented, "It really makes it tough on us single girls. What are we supposed to do? I need a job badly. I'm on my own." According to a Women's Bureau survey, 22 percent of the women employed in the Seattle-Tacoma area who lived in family groups and who planned to continue working were the sole support of themselves or their families; the figures for Baltimore and Detroit were 13 and 11 percent, respectively. For these women the postwar choices involved, at best, which job to take and, at worst, whether to accept a low-paying job and see much of their earnings going for child care and other expenses or to go on welfare and stay at home with their children. That some women either could not find jobs or preferred the latter option was reflected in the steadily increasing number of women receiving assistance in the Aid to Dependent Children program.[20]

Many other women, including many whose contributions to family incomes had become quite important during the war years, also desired to remain in the labor force. In the ten defense centers surveyed by the Women's Bureau, an average of 75 percent of the women employed in 1944–45 planned to continue working. Seattle and Wichita, with only 61 percent of the female wartime workers expressing their intention to continue working, had the lowest proportion wanting postwar work. By contrast, 78 percent of the women workers surveyed in Detroit and 81 percent in Baltimore planned to work after the war. Seattle's lower figures cannot be explained with reference to any particular subgroup within the female labor force; single and married women, older women and younger women were all less likely to stay in the labor force than in the other major war production areas. Although it is difficult to explain precisely why Seattle diverged from the national pattern in the expressed aspirations of women workers, the numerical importance of white-collar workers in the area economy and the high level of per capita income in the community fostered a rather conventional middle-class consensus regarding women's roles and provided the income structure to sustain it. Moreover, the large numbers of servicemen in the area promoted a very high marriage rate during and after the war, promoting a focus on family goals rather than on labor force participation on the part on many women. If work decisions were at least partly a response to the level of opportunity, so were those involving marriage and family.[21]

Of those women who hoped to continue working, the majority also wanted to remain in the same occupational group, especially those employed in manufacturing or by the government, areas which had been disproportionately expanded by wartime needs and which were particularly vulnerable to postwar cutbacks. In Baltimore, 86 percent of those women employed in manufacturing who planned to remain in the labor force hoped to continue in the same kind of work; the figures for Detroit and Seattle were 85 and 77 percent, respectively. The vulnerability of women working in the manufacturing sector was underscored by a 1944 survey of 208 manufacturing employers in Washington which indicated that they expected women to account for a disproportionate amount of their postwar cutbacks, retaining only 3,244 of the 28,493 jobs they held in July 1944.[22]

Whatever the wishes or plans of the women workers, they bore the brunt of the reconversion cutbacks, which began much earlier for them than for male workers. Even in the mid-war period, women represented 40 to 50 percent of those laid off by war industries, even though they were only 35 percent of the employees in the affected plants. From June through August 1945, women in manufacturing were discharged at a rate of 72 per 1,000 workers, while men were fired at a rate of 42 per 1,000. In the summer of 1945, three-fourths of the women employed in aircraft and shipbuilding lost their jobs. Not surprisingly, women were overrepresented among the unemployed at this time. In July 1945, women accounted for 49 percent of Americans seeking work. Their share declined to 40 percent by October 1945, and 19 percent by March 1946, reflecting the fact that the layoffs included increasing proportions of men as time passed and that more veterans were returning to the civilian labor force.[23]

This pattern was mirrored in the major defense centers. In Detroit, where significant numbers of women were unemployed as early as January 1944, women experienced particular difficulties in retaining their jobs or finding new ones in the months before V-J Day. A survey of 20,000 unemployed Detroit women taken in early 1945 revealed that 72 percent of them had no jobs weeks after their layoffs even though they wanted to work. In the first two weeks after the war ended, women contributed 57 percent of the initial claims for unemployment compensation in Detroit. As elsewhere, employment officials reported special difficulties in placing these women in jobs commensurate with their skills and preferences.[24]

In the Motor City automakers' policies would largely determine the labor force status of women in the postwar period. Never enthusiastic about the wartime necessity to hire women, they led the effort there to return women to prewar employment patterns. Even before the war ended, they had released large numbers of women employees. After V-J Day, the auto industry accelerated its layoffs and transferred some women production workers to other types of work. Wartime seniority agreements between the UAW and the automakers guaranteed that those few women in production work before the war who had sufficient seniority to be retained after the war would return to their prewar jobs rather than continuing in their wartime assignments. Once the auto industries began their postwar callbacks, they ignored the skills and seniority of the women workers, reasserting their preference for young white male workers. As a result, women workers, who had claimed one-fourth of the production jobs in the auto plants of Detroit during the war, held only 7.5 percent of such positions in April 1946.[25]

Having been told by the UAW during the war that they could rely on the union to safeguard the interests of all workers, women members soon found out how meaningful union protection was when the victims of management discrimination were female. When the automakers ignored the seniority provisions of their contracts with the UAW in order to limit women's access to industry jobs, the union ignored the situation, filing no grievance actions. After their union proved of little help in fighting postwar discrimination, the dispossessed women autoworkers took action on their own, setting up picket lines outside of the Ford Highland Park plant in November 1945. Bearing placards reading "Stop Discrimination Because of Sex" and warning male workers that their seniority could also be threatened, women members of UAW Locals 400, 50, and 600 claimed that 2,200 men without seniority had been hired at the plant while 5,000 experienced women remained idle. Officials at Ford justified their refusal to hire women for the plant, where they had cut the female work force from a wartime peak of 5,849 to 300, on the grounds that the work had become too heavy for women when the factory shifted to the production of tractors. The company denied a charge by the women that the job classification system had been manipulated so that entry-level jobs involved heavy work and served to exclude women. In response to the women's action, John C. Carney, president of Local 400, promised to put the matter before the union's executive board. In fact, however, UAW officials, who were engaged in contract negotiations with General Motors, preferred to concentrate only on the rights of male workers and privately reassured Ford management that it need not worry about the women's protest. Abandoned by their union, the women failed to challenge successfully the discriminatory practices that excluded them from the vast majority of jobs in the industry that dominated their local economy.[26]

In Baltimore, many women working in war industries experienced a similar fate. Because the cutbacks in Baltimore were limited primarily to aircraft and shipbuilding, where the layoffs included a large proportion of women, women constituted one-third to one-half of the area's unemployed in the postwar period. The shipbuilding industry, which had hired only limited numbers of women workers during the war, fired them almost immediately after V-J Day. At Martin Aircraft, the area's largest wartime employer of women, the percentage of jobs held by men increased from 63 percent to 82 percent in the early postwar period. In the machine industries, where women had made considerable gains during the war years, women retained a share of the work significantly above prewar levels despite the fact that they accounted for two-thirds of the postwar separations. Even in machine industries, however, several employers justified discriminating against women on the grounds that the nature of their work had changed after the war so that it had become too heavy or skilled for women to handle. As a result of the lack of postwar opportunity, Baltimore women had great difficulty finding acceptable work.[27]

A special postwar survey done by the Women's Bureau in 1946 of 300 Baltimore women who had held jobs in war industries provides a detailed picture of the fate of "Rosie the Riveter" in that community. Of the women included in the study, only 11 percent had withdrawn voluntarily from the labor force by the end of the war. An additional 7 percent had surveyed the postwar job situation for a while and then decided to return to domestic responsibilities. Of the 300 women, sixty-three kept their war jobs, and an additional twenty-seven were recalled at a later date; the rest shifted to other jobs or remained unemployed. According to the study, the women riveters and welders who had symbolized the female work experience during the war had the greatest difficulty retaining their jobs. Although 40 percent preferred to stay in their wartime jobs, only two of the forty-two who had held such jobs managed to keep them after the war. By contrast, women engaged in machine industries, assembly work, or testing and inspection had greater success in continuing their wartime employment.

As the Baltimore study shows, some of the shifts to traditional women's jobs in the postwar period were voluntary; many women found their war jobs too strenuous, tedious, and exhausting or objected to the long hours or poor working conditions, claiming that the workplace was too hot, dirty, or noisy. Many middle-class women preferred jobs that were white-collar, and others expressed a desire for more "womanly" work, indicating once again that the wartime experience could create anxieties among women workers about their femininity. A woman who had been a timekeeper in a factory during the war expressed pleasure at her postwar sales job, noting that it was "much higher class" than her war work and "clean, nice, and refined." In addition, she commented that the pace was more leisurely whereas during the war employees were "hounded and driven." Some women who returned to work as waitresses after the war commented that they found that work more clean, more relaxed, and more varied than their war work. Not all agreed, however; a former machinist commented that "a waitress' brains are in her feet."[28]

In the Puget Sound area, management discrimination aided by union acquiescence also served to deprive women workers of their postwar employment rights. Because they had received only a temporary certification from their union during the war, most women employed in the shipyards lost their jobs within two weeks of V-J Day. In a patronizing editorial in the *104 Reporter*, A. F. O'Neill, business agent for Local 104 of the Boilermakers, explained the need for "benching" the women as follows:

Our hats are off to the women. Yours is a job all well done. We have never heard you complain, after going home from your eight-hour shift in the shipyards, about doing your household work and raising your family. You have made mere man ashamed of himself when it came to sacrifices. Your record for loyalty to your employers, your job and your Union can never be questioned. Your production record as a war worker will never be forgotten.

Now we are faced with cutbacks in shipbuilding, and you are being taken off the production team. You are being benched. Competition for playing positions on the team is great. We know some of you don't like it, but the majority feel theirs is a rest well earned. They feel they have fulfilled their part in winning the war. You have more than done your part. Let the lowly male species do the work (they don't know any better), and you see that he provides the American standard of living to which you are entitled.

We are proud to have had you as members of our Union. You are tops in any language, and we hate to see you go.[29]

Of the major wartime employers only Boeing retained any of its women production workers, and even there the numbers involved were negligible until 1951, when war contracts once again created substantial numbers of jobs in the aircraft industry. In the late 1940s Boeing would not consider hiring a woman unless she had previous Boeing or other aircraft industrial experience, and even then she was much less likely to be hired than a man. According to a study examining applicants rejected by Boeing's personnel office in late 1948, 20 percent of the women denied employment had previous Boeing employment while only 3.8 percent of the men were similarly experienced.[30]

As elsewhere, women contributed more than their share to the growing ranks of the unemployed in the postwar period. In September 1945, women filed 41.1 percent of the initial claims for unemployment compensation. By January 1946, the problem of placing women workers in new jobs had become so acute that A. F. Hardy, manager of the Washington State Employment Service, reported that the provision of work for women permanently in the labor force had become a serious problem. A few months later, employment officials revealed that out-of-work women represented a majority of those drawing unemployment compensation within the state and a majority of those who had already exhausted their benefits.[31]

For many of the women who had lost their war jobs, the issue of access to unemployment benefits posed special difficulties. In order to qualify for unemployment compensation according to the regulations of the U.S. Employment Service, a person had to have been involuntarily terminated from his or her job and available for and actively seeking "suitable" work. Although established procedures usually classified job seekers into occupational categories according to their last previous employment, they also involved the use of sex-segregated job classifications which divided manufacturing, clerical, sales, and other fields into "male" and "female" subdivisions. When women came in seeking jobs as welders, riveters, and in other industrial occupations, the USES was at a loss as to how to handle them. Because of the cutbacks and discriminatory employment policies, there were few industrial jobs available for women. Yet job seekers had up to that time been allowed to refuse employment outside of their classifications and still receive their unemployment compensation benefits. When women refused job referrals on this basis, however, they frequently had their unemployment compensation terminated on the grounds that they were so limiting their employability as to be in fact unavailable for work and consequently not eligible under the law.[32]

Although detailed information as to the number of women who were denied compensation for this reason is not available, it is clear that this practice contributed significantly to the return of women workers to traditional "women's" jobs at lower pay levels. In May 1946, when local canneries needed seasonal workers, Seattle employment officials disqualified over 1,000 women job seekers from benefits because they refused cannery or other "suitable" work. According to the Women's Bureau study of Baltimore women workers in the postwar period, 18 percent of the women who had unemployment compensation payments suspended lost their benefits because they had rejected jobs offered them. Statistics for the State of Washington for the month of November 1945 show that more women were disqualified for benefits than men, although there were fewer women applying for compensation.[33]

Although many women must have accepted whatever work was immediately available because they feared losing their benefits, they did so reluctantly. According to a USES survey of 535 women laid off in

Detroit in early 1945, 275 would only accept work in a war industry, while 197 preferred such work but would take anything with a suitable salary. Given the nature of the work available to women once reconversion began and its low pay level, the determination of many working women to retain their wartime gains was understandable. In Seattle, for example, the women who refused cannery work at $.71 an hour included a forty-three-year-old former shipyard worker, whose wartime earnings had been $1.20 an hour. Of the former Baltimore war workers surveyed by the Women's Bureau, those who still retained their war jobs in 1946 earned $44 a week, while those working for other employers averaged only $31 a week. Thus, it is not surprising that women job seekers in Baltimore were more likely to refuse referrals than men.[34]

As they did during the war, USES officials generally acquiesced in discriminatory job requests from area employers, thus cooperating in the reimposition of the sex-segregated labor force of the prewar period. As the records of the Detroit employment office indicate, they were willing to do so despite the expressed wishes of both male and female job seekers. In the summer of 1946, Detroit officials found themselves confronted with an unexpected problem—the number of men, mostly veterans, who expressed interest in white-collar jobs in either clerical or service work was increasing dramatically. Many of the returning veterans, large numbers of whom had done clerical work in the military, stated that they preferred such work to factory jobs, which they contended were too monotonous or confining. At the same time, women workers continued to hope that they could utilize the skills they had developed in war industries. As a result, the Detroit applications for clerical and service work in July 1946 included 2,770 women and 3,572 veterans, while the applicants for semiskilled and unskilled work included 8,137 women and 4,531 veterans. Moreover, the veterans proved as obdurate as the women regarding their occupational preferences; 35 percent of them refused jobs offered them.[35]

In order to fit the job seekers to employer specifications, the Detroit USES denied benefits to women who refused the clerical and service jobs requested by the veterans and sent letters to the men who had indicated a white-collar preference, contending that opportunities in the field were limited and that pay levels were inappropriately low for men. They also prepared a second job preference card for such men indicating their availability for more traditional "men's" work. The men, however, did not lose their benefits for pursuing work deemed unsuitable. In the meantime, employment officials alerted manufacturing employers, including the automakers, to the availability of women for the jobs being spurned by many men, but to no avail. In order that traditional sex divisions could be maintained within the labor force, official employment policies encouraged the development of a situation where high unemployment was allowed to coexist with high labor demand.[36]

Although the vast majority of women victimized by the USES accepted their discriminatory treatment, Seattle USES records include the appeals of four women who had been employed at Todd Pacific Shipyards until early 1946, when the ending of ship repair work dictated large cutbacks. All four women refused to accept employment involving pay levels substantially lower than they had been accustomed to and were consequently denied benefits. Wilhelmina Isaacson, for example, had been making a base wage of $1.20 an hour and refused a referral to the Seattle Army Service Forces Depot at $.92 an hour, saying she would not work for less than $1.05 an hour. When the Seattle office called Welders Local 541 to inquire as to her employment prospects as a welder, a union official told them she was a member in good standing but that all job requests being received by the union at that time were for men and that 200 men in the union were unemployed at the time. On that basis the Seattle office disqualified her. When the appeal investigation was held, however, the union, which supposedly had a nondiscriminatory employment policy, stated that Isaacson was in as good a position to get a job as anyone else among the union's unemployed. The Washington State Office of Unemployment Compensation and Placement thus determined that she was available for work and justified in refusing referrals, reversing the local office's action. In the case of Minna Hinkle, which closely paralleled that of Isaacson, a similar decision was reached. By the time these precedents were established, however, it was June 1946, and the issue had long been settled for most women workers.[37]

The scarcity of jobs for women after the war created special difficulties for older women and black women as employers reestablished prewar employment barriers. In factory work, where their gains even in a time of labor shortage had been constrained by employer reluctance to hire them, older women were virtually eliminated from many industries. In Baltimore an electrical equipment plant told Women's Bureau representatives that it refused to hire women over thirty-five on the grounds that test results indicated that "their muscles stiffen" after that age. Other industrial employers stated that "older women can't stand the pace" or, significantly, "the younger ones don't generally have previous standards and therefore are not so critical or likely to complain." In the clerical sector, which was chronically short of workers after the war, older women suffered from employer preferences for young, attractive women for office positions. In an anonymous letter to the editor in the *Seattle Times*, one woman who had suffered from such age discrimination in office work contended that she could "outshine any young sweet thing when it comes to work and keeping a boss's feathers unruffled."[38]

As the victims of both race and sex discrimination, black women found the postwar employment situation especially difficult. When the wartime labor shortage was ended and the legal protection provided by wartime manpower policies was abandoned, barriers against black job seekers were reimposed. Despite the persistence of discrimination, black women were able to retain their foothold in their wartime jobs to a surprising extent, largely because their gains in the wartime economy had been confined largely to an increase in service jobs and some less desirable jobs in the manufacturing category. Most importantly, their exodus from agricultural work and domestic service, the categories which had claimed the vast majority of black women workers before the war, actually continued in the postwar period. The urban migration of blacks, which had been interrupted by the Depression, resumed and accelerated during and after the war. As a result, the proportion of all employed black women in farm occupations declined from 20.9 percent in 1940 to 7.2 percent in 1947. Although domestic service remained their largest occupational group, it declined in importance as a source of work within the urban economy, claiming less than one-half of the black women wage earners by 1947. Their gains in service work outside of the personal household accounted for much of the change, although they also managed to retain a surprising proportion of their industrial work once the war was over. Despite these advances, discrimination against black women continued to limit their mobility and contributed to unemployment rates which persisted at levels higher than those for other workers.[39]

In the postwar period, the rapid and consistent resort to white male workers, which was abridged only in times of serious labor shortage, raises the question of whether the war actually undermined employer prejudices to any appreciable extent. After the war, employers once again claimed that their work was too physically demanding, too skilled, or too responsible for women workers to handle. No longer forced to cajole reluctant women into the labor force with empty rhetoric, they criticized women's record of performance during the war, claiming that women's work attitude was bad, that they were guilty of excessive absenteeism, and that the presence of women distracted male workers and lowered their productivity. Such generalizations justified their discriminatory polilcies and relieved them of the obligation to treat women workers as individuals. Despite a serious problem with turnover among veterans hired in many postwar industries, employers continued to act on the assumption that male workers were more competent, reliable, and in need of work than women employees.[40]

Despite the temporary gains of the war years, women's status within the labor force was not much better than it had been before the war. Although improvements were made in some areas, women remained a cheap labor force to be kept in reserve in anticipation of future needs and to be otherwise discriminated against in hiring, pay, and promotion. The economic advances experienced by women during the war had been predicated on a rate of economic growth high enough to accommodate millions of new women workers and provide them with opportunities in traditionally male fields in industry and the professions. Given the return to the prewar economic structure, the retention of those wartime gains became dependent on the articulation of new values regarding the status of women in American society. In the absence of a new commitment to change, the postwar shift of women from high-paying industrial work to low-skill, low-paying, dead-end jobs in traditional "women's" categories became inevitable.

In all three cities under study, the increase in the female labor force between 1940 and 1947, which mirrored national trends, was predicated on the expansion of jobs in clerical and sales work. In Baltimore, where the large number of jobs in woman-employing industries and in clerical work provided an economic structure hospitable to women workers, the work rates for women exceeded national averages both before and after the war, although the rate of increase was comparable. Despite the fact that women's share of industrial jobs in Detroit increased as a result of the war, increases in nonmanufacturing work accounted for most of the growth in female employment there in the postwar period. Because of the failure of the manufacturing sector there to generate as much opportunity for women after the war as it did for men, the expansion of the female labor force was constrained, and participation levels for women remained low. In Seattle, the proportion of women workers engaged in clerical and sales work increased from 40 to 47 percent in the 1940s.[41]

Because it greatly accelerated the tendency of women to seek paid employment, especially including those with family responsibilities, World War II was a profoundly important event in American social history. The influx of large numbers of married women into the labor force marked an important turning point for women, involving as it did the implicit rejection of the idea that a woman's household responsibilities could not be reconciled with outside employment. By removing some prescriptive barriers against married women working, the wartime experience began the process of accommodation between family and work and pointed the way to a greater degree of choice for American women. As the quality of family life came to be defined to some extent in terms of financial security and material circumstances in the post-Depression decades, women's work and family responsibilities became compatible rather than antagonistic. The materialism of the years after 1945 was probably an even more significant cultural value than the veneration of domesticity; the good life was expensive and women had to contribute their share. Once begun, the process of qualifying hitherto unequivocal social norms and expectations regarding the appropriate roles of women continued unabated in the postwar era.[42]

Nevertheless, it is important to note just how much the change begun in the war years was thwarted in the postwar period. Because the war had promoted changes in the circumstances and experiences of both men and women, demobilization was thought to involve social as well as economic readjustments. As Susan Hartmann has pointed out, the postwar period produced a considerable body of literature concerned with returning military men to civilian life and working women to domestic responsibilities. For many of the servicemen's wives to whom the literature was addressed, the essential challenge was to reconcile the autonomy and competence they had demonstrated while on their own with the needs and wishes of their returning husbands. In order to promote domestic harmony, they were told to subordinate their interests and needs to those of their husbands. Wives who had emerged from their wartime experiences with increased self-confidence and self-reliance were urged to deny those capacities if such duplicity and self-abnegation was necessary to restore diminished male egos. With their stress on manipulative femininity and the importance of purchasing marital harmony at the cost of a woman's individuality, the postwar themes resembled closely those of the nineteenth-century cult of domesticity.[43]

In some ways, however, the literature of the postwar period represented a more frank avowal of the nature and reasons for women's subordination—essentially acknowledging that it served men only—than past and future such works. There was a frequent recognition that work had often met women's needs, including those for sociability, a sense of self-worth, pride in work, independence, and relief from household monotony. A War Department manual for servicemen, for example, expressed the opinion that traditional definitions of women's place had been too constricting, as women's interests and abilities varied. It also noted that motherhood was not a lifelong vocation and that not all women were equally fond of children. Thus, some writers acknowledged a conflict between women's aspirations and inner needs and their family duties; they also recognized a broader definition of feminine personality while advocating its repression.[44]

On the other hand, the attention given male accomplishments and contributions by postwar writers and the conviction that such sacrifices necessitated compensatory concessions from civilians justified the encouragement and subsidizing of male mobility in the postwar period. Under the GI Bill, passed in 1944, over 2 million veterans (97 percent of them men) received financial assistance in meeting educational expenses. Because the benefits under the law were frequently insufficient for family support, the importance of a working wife was increased for the veteran students, many of whom were married. The lessened insistence on the necessity for a man to be able to support a family before assuming family responsibilities contributed to the increasing work rate of married women, the trends toward younger marriages and a higher marriage rate, and the increasing expectation that a woman's education and work decisions should underwrite male mobility regardless of her own aspirations or needs. The effect of such changing expectations on young women was indicated by the declining importance of women on college campuses after the war. In Seattle, for example, the proportion of women aged eighteen to twenty-four who were in school declined from 20 percent in 1940 to 14 percent in 1947.[45]

In contrast to the demobilization literature, the psychological and child development theories of the 1940s and 1950s placed women solely and securely in a domestic setting and assumed that a woman's personality was completely defined by her sex and that the needs of a woman and her family were basically compatible. Beginning with the 1947 publication of *Modern Woman: The Lost Sex*, by Marynia Farnham and Ferdinand Lundberg, Freudian psychology became a significant element in the definition of womanhood, its "insights" finding expression in marriage manuals, women's magazines, and other forms of popular literature. According to the new experts, wartime changes had fostered the development of widespread individual neuroses and social maladjustments largely caused by the failure of women to accept their femininity, by which they meant accepting a subordinate and dependent status. "Rosie the Riveter" was thus transformed with dizzying speed from a wartime heroine to a neurotic, castrating victim of penis envy.[46]

Having diagnosed the problem, the psychology profession had also developed the tools to deal with it. According to Rebecca Greene, the increased role of psychiatry in the American military during the war caused the functions of the psychiatric profession to change and expand. In order to promote harmony, unity, and discipline in close military situations, military psychiatrists developed a stricter definition of mental illness, stressing the elimination of minor personality idiosyncrasies that might otherwise have strained interpersonal relations. As a result, the focus of psychiatric concern shifted from a prewar stress on psychosis to a wartime preoccupation with neurosis and adjusting the individual to society's role expectations. Having greatly expanded its purposes during the war, psychiatry was loathe to lose its new role once the conflict had ended. The 1940s thus witnessed a rise in the numbers engaged in psychiatry and related professions and a shift in the locus of their activities from mental hospitals, which employed 80 percent of psychiatrists prior to the war, to private practice, which claimed a majority of psychiatrists after the war.[47]

While the psychiatrists reasserted the primacy of the "maternal instinct" in the feminine personality, postwar childrearing experts proclaimed the importance of maternal care for children, especially during infancy and early childhood. Despite the wartime experiment with group child care, most child welfare authorities remained convinced that such programs were lesser substitutes for the preferred system of privatized, individualized care by the mother. In fact, the war generated a considerable literature on the damage done to children cared for in institutional settings. After the war, Dr. Benjamin Spock and others joined the ranks of those popularizing the idea that the healthy physical and emotional development of a child required a maternal involvement so thoroughgoing that it precluded any significant outside activities, including paid employment.[48]

As a result of such ideas, the resumption of child care responsibilities by mothers became an important part of the postwar agenda for many Americans. An early casualty of this hostility to alternative modes of childrearing was the wartime day-care program, which was further undermined by the lack of work for women in the reconversion economy. In order to ease the transition to peacetime patterns, Lanham Act funds were continued until March 1946, largely as a result of protests from day-care officials, working women, labor unions, and others. Once federal funds were withdrawn, communities were forced to close the centers, raise parent fees considerably, or find alternative sources of public funding. Although a few state and local governments were willing to allocate funds for day care, if only for a short while, most allowed the system to fold. By the summer of 1946 most centers were closed, while those few still open had curtailed their hours and raised their fees substantially.[49]

The postwar stress on traditional family roles and values for women did not constitute a dramatic break with wartime themes. Both during and after the war the importance of women being supportive and subordinating their own goals to the requirements of family and society was emphasized. Wartime publicity stressed the need for women to take a war job or otherwise support the war effort as a means of aiding their husbands, fathers, and brothers overseas. In the postwar period women who voluntarily left their jobs received approbation in the press because their actions meant more jobs for men. In addition, the disruptions of family life during the war, especially including the deferral of marriage or childbearing, had caused family life to be more highly valued, prompting a renewed emphasis on it in the postwar period.

Thus, the exaggerated emphasis on family life in the postwar era could also be considered a part of the legacy of the war experience. Despite the changes wrought by the war, conventional attitudes regarding the role of women within the family retained their appeal. As a result, social norms had hardly begun to accommodate the new content in women's lives, contributing to an ambiguity that could be resolved for many women by a glorification of traditional femininity and family roles. Although the gap between normative expectations and actual behavior had widened considerably during the war years, the war generated no ideological or institutional legacy that could aid in resolving the growing contradictions in women's lives. As a result, the women of postwar America embodied the fundamental dilemma of the modern women—that she is, in the words of Simone de Beauvoir, "torn between the past and the future."[50]

Notes

1. Clive, pp. 223, 581; Polenberg, pp. 235-36; Jerome Beatty, "Detroit Gets Shrinking Pains," *American Magazine* 140 (October 1945): 21-22, 114-15.

2. Clive, pp. 594-95; *Baltimore Evening Sun*, February 4, 1943; *Baltimore Sun*, August 16, 1945, August 17, 1945; *Seattle Times*, April 19, 1944; Ramsey Oppenheim, "What Are the Postwar Marketing Opportunities in the Western States?" in Pacific Advertising Association, *How the War is Changing Pacific Area Markets* (San Francisco: Pacific Advertising Association, 1943); U.S., War Manpower Commission, "Postwar Employment in Washington State and Puget Sound Area," (Seattle, 1944), pp. 1, 2.

3. U.S., War Manpower Commission, "Postwar Employment," pp. 3-4; *Seattle Times*, December 25, 1944; WBB 209; *War Program News*, September-October 1944, OCWS, General Classified, Region IV, RG 215, Box 9, NA; "Women's Postwar Job Plans," *Monthly Labor Review* 58 (May 1944): 1030.

4. Clive, pp. 578-79; Seattle Chamber of Commerce, *The Postwar Labor Market in the Seattle Area*, (Seattle: Chamber of Commerce, 1944); *Seattle Times*, April 19, 1944; "Minutes, Washington State Advisory Committee on War and Postwar Readjustments," May 4, 1943, Records of Washington State Planning Commission [hereafter cited as WSPC], RG 71, Box 32, Washington State Archives, [hereafter cited as WSA]; *Baltimore Evening Sun*, February 4, 1943, March 23, 1943.

5. Memo, Mary Woods to Regional Federal Council, June 20, 1945, OCWS, Community Reports, RG 215, Box 5, NA; "Special Survey of Labor Market Conditions in Michigan," March 1949, BES, RG 183, Box 180, NA; Clive, pp. 587-91.

6. Clive, pp. 591–604; *Detroit News*, August 21, 1945, September 20, 1945; *Detroit Free Press*, November 12, 1945; "Labor Market Developments Report, Detroit Labor Market Area," Month Ending July 31, 1946, BES, RG 183, Box 184, NA.

7. Warwick Carpenter, "What the War Is Doing to Western Consumer Incomes," in Pacific Advertising Association, *How the War Is Changing Pacific Area Markets* (San Francisco: Pacific Advertising Association, 1943); U.S., War Manpower Commission, "Postwar Employment," pp. 1, 2.

8. "Social and Economic Changes Affecting the Welfare of a County: Pierce County," May 1, 1944, September 30, 1945, DSS, RG 75, WSA; *Seattle Times*, March 7, 1944, August 26, 1945, September 17, 1945; *Tacoma News-Tribune*, August 24, 1945.

9. Grant Butterbaugh, "Highlights of Pacific Northwest Business in 1945," *Northwest Industry* (December 1945), 47; *Seattle Times*, August 15, 1945, August 18, 1945, September 6, 1945, September 7, 1945; *Seattle Business*, September 13, 1945; *Aero Mechanic*, August 23, 1945.

10. Seattle First National Bank, *Summary of Pacific Northwest Industries* (Seattle: First National Bank, 1946), pp. 7–8; *Seattle Times*, January 14, 1946; *Northwest Industry*, (March 1948), p. 108; Paul Simpson, *Regional Aspects of Business Cycles and Special Studies of the Pacific Northwest* (Eugene, Oregon: University of Oregon, 1953), p. 46; State of Washington, Employment Security Department, "Labor Force and Employment in Tacoma Area (Pierce County)," 1940-47.

11. *Baltimore Sun*, March 14, 1944; "Labor Market Developments Report, Baltimore," September, 1945, November, 1945, BES, RG 183, Box 162, NA.

12. "Labor Market Developments Report, Baltimore," November, 1945, BES, RG 183, Box 162, NA; *Baltimore Sun*, August 16, 1945; *Baltimore Evening Sun*, November 2, 1945, December 5, 1946.

13. "Labor Market Developments Report, Baltimore," November 1945, BES, RG 183, Box 162, NA; Glenn L. Martin Company, Public Relations Department, Release No. 1100, July 29, 1946, WRC, RG 2010, Box 102, MHS; U.S., Department of Commerce, Bureau of the Census, Series P-LF, No. 5, "Report on the Labor Force of Baltimore, Maryland: October, 1946," p. 5.

14. Dun and Bradstreet, pp. 14, 20, 23; "Job Opportunities in Clerical Occupations in Detroit," November 13, 1946, BES, RG 183, Box 183, NA; U.S., Department of Commerce, Bureau of the Census, *Current Population Reports: Labor Force*, Series P-51, No. 28, August 13, 1947, "Labor Force Characteristics of the Baltimore, Maryland, Metropolitan District," April 1947, p. 6.

15. Trey, pp. 48–50; Waggaman, pp. 4–9; Mary Pidgeon, "Reconversion and the Employment of Women," *Public Affairs* (Winter 1946): 103-5; "Employment of Women—Notes for Use of Staff," February 11, 1946, WBA, RG 86, Box 1536, NA; Tobias and Anderson, pp. 93–95.

16. Rupp, pp. 143–66; *Detroit News,* May 16, 1943, November 26, 1943, August 28, 1945; *Seattle Times,* December 25, 1944.

17. *Baltimore Sun,* August 17, 1945, August 18, 1945; *Baltimore Evening Sun,* August 20, 1945; *Seattle Times,* August 23, 1945, September 16, 1945; *Seattle Business,* August 30, 1945.

18. *Seattle Times,* August 15, 1945, August 18, 1945; *Tacoma News-Tribune,* August 19, 1945; *Navy Yard Salute,* February 11, 1944; *Detroit News,* August 22, 1945; *Baltimore Sun,* August 12, 1945.

19. *Seattle Times,* December 25, 1944, August 18, 1945; *Tacoma News-Tribune,* August 19, 1945; *Navy Yard Salute,* August 31, 1945; *Baltimore Evening Sun,* August 22, 1945.

20. *Baltimore Sun,* August 18, 1945; "Field Report, Pierce County," September, 1945–March, 1946, DSS, RG 75, WSA; WBB 209, p. 53.

21. WBB 209, p. 31.

22. Ibid., p. 42; State of Washington, Office of Unemployment Compensation and Placement, "Postwar Reconversion Problems," December 1944, WSPC, RG 71, Box 32, WSA.

23. Waggaman, pp. 4–5; Pidgeon, pp. 103–4; U.S., Department of Commerce, Bureau of the Census, *Current Population Reports: Labor Force,* Series P-57, No. 60, "The Monthly Report of the Labor Force," June 10, 1947, p. 7; *New York Times,* February 26, 1944.

24. Mezerik, p. 82; Beatty, p. 22; "Employment Cut-backs of Women Since V-J Day," WBA, RG 86, Box 1536, NA.

25. "Seniority in the Automobile Industry," *Monthly Labor Review* 59 (September 1944): 463-64; "Recent Trends Affecting the Employment of Women in Automobile Manufacture in Detroit," July 26, 1946, WBA, RG 86, Box 1290, NA.

26. *Detroit News,* November 8, 1945; *New York Times,* November 9, 1945; *Detroit Free Press,* November 9, 1945.

27. "Baltimore Women War Workers in the Postwar Period," WBA, RG 86, Box 1350, NA; "Labor Market Developments Report, Baltimore," November, 1945, BES, RG 183, Box 162, NA; U.S., Department of Commerce, Bureau of the Census, "Report on the Labor Force of Baltimore, Maryland: October, 1946," p. 5.

28. "Baltimore Women War Workers in the Postwar Period," WBA, RG 86, Box 1350, NA.

29. *Seattle Times,* August 19, 1945, August 28, 1945; *104 Reporter,* August 23, 1945.

30. "Interviews—Seattle," L. Isaacson, March 18, 1951, WBA, RG 86, Box 1423, NA; John Broussard, "The Rejected Applicant: A Study of the Unsuccessful Factory Job Seeker" (M.A. thesis, University of Washington, 1951), p. 23.

31. "The Washington Labor Market," June 1946, BES, RG 183, Box 413, NA; *Seattle Times*, January 22, 1945; State of Washington, Office of Unemployment Compensation and Placement, *Statistical Bulletin*, September 1945, p. 112.

32. *New York Times*, February 26, 1944; "Employment of Women—Notes for Use of Staff," February 11, 1946, WBA, RG 86, Box 1536, NA; Pidgeon, p. 105; *Aero Mechanic*, October 11, 1945; "The Washington Labor Market," June, 1946, BES, RG 183, Box 413, NA; *Detroit Free Press*, August 17, 1945.

33. "The Washington Labor Market," June 1946, BES, RG 183, Box 413, NA; "Baltimore Women War Workers in the Postwar Period," WBA, RG 86, Box 1350, NA; State of Washington, Office of Unemployment Compensation and Placement, *Statistical Bulletin*, November 1945, p. 140.

34. *Detroit News*, February 28, 1945; "The Washington Labor Market," June 1946, BES, RG 183, Box 413, NA; "Baltimore Women War Workers in the Postwar Period," WBA, RG 86, Box 1350, NA.

35. "Labor Market Developments Report, Detroit Labor Market Area," Month Ending July 31, 1946, BES, RG 183, Box 184, NA; "Job Opportunities in Clerical Occupations in Detroit," USES, November 13, 1946, BES, RG 183, Box 183, NA.

36. Ibid.

37. "Appeal of Wilhelmina Isaacson to USES," April 13, 1946, Papers of the Boilermakers Union [hereafter cited as BU], Box 5, University of Washington Archives, [hereafter cited as UWA]; "Appeal of Susan Walker," BU, Box 5, UWA; "Notice of Decision, Case of Wilhelmina Isaacson," June 7, 1946, BU, Box 5, UWA; "Notice of Appeal, Marian Olsen," May 14, 1946, BU, Box 5, UWA; "Notice of Decision, Case of Minna Hinkle," June 7, 1946, BU, Box 5, UWA.

38. "Baltimore Women War Workers in the Postwar Period," WBA, RG 86, Box 1350, NA; *Seattle Times*, January 29, 1946.

39. "Negro Women Workers," December 5, 1950, WBA, RG 86, Box 1601, NA.

40. "Labor Market Developments Report, Detroit Labor Market Area," Month Ending July 31, 1946, BES, RG 183, Box 184, NA; "Baltimore Women War Workers in the Postwar Period," WBA, RG 86, Box 1350, NA.

41. "Labor Market Developments Report, Detroit Labor Market Area," Month Ending September 30, 1946, BES, RG 183, Box 180, NA; U.S., Department of Commerce, Bureau of the Census, *Current Population Reports: Labor Force*, Series P-51, No. 35, "Labor Force Characteristics of the Metropolitan Districts: April, 1947," p. 5; U.S., Department of Commerce, Bureau of the Census, *Sixteenth Census*, Vol. 3, Part 5, p. 856; U.S., Department of Commerce, Bureau of the Census, *Seventeenth Census*, Vol. 2, Part 47, p. 179; U.S., Depart-

ment of Commerce, Bureau of the Census, *Current Population Reports: Labor Force*, "Labor Force Characteristics of the Baltimore, Maryland, Metropolitan District," p. 6.

42. Chafe, pp. 183–84, 194–95.

43. Hartmann, "Prescriptions for Penelope," 223–39.

44. Ibid.; "Do You Want Your Wife to Work After War?" War Department, Educational Manual EM-31, GI Roundtable Series, WBA, RG 86, Box 1545, NA.

45. Keith Olson, *The G.I. Bill, the Veterans and the Colleges* (Lexington: University Press of Kentucky, 1974) pp. 43–44; U.S., Department of Commerce, Bureau of the Census, "Population Characteristics of the Metropolitan Districts: April, 1947," p. 9; Hartmann, "Prescriptions for Penelope," pp. 224–36.

46. Chafe, pp. 202–10.

47. Rebecca S. Greene, "Everyone Has His Breaking Point: World War II and the Emergence of Modern American Psychiatry" (paper presented at the University of Maryland, College Park, Md., April 23, 1979.)

48. Nancy P. Weiss, "Mother, the Invention of Necessity: Dr. Benjamin Spock's Baby and Child Care," *American Quarterly* 29 (Winter 1977): 543; Kerr, p. 166; Zucker, p. 43.

49. Kerr, p. 165; Dratch, pp. 179–81; *Detroit News*, September 26, 1945.

50. Simone de Beauvoir, *The Second Sex* (New York: Bantam, 1952), p. 683.

BIBLIOGRAPHY

Manuscripts

Boilermakers Union, papers of. University of Washington Archives, Seattle.
Arthur B. Langlie, papers of. Washington State Archives, Olympia.
Dietrich Schmitz, papers of. University of Washington Archives, Seattle.
U.S. Children's Bureau, papers of. Federal Records Center, Suitland, Maryland.
U.S. Committee for Congested Production Areas, papers of. National Archives, Washington, D.C.
U.S. Office of Community War Services, papers of. National Archives, Washington, D.C.
U.S. Bureau of Employment Security, papers of. National Archives, Washington, D.C.
U.S. Women's Bureau, papers of. National Archives, Washington, D.C.
Mon C. Wallgren, papers of. Washington State Archives, Olympia.
Washington State Department of Conservation, papers of. Washington State Archives, Olympia.
Washington State Department of Social Security, papers of. Washington State Archives, Olympia.
Washington State Planning Council, papers of. Washington State Archives, Olympia.
Washington State Superintendent of Public Instruction, papers of. Washington State Archives, Olympia.
War Records Collection. Maryland State Historical Society, Baltimore.

Public Documents

City of Seattle. Civilian War Commission. *Annual Report*, 1943.

————. *Final Report: Seattle Went to War.*

————. *Minutes,* 1941–45.

City of Seattle. Education Board. *Annual Report,* 1940–45.

————. Report of the Public Schools, Years Ending June 30, 1942 and June 30, 1943.

————. *The Seattle Schools and Character Education,* March 3, 1944.

City of Seattle. Police Department. *Annual Reports,* 1939–45.

City of Tacoma. School District No. 10. *Annual Reports,* 1940–45.

State of Washington. Department of Conservation and Development. *A Survey of Employment Levels in the State of Washington During the War and Postwar Period, 1948.*

State of Washington. Department of Labor and Industries. *Reports,* 1940–41 to 1948–49.

State of Washington. Department of Social Security. Division for Children. *Standards for Day Nurseries,* Publication No. 7, 1942.

State of Washington. Employment Security Department. *Labor Force and Employment,* August 1947.

————. *Labor Market Bulletins,* 1945–46.

————. *Labor Market Reports,* 1951.

State of Washington. Governor's Commission on the Status of Women. *Report,* December 1963.

State of Washington. Office of Unemployment Compensation and Placement. *Employment and Payrolls in Washington State, 1938-1942,* April 1944.

————. *Statistical Bulletins,* 1944–45.

State of Washington. Secretary of State. *The Counties of Washington,* September 1943.

State of Washington. Superintendent of Public Instruction. *Biennial Report,* 1940–42.

State of Washington. Unemployment Compensation Division. *Reports,* 1940–46.

U.S. Department of Commerce. Bureau of the Census. *Current Population Reports: Housing.* Series P-71, No. 28, "Housing Characteristics of the Baltimore, Maryland Metropolitan District." August 19, 1947.

————. *Current Population Reports: Labor Force.* Series P-51, No. 28, "Labor Force Characteristics of the Baltimore, Maryland, Metropolitan District." August 13, 1947.

————. *Current Population Reports: Labor Force,* Series P-51, No. 35, "Labor Force Characteristics of the Metropolitan Districts: April, 1947."

————. *Current Population Reports: Labor Force.* Series P-57, No. 60, "The Monthly Report of the Labor Force." June 10, 1947.

————. *Current Population Reports,* Series P-LF, No. 5, "Report on the Labor

Force of Baltimore, Maryland: October, 1946." 1947.

_____. *Current Population Reports*, Series P-21, No. 35, "Population Character-
istics of the Metropolitan Districts: April, 1947." 1947.

_____. *Current Population Reports*, Series P-46, No. 2, "Estimated Population
of the United States, By Age, Color, and Sex: 1945 and 1944." January
27, 1946.

_____. *Population*. Series PM-1, No. 3, "The Wartime Marriage Surplus."
November 12, 1944.

_____. *Current Population Reports*, Series P-S, No. 9, "School Attendance of
the Civilian Population; October, 1945." July 23, 1946.

_____. Population Series CA-3, No. 8, "Characteristics of the Population,
Labor Force, Families, and Housing, Puget Sound Congested Production
Area: June, 1944." Washington, D.C.: Government Printing Office,
1944.

_____. Population Series CA-3, No. 9, "Characteristics of the Population,
Labor Force, Families, and Housing, Detroit-Willow Run Congested
Production Area: June, 1944." Washington, D.C.: Government Printing
Office, 1944.

_____. *Population*. Series PM-1, No. 4, December 14, 1945. "Marriage Licenses
Issued in Cities of 100,000 Inhabitants or More, 1939–44, with Statistics
by Months, 1941–44."

_____. *Sixteenth Census of the United States: 1940*. Vol. 3, Part 5. 1943.

_____. *Seventeenth Census of the United States: 1950*. Vol. 2, Part 47. 1952.

U.S. Department of Labor, Bureau of Labor Statistics, *Handbook of Labor
Statistics* (Washington, D.C.: Government Printing Office, 1973).

U.S. Department of Labor. Bureau of Labor Statistics, Industrial Area Study
No. 10, "The Impact of the War on the Detroit Area," July 1943.

U.S. Department of Labor. Bureau of Labor Statistics. Industrial Area Study
No. 19, "The Impact of the War on the Seattle-Tacoma Area," January
1945.

U.S. Department of Labor. Women's Bureau. Bulletin No. 209, "Women
Workers in Ten War Production Areas and Their Postwar Employment
Plans." Washington, D.C.: Government Printing Office, 1946.

_____. Bulletin No. 211, "Employment of Women in the Early Post-war
Period with Background of Prewar and War Data." Washington, D.C.:
Government Printing Office, 1946.

_____. Bulletin No. 294, "Handbook of Women Workers." Washington,
D.C.: Government Printing Office, 1969.

U.S. Department of Labor, Women's Bureau, Special Bulletin No. 20, "Changes
in Women's Employment During the War." Washington, D.C.: Government Printing Office, 1944.

186   Bibliography

U.S. War Manpower Commission. "Adequacy of Labor Supply in Important Labor Market Areas." 1944-45.
_____. "America at War Needs Women at Work." 1943.
_____. "Postwar Employment in Washington State and Puget Sound Area." Seattle, 1944.
U.S. Works Progress Administration, "Washington at War." Seattle: War Information Service of War Services Clerical Project, 1942.

Newspapers and Periodicals

Aero Mechanic
Ammunition
Baltimore Afro-American
Baltimore Evening Sun
Baltimore Sun
Bendix Beam
Boeing News (later *Boeing Magazine*)
Bremerton Sun
Catholic Northwest Progess
CIO News
Detroit Free Press
Detroit News
For Your Information (official weekly bulletin of the Washington State Defense Council)
IAM Local 79 Bulletin
Martin Star
Navy Yard Salute
New York Times
Northwest Industry
104 Reporter
Seattle Business
Seattle Post-Intelligencer
Seattle Star
Seattle Times
Tacoma News-Tribune
Washington Athletic Club News
Washington Clubwoman
Washington State CIO News
Washington State Labor News

Books

Arnow, Harriet, *The Dollmaker*. New York: Avon, 1954.

Baker, Helen. *Women in War Industries*. Princeton, N.J.: Princeton University Press, 1942.

Cain, Glen. *Married Women in the Labor Force: An Economic Analysis*. Chicago: University of Chicago Press, 1966.

Caplow, Theodore. *The Sociology of Work*. Minneapolis: University of Minnesota Press, 1964.

Carr, Lowell, and Stermer, James. *Willow Run: A Study of Industrialization and Cultural Inadequacy*. New York: Harper & Bros., 1952.

Chafe, William. *The American Woman: Her Changing Social, Economic, and Political Roles, 1920-1970*. New York: Oxford University Press, 1972.

Consolidated Gas Electric Light and Power Company of Baltimore. *Second Industrial Survey of Baltimore*. Baltimore: CGELPCB, 1939.

de Beauvoir, Simone. *The Second Sex*. New York: Bantam, 1952.

Dos Passos, John. *State of the Nation*. Boston: Houghton-Mifflin, 1944.

Dun and Bradstreet, Inc. *Study of Economic and Financial History of Seattle*. Seattle: Dun and Bradstreet, 1948.

Ferriss, Abbott L. *Indicators of Change in the American Family*. New York: Russell Sage Foundation, 1970.

Ginzberg, Eli. *The Development of Human Resources*. New York: McGraw-Hill, 1966.

Gruenberg, Sidonie, ed. *The Family in a World at War*. New York: Harper & Brothers, 1942.

Hacker, Andrew. *The End of the American Era*. New York: Atheneum, 1971.

International Labour Office. *The War and Women's Employment: The Experience of the United Kingdom and the United States*. Montreal: International Labour Office, 1946.

Kinsey, Alfred C. *Sexual Behavior in the Human Female*. Philadelphia: Saunders, 1953.

Komarovsky, Mirra. *Blue-Collar Marriage*. New York: Random House, 1964.

Kreps, Juanita. *Sex in the Marketplace: American Women at Work*. Baltimore: Johns Hopkins University Press, 1971.

Long, Clarence D. *The Labor Force Under Changing Income and Employment*. Princeton: Princeton University Press, 1958.

Maryland Historical Society. War Records Division. *Maryland in World War II*. Vol. 3. Baltimore: Maryland Historical Society, 1958.

Merrill, Francis. *Social Problems on the Home Front*. New York: Harper and Brothers, 1948.

Morgan, James; Sirageldin, Ismail; and Baerwaldt, Nancy. *Productive Americans*. Ann Arbor: University of Michigan Press, 1966.

Myer, Agnes. *Journey Through Chaos*. New York: Harcourt, Brace, 1943.

National Manpower Council. *Womanpower*. New York: Columbia University Press, 1957.

Ogburn, William, ed. *American Society in Wartime*. Chicago: University of Chicago Press, 1943.

Olson, Keith. *The G.I. Bill, the Veterans and the Colleges*. Lexington: University Press of Kentucky, 1974.

Oppenheimer, Valerie K. *The Female Labor Force in the United States*. Berkeley: University of California Press, 1970.

Owens, Hamilton. *Baltimore on the Chesapeake*. Garden City, N.Y.: Doubleday, Doran, 1941.

Pacific Advertising Association. *How the War Is Changing Pacific Area Markets*. San Francisco: Pacific Advertising Association, 1943.

Polenberg, Richard. *The U.S., War and Society: 1941-1945*. Philadelphia: Lippincott, 1972.

Rupp, Leila. *Mobilizing Women for War: German and American Propaganda, 1939-1945*. Princeton: Princeton University Press, 1978.

Schneider, David M., and Smith, Raymond T. *Class Differences in American Kinship*. Ann Arbor: University of Michigan Press, 1978.

Seattle Chamber of Commerce. *Estimate of Postwar Employment in King County*. Seattle: Chamber of Commerce, 1945.

――――. *The Postwar Labor Market in the Seattle Area*. Seattle: Chamber of Commerce, 1944.

――――. *Seattle: Industrial Horizons Unlimited*. Seattle: Chamber of Commerce, 1948.

――――. *Where We Stand on Postwar Planning*. Seattle: Chamber of Commerce, 1945.

Seattle First National Bank. *Summary of Pacific Northwest Industries*. Seattle: First National Bank, 1946.

Simpson, Paul. *Regional Aspects of Business Cycles and Special Studies of the Pacific Northwest*. Eugene, Oregon: University of Oregon Press, 1953.

Turner, Marjorie. *Women and Work*. Los Angeles: UCLA Institute of Industrial Relations, 1964.

University of Washington. Institute of Labor Economics. *Job Opportunities for Racial Minorities in the Seattle Area*. Seattle: University of Washington Press, 1948.

University of Washington. Bureau of Business Research. *An Analysis of Manufacturing in the Puget Sound Area*. Seattle: University of Washington Press, 1955.

_____. *Federal Expenditures in Washington*. Seattle: University of Washington Press, 1956.

Waggaman, Mary. *Women Workers in Wartime and Reconversion*. New York: Paulist Press, 1947.

Weaver, Robert. *Negro Labor: A National Problem*. New York: Harcourt, Brace, 1946.

Articles

Abbott, Josephine. "What of Youth in Wartime?" *Survey Midmonthly* 79 (October 1943): 265–67.

Beatty, Jerome. "Detroit Gets Shrinking Pains." *American Magazine* 140 (October 1945): 21–22, 114–15.

"Boeing's Role in the War—1943. . . ." *Northwest Industry* 2 (September 1943).

Bossard, James H. S. "Family Backgrounds of Wartime Adolescents." *Annals of the American Academy of Political and Social Science* 236 (November 1944): 33–42.

Buechel, Henry. "Absenteeism in Seattle War Plants." *Northwest Industry* 2 (September 1943).

Butterbaugh, Grant. "Highlights of Pacific Northwest Business in 1945." *Northwest Industry* (December 1945).

Clapp, Raymond F. "Social Treatment of Prostitutes and Promiscuous Women." *Federal Probation* 7 (April-June 1943): 23–27.

Cuber, John F. "The Adjustment of College Men to Military Life: Case Data." *Sociology and Social Research* 27 (March-April 1943): 267–76.

Degler, Carl. "The Changing Place of Women in America." In *The Woman Question in American History*, edited by Barbara Welter. Hinsdale, Ill.: Dryden, 1973.

"Detroit Is Dynamite." *Life* 13 (August 17, 1942): 15–20.

"Detroit: Six Months After." *Life* 14 (March 1, 1943): 28–29.

Dratch, Howard. "The Politics of Child Care in the 1940's." *Science and Society* 38 (Summer 1974): 167–204.

Engel, Nathanael. "Jobs After Victory." *Northwest Industry* 3 (October 1943): 5–9.

_____. "1946 Business Outlook for Western Washington." *Northwest Industry* 5 (December 1945): 46–51.

" 'Extra' Workers in the Postwar Labor Force." *Monthly Labor Review* 61 (November 1945): 841–47.

Fletcher, Ralph Carr. "Runaway Youth to Detroit During the War." *Social Service Review* 22 (September 1948): 349–54.

Gaylord, Gladys. "Marriage Counseling in Wartime." *Annals of the American Academy of Political and Social Science* 229 (September 1943): 39–45.

"Girls in Uniform." *Life* (July 6, 1942): 41.

Hartmann, Susan. "Prescriptions for Penelope: Literature on Women's Obligations to Returning World War II Veterans." *Women Studies* 5 (1978): 223–39.

Hayner, Norman. "Women in a Changing World." *Marriage and Family Living* 5 (August 1943): 55.

Heer, David M. "Dominance and the Working Wife." In *The Employed Mother in America*, edited by F. Ivan Nye and Lois W. Hoffman. Chicago: Rand McNally, 1963.

"Increases in Number of Child Workers." *Monthly Labor Review* (November 1943): 942.

Kerr, Virginia. "One Step Forward—Two Steps Back: Child Care's Long American History." In *Child Care—Who Cares?*, edited by Pamela Roby. New York: Basic Books, 1973.

Locke, H. J. "Family Behavior in Wartime." *Sociology and Social Research* 27 (March–April 1943): 277–84.

Magee, Elizabeth S. "Impact of War on Child Labor." *Annals of the American Academy of Political and Social Science* 236 (November 1944): 101–5.

Mezerik, A. G. "Getting Rid of the Women." *Atlantic* (June 1945): 79–82.

Murphy, Irene E. "Detroit's Experience With the Wartime Care of Children." *Proceedings of the National Conference of Social Work*. New York: Columbia University Press, 1943.

Nottingham, Elizabeth. "Toward An Analysis of the Effects of Two World Wars on the Role and Status of Middle-Class Women in the English-Speaking World." *American Sociological Review* 12 (December 1947): 666–75.

Olson, Louise, and Schrader, Ruth. "The Trailer Population in a Defense Area." *Sociology and Social Research* 27 (March–April 1943): 295–302.

Ostrander, Gilman. "The Revolution in Morals." In *The Twenties: The Critical Issues*, edited by Joan Hoff Wilson. Boston: Little, Brown, 1972.

Pidgeon, Mary. "Reconversion and the Employment of Women." *Public Affairs* (Winter 1946).

Quick, Paddy. "Rosie the Riveter: Myths and Realities." *Radical America* 9 (July–August 1975): 115–32.

Rappaport, Mazie. "A Protective Service for Promiscuous Girls." *Federal Probation* 9 (January–March 1945): 33–36.

Redl, Fritz. "Zoot Suits: An Interpretation." *Survey Midmonthly* 79 (October 1943): 259–62.

Sanday, Peggy R. "Female Status in the Public Domain." In *Woman, Culture, and Society*, edited by Michelle Rosaldo and Louise Lamphere. Stanford: Stanford University Press, 1974.

"Seattle—A Boom Comes Back." *Business Week* (June 20, 1942):26–32.

"Seniority in the Automobile Industry." *Monthly Labor Review* 59 (September 1944): 463–74.

Simpich, Frederick. "Wartime in the Pacific Northwest." *National Geographic* 82 (October 1942): 424–36.

Straub, Eleanor. "United States Government Policy Toward Civilian Women During World War II," *Prologue* (Winter 1973).

Sutermeister, Robert. "The Status of Personnel Practices in the Pacific Northwest." *Northwest Industry* 1 (April 1942): 1–7.

Trey, Joan Ellen. "Women in the War Economy." *Review of Radical Political Economics* 4 (July 1972): 40–57.

Tobias, Sheila, and Anderson, Lisa. "Whatever Happened to Rosie the Riveter?" *Ms.* 1 (June 1973).

Weiss, Nancy. "Mother, the Invention of Necessity: Dr. Benjamin Spock's Baby and Child Care." *American Quarterly* 29 (Winter 1977): 519–46.

"Women's Post-War Job Plans." *Monthly Labor Review* 58 (May 1944): 1030.

"Work and Wage Experience of Willow Run Workers." *Monthly Labor Review* 61 (December 1945): 1074–1090.

Znaniecki, Florian. "The Impact of War on Personality Organization." *Sociology and Social Research* 27 (January-February 1943): 167–80.

Zucker, Henry L. "Working Parents and Latchkey Children." *Annals of the American Academy of Political and Social Science* 236 (November 1944): 43–48.

Unpublished Materials

Anderson, Karen. "The Victory Girl in Wartime America." Paper presented at the conference of the Southeastern Women Studies Association, Johnson City, Tennessee, February 1979.

Bolin, Winifred. "Past Ideals and Present Pleasures: Women, Work and the Family, 1920–1940." Ph.D. dissertation, University of Minnesota, 1976.

Broussard, John. "The Rejected Applicant: A Study of the Unsuccessful Factory Job Seeker." Master's thesis, University of Washington, 1951.

Campbell, D'Ann. "Unorganized Women: Housewives in World War II." Paper presented at the convention of the Organization of American Historians, New York, April 1978.

Clive, Alan. "The Society and Economy of Wartime Michigan, 1939–1945."
    Ph.D. dissertation, University of Michigan, 1976.
Hartmann, Susan. "Women's Organizations During World War II: The Inter-
    action of Class, Race, and Feminism." Paper presented at the convention
    of the Organization of American Historians, New York, April 1978.
Scharf, Lois. "The Employment of Married Women During the Depression,
    1929-1941." Ph.D. dissertation, Case Western Reserve University, 1977.
Straub, Eleanor. "Government Policy Toward Civilian Women During World
    War II." Ph.D. dissertation, Emory University, 1973.

INDEX

About the Author

KAREN ANDERSON is Assistant Professor of History at the University of Arizona at Tucson. A specialist in women's studies, she is a contributor to *Values of the American Heritage: Challenges, Case Studies, and Teaching Strategies*.